Mahatma Gandhi

MAHATMA GANDHI

Series Editor
Dr. M.H. Syed

Editor
Anil Kathuria **Bharat Singh**

Himalaya Books Pvt. Ltd.
'Ramdoot', Dr. Bhalerao Marg, Girgaon, Mumbai - 400 004
Tel : (022) 23863863, Fax : (022) 23877178
Email : himpub@vsnl.com

Edition : 2013

Published by : **H.B.P.L.**
"Pooja Apartments", 4-B, Murari Lal Street, Ansari Road,
Darya Ganj, New Delhi-110 002
Phones : 23270392, 23278631 Reliance : 30180392 to 396
Fax : 011-23256286 Email : hphdel@vsnl.com

Sole Distributers : HIMALAYA PUBLISHING HOUSE PVT. LTD.

Branch Offices

Mumbai : "Ramdoot", Dr. Bhalerao Marg, Girgaon, Mumbai-400 004.
Phones : 23860170/23863863 Fax : 022-23877178
Email : himpub@vsnl.com
Website : www.himpub.com

Nagpur : Kundanlal Chandak Industrial Estate, Ghat Road, **Nagpur - 440 018.**
Phone: 2738731, 3296733 Telefax : 0712-2721215

Bengaluru : No. 16/1 (Old 12/1), 1st Floor, Next to Hotel Highlands,
Madhava Nagar, Race Course Road, **Bengaluru - 560 001.**
Phone : 22281541, 22385461, Telefax: 080-22286611

Hyderabad : No. 3-4-184, Lingampally, Besides Raghavendra Swamy Matham,
Kachiguda, **Hyderabad - 500 027.** Phone: 040-27560041, 27550139,
Mobile:- 09848130433 Telefax: 040-27560041

Chennai : No. 85/50, Bazullah Road, T. Nagar, **Chennai - 600 017.**
Phone: 044-28344020, 32463737, 42124860

Pune : No. 527, "Laksha" Apartment, First Floor, Mehunpura, Shaniwarpeth,
(Near Prabhat Theatre), **Pune - 411 030.**
Phone: 020-24496323/24496333/32326733

Lucknow : House No. 731, Sehkhupura Colony, Near B.D. Convent School,
Lucknow - 226 024. Mobile : 09307501549

Ahmedabad : No. 114, "SHAIL", 1st Floor, Opp. Madhu Sudan House, C.G.Road,
Navrang Pura, **Ahmedabad – 380 009.**
Phone: 079-26560126, Mobiles: 09327324149, 09314679413

Ernakulam : No. 39/104 A, Lakshmi Apartment, Karikkamuri Cross Rd.,
Ernakulam, **Cochin – 682011**, Kerala.
Phone: 0484-2378012, 2378016, Mob.: 09344199799

Bhubaneswar : 5 Station Square, **Bhubaneswar (Orissa) - 751 001.**
Mobile: 9861046007, E-mail:- orissa@himpub.com

Indore : Kesardeep Avenue Extension, 73, Narayan Bagh.Flat No. 302,
IIIrd Floor, Near Humpty Dumpty School, Narayan Bagh,
Indore (M.P.) 452 007 Mobile: 09301386468

Kolkata : 108/4, Beliaghata, Main Road, Near ID Hospital, Opp. SBI Bank
Kolkata - 700 010.
Mobile: 09910440956, E-mail:- nkmitra@himpub.com

Guwahati : House No. 15, Behind Prajjyotish College, Near Sharma
Printing Press, P.O. Bharalumukh, Guwahati - 781009 (Assam)
Mobile: 07439040301; 07439040302

Printed by : Printed at : Sri Prints & Sales, Delhi Ph. : 23262724

Preface

Biography, is now a form of literature, very much in vogue. In fact, biography is a description or account of someone's life and the times, which is usually published in the form of a book. A biography is more than a mention of personal facts (life, education, work, relationships and death), it also portrays the subject's experience of events. Technically speaking, a work is biographical, if it covers, all of a person's life. Biography writing has a long history. A biography is real. Ancient Greeks developed the biographical tradition, which we have inherited, although until the 5th century AD, when the word 'biographia' first appeared, in Damascius' "Life of Isodorus," biographical pieces were called simply "lives". It is quite likely that the Greeks were drawing on a pre-existing eastern tradition. Certainly Herodotus' "Histories" contains more detailed biographical information on Persian kings and subjects. The earliest surviving pieces, which we would identify as biographical are Isocrates' "Life of Evagoras" and Xenophon's "Life of Agesilaos," both from the fifth century BC. "Parallel Lives" by Plutarch, a Greek writing under the Roman empire, is a series of short biographies of eminent men.

The Golden Age of English biography emerged in late eighteenth century, the century in which the terms "biography" and "autobiography" entered English lexicon. The classic works of the period were Samuel Johnson's "Critical Lives of the Poets" and James Boswell's "Massive Life of Johnson". Generally American biography followed English model. By World War I, cheap hardcover reprints had become popular. The decade of the 1920s witnessed a biographical 'boom'. Later, biographical writings developed a lot and today biographies are written and compiled in the finest form of the genre. In India too, biography, as a form of literature has been evolved, cultivated and polished over the years. Here is an effort to promote this tradition further.

This series of biographies of great men, great women and celebrities in all walks of life is an adventurous academic endeavour, in its own right. A team of researchers and compilers has worked for a good period of time to accomplish the project. For this purpose, hundreds of books by eminent authors and editors have been consulted and referred to. We have benefited from various works, liberally, in order to illustrate and enrich this effort of ours. Present book is devoted to the great personality of Mohandas Karamchand Gandhi.

Mohandas Karamchand Gandhi was the pre-eminent political and spiritual leader of our country, during the Indian independence movement. He was the pioneer of satyagraha-resistance to tyranny, through mass civil disobedience, a philosophy, firmly founded upon *ahimsa* or total nonviolence — which led India to independence and inspired movements for civil rights and freedom across the world. As a practitioner of *ahimsa,* he swore to speak the truth and advocated that others do the same. Gandhi is commonly known around the world as Mahatma Gandhi. He is officially honoured in India as the Father of the Nation; his birthday, 2 October, is commemorated here as Gandhi Jayanti, a national holiday, and worldwide as the International Day of Nonviolence.

This is a compact and comprehensive account of the above mentioned great life, which is bound to attract the attention of scholars, researchers, students and the general readers alike. Let's hope this humble effort would receive a warm welcome and due applause.

— ***Editors***

Contents

1

An Illustrious Life

Father of the Nation, Mohandas Karamchand Gandhi's figure is today a transfigured presence in the eyes of his countrymen. Like the unveiling of some sanctuary, where the high gods sit in session, or like some romance of the soul, is his career. The loftiest ideals of conduct of which man has dreamed are in him translated into actuality. He is the latest, though not the least, of the world's apostles. He seems for ever robed in vestments of shining white. Infinitely gentle, to the inner ear, is his foot-fall upon earth. His accents have the dewy freshness of the dawn. His brows are steeped in serenity and calm. His head is crowned with the martyr's crown. The radiance of the light spiritual encircles his whole being.

A Whole World Gained

What shall it profit a man if he gains the whole world and loses his own soul! Returns good for evil. Hatred ceases not by hatred but by love. How often has humanity in its long history listened to such exhortations! And yet how few are the souls to whom they have ever carried the waters of life! To all men, surely, come glimpses of the highest. At the moment they touch our being with ecstasy and fade even before they are recognised. Not so with the great Ones of earth, the elect of God. They live their lives as ever before the altar. A divine inebriation is upon them and they can know no rest till they have drained the immortal cup to the dregs. The steeps they sight they needs must climb: and far down in the valley there kneels before them an adoring host of mortals.

The spontaneous and heartfelt reverence which Mr. Gandhi's name inspires today is a token that in him also India has recognised one such born priest of the ideal. The Sermon on the Mount may appear to many as gloriously impractical, but to Mr. Gandhi at least nothing is or ought to be more practical. To turn the left cheek when the right is beaten; to bless those that curse; to suffer for righteousness' sake; these are the very ideals to which he has surrendered his whole being. And by impassioned devotion to them he has developed a character before which men stand in awe. To the self-discipline of the ascetic he adds the sweetness and simplicity of a saint.

The hero's will is in him wedged to the heart of a child. It was of such that it was said: Ye are the salt of the earth. But how to write the life of such a man? How to tell the story of the soul's development? The task is impossible. The hopes and strivings of millions fulfil themselves in a single perfected character and to that extent the common man makes the hero and the apostle. The events of the personal drama simply register the rise and fall of consciousness; their explanation is outside them. In Mr. Gandhi's case, such a revelation came in the shape of the South African struggle. It was then that he burst upon the world as a moral force of the first order. That force itself had been long in preparing: how long who shall say?

The story of that struggle with its shining roil of martyrs, both men and women, its thrilling incidents, marvellous pathos, and divine inspiration still waits for its destined chronicler. When he comes and throws it into terms of immortal literature it will assuredly take rank with the most memorable and resplendent chapters of its kind in history. It was an example and a demonstration of what one man can do by the sheer force of his character, It was likewise a demonstration of how masses of men and women, apparently lifeless and downtrodden, can develop astounding heroism under the impulsion of a truly great and self-less leader. The work done by Mr. Gandhi in South Africa must ever be reckoned amongst the greatest things accomplished by any single man. His life prior to his emergence on the South

African stage was comparatively uneventful except for one or two glimpses of the coming greatness.

Youngest Child

Mohandas Karamchand Gandhi was born as the youngest of three children in a Vaishya family, at Porbandar, a city of Kathiawar in Gujarat. Courage, administrative capacity, and piety were hereditary in the family. His immediate ancestors were in their way quite remarkable. His grandfather was Dewan of the Hana of Porbandar. Incurring the displeasure of the Queen who was acting as Regent for her son, he had actually to flee the Court of Porbandar and take refuge with the Nawab of Junagadh who received him with great kindness.

The courtiers of the Nawab observed and remarked that the ex-Dewan of Porbandar gave his salute to the Nawab with his left hand in outrage of all convention. But the intrepid man replied, "In spite of all that I have suffered I keep my right hand for Porbandar still." Mr. Gandhi's father was no less distinguished. Succeeding his father as Dewan of Porbandar and losing like him the favour of the Ruling Chief, he repaired to Rajkot where he was entertained as Dewan. Here he rose rapidly in favour and such was the high regard which the Thakore Saheb of Rajkot came to have for him that he (the Thakore Saheb) pressed his minister to accept a large grant of land in token of his esteem. But wealth had no attractions for him, and at first he declined the generous offer.

Even when the entreaties of friends and relatives prevailed at last it was only a fraction of what was offered that he could be persuaded to accept. Even more interesting is another incident told of him. Happening to hear one day the Assistant Political Agent hold abusive language regarding the Thakore Sahib, he indignantly repudiated it. His Omnipotence the Political Agent demanded an apology which was stoutly refused. To rehabilitate his dignity the Assistant Political Agent thereupon ordered the offending Dewan to be arrested and detained under a tree for some hours! The apology was eventually waived and a reconciliation effected. Comment is needless. Mr. Gandhi's father was also a man of severe piety and could repeat the Baghavad Gita from end to end. His mother, however, was the most remarkable of all. Her influence on the character of her son has been profound and ineffaceable. Religion was the breath of her life. Long and rigorous were her fasts; many and lavish were her charities; and never could she brook to see a starving soul in her neighbourhood. Though in these respects she was typical of the Hindu woman, yet one feels that there must have been something unique about her. How else could she have been the mother of a Gandhi?

Education

In a home presided over by such a mother was his childhood passed. He was duly put to school at Porbandar but a change occurring in its fortunes the whole family moved to Rajkot. Here the boy studied at first in a Vernacular School, and afterwards in the Kathiawar High School, whence he passed the matriculation examination at the age of seventeen. It may here be said that Mr. Gandhi was married as a boy of twelve to the noble soul who was his partner in life and the glorified participator in all his sufferings and struggles. An incident in his school life deserves more than ordinary mention.

Born and bred in an atmosphere of uncompromising Vaishnavism, he had learned to perfection its ritual and worship, if not also to some extent, its rationale and doctrine. The principle of Ahimsa, non-killing (non-resistance to evil generally), is one of the keynotes of this teaching and Vaishnavas are, as a rule, strict vegetarians. But those were the days when even a schoolboy unconsciously imbibed a contempt for religion in general and for the ways of his forefathers in particular. Mr. Gandhi seems to have been no exception to this rule.

Truth to say, the young Gandhi became a veritable sceptic even at the stage of his school career. This wreck of faith brought one disastrous consequence in its train. He and some school-companions of his came sincerely to believe that vegetarianism was a folly and superstition, and that to be civilised, the eating of flesh was essential. Nor were the boys slow to put their belief into action. Buying some flesh in secret every evening, they went to a secluded spot on the bank of a stream, cooked it and made a convivial meal. But Mr. Gandhi's conscience was all the while never at peace. At home he had to tell lies to excuse his lack of appetite and one subterfuge led to another. The boy loved truth and hated falsehood, and simply to avoid telling lies he abjured flesh-eating for ever. Truly the boy is father of the man!

After he passed the matriculation examination he was advised by a friend of the family to go to England and qualify himself for the Bar. His mother, however, would not listen to any such thing. Many a gruesome tale had the good woman heard of the abandoned nature of life in England and she shrank from the prospect of exposing her son to all its temptations as from the thought of hell. But the son was firm and the mother had to yield. But not until she had taken her son to a Jain Sanyasin and made him swear three solemn vows forswearing wine, flesh and women, did she *give* her consent.

Exposure to West

Once in England Mr. Gandhi set about to make of himself a thorough 'English gentleman.' An Indian friend of his, then in England, who gloried in his anglicised ways took him in hand and gave lessons in fashion. Under his leadership he began to school himself in dancing. English music, and French, in fact in all the accomplishments needed for the great role of the ' English gentleman.' His heart, however, was never in the matter.

The vows he had taken at his mother's instance haunted him strangely. One day he went to a party and there was served with flesh soup. It was a critical moment. His conscience swelled in protest and bade him make his choice on the spot between his three vows and the character of the English gentleman. And conscience won. Much to the chagrin of his friend before alluded to, he rose from the table and committed the great social sin of quitting the party abruptly. A great triumph for a youth! He thereafter bade adieu to all his new-fangled ways: his feet ceased to dance, his fingers knew the violin no more, and the possibilities of 'the English gentleman' in him were lost for ever.

All this proved to be but the beginning of a keen spiritual struggle which stirred his being to its depths and out of which he emerged into an assured self-consciousness and abiding peace of soul. The eternal problems of existence now faced him and pressed for an answer. That this struggle was not merely intellectual, that it was no passing spasm such as even inferior men have known is proved by his subsequent career. As in the case of all great souls, his entire being was, we may take it, cast into the crucible to be melted and poured into divine moulds. The sense of an insufferable void within and without, that tribulation of the spirit which lays hands of torture upon the barred doors of the heart and unseals the inner vision — this it was that assailed him. At this critical time, friends were not wanting who tried to persuade him that in Christianity he would find the light for which he yearned. But these apparently did not meet with much success. At the same time he began to make a close study of the Bhagavad Gita, and it was the spiritual panorama which here was unveiled before him that finally stilled the commotion of his soul. It was here that he found the staff upon which he could lean. The void was now filled, light flooded his being and he had sensed the peace that passes understanding. Hereafter the soul's endeavour was to be one, not of search, but realisation.

Mr. Gandhi's stay in England was otherwise uneventful. He passed the London Matriculation Examination, qualified himself for the Bar, and returned to India.

Melancholy news awaited his arrival in Bombay. Unknown to himself a calamity which to a Indian at least is one of the great calamities of life, had befallen him. His mother who had loved him as perhaps only an Indian mother could, who had saved him from moral ruin, and who had doubtless winged ceaseless thoughts of love and prayer for her faraway son in England, that angel of a mother was no more. She had been dead sometime and the occurrence had been purposely kept a secret from him. We shall not attempt to describe his feelings when at last the news was disclosed to him.

Preparation for the Great Mission

The next eighteen months Mr. Gandhi spent, partly at Bombay and partly at Rajkot, devoting himself to a deeper study of love and the Hindu scriptures. He also set up practice in the Bombay High Court. But there was other work to do for him in a different part of the world and the fates thus fulfilled themselves. A firm at Porbandar which had a branch at Pretoria had an important lawsuit in South Africa in which several Indians were concerned. The conduct of this suit expected to last for over a year being offered to him, he accepted it and proceeded to South Africa.

And here perhaps it will be fitting to envisage in general outline the position of the Indian immigrant in South Africa at the time. That position was frankly one of the utmost ignominy and injustice. More than half a century ago the colony of Natal wanted cheap labour for the development of its resources, and its eyes were turned to India as the best market for this supply. Representations were accordingly made to the Government of India through the Imperial Government and the indenture system was inaugurated.

One gathers that in the early negotiations that went on between the Imperial and the Indian Governments on the question, solemn promises were made by the Imperial Government that the indentured immigrant would be treated with every consideration during the term of indenture and thereafter be accorded every facility to settle in South Africa if he so chose. But the way to a certain place is paved with good intentions, and after a time the indenture system fast proved itself an abomination. Thousands of sturdy peasants from all parts of India, simple souls caught in the meshes of the recruiting agents by specious promises of a land flowing with milk and honey, found themselves on landing in South Africa waking up to a hopeless sense of anguish and disillusionment.

The physical and moral conditions of life on the estates were ideally calculated to turn the very angels into brutes. The treatment accorded to the indentured labourer by his master way, to be as mild as possible, revolting in the extreme. The slave-owner was at least compelled by his selfishness to take care of the physical comfort of his human chattels but the employer of indentured labour was destitute of even this consideration ! The tales of cruelty and individual suffering that has been collected and published almost tempt us to think that man was made not in the image of God bat in that of His Ancient Enemy. And the most hopeless feature of the situation was that these victims of colonial greed were bound to serve their term and that they had no chance of laying, and much less of making good, any case against their masters. The laws themselves were unjust to the indentured labourer and were atrociously administered.

The position of the indentured labourer who had served his term and did not desire to re-enlist was one of calculated invidiousness. At every step he was hemmed in by a thousand obstacles thrown in his way and intended to frustrate any attempt to acquire a livelihood in freedom. Law and society conspired together to fix the brand of helotry to his brow. It was brought home to him in numberless ways that he was regarded as the member of some subhuman species, in whom it was sacrilege to defile the earth occupied by the white man, except as his hewer of wood and drawer of water. The law of the land here also did but reflect this dominant spirit of exclusiveness. It made distinctions between man and man on the ground of colour and race. In Natal, for instance, every ex-indentured Indian, man, woman, and child (boys and girls over a certain age) had to pay a poll tax of £3 per head. It is unnecessary, however to catalogue in detail the various disabilities legal, economic, political and social under which the Indian laboured.

The small body of professional people, lawyers, doctors, merchants, religious teachers, who followed in the wake of the indentured Indian, these also, whatever their position and culture, fell equally under the same ban. The coloured man was in the eyes of the white colonist in South Africa a vile and accursed thing. There could be no distinction here of high and low. If these colonials had been asked to paint God they would have painted him white! There were certain differences in the position of the Indian between one province and another, in South Africa itself, the ideal m this line having been attained in the Transvaal and the Orange Free State, then independent Not to labour the tale throughout South Africa the law was unjust to the Indian and man inhuman.

It is however interesting to think what a medley of elements contributed to this attitude. First and foremost, there was the antipathy of colour and race — to what lengths this can go in the modern civilized West, the American institution of lynching sufficiently illustrates. Secondly, there was the economic factor — the free Indian was a formidable competitor in trade to the small white dealer. His habits were simple, his life temperate, and he was able to sell things much more cheaply. Thirdly, there was the instinct of earth-monopoly — South Africa must be and continue to remain a white man's land. Lastly, there was a vague feeling that the influx of the coloured man was a growing menace to the civilization of the white. The solution of the problem from the point of view of the South African colonist was very simple — to prohibit all immigration in the future, and to make the position of those that already had come so intolerable as to drive them to repatriate themselves. And towards this end, forces were inwardly making in South Africa when Mr. Gandhi first landed there.

The paradox of the whole thing lay in the fact, that while India had been asking for the Indian, in South Africa, the elementary rights of a British citizen, the colonial was all the while thinking of casting him out for ever as an unclean thing. From the very day that Mr. Gandhi set foot at Natal he had to taste of the bitter cup of humiliation which was then the Indian's portion. At court he was rudely ordered to remove the barrister's turban he had on, and he left the court at once burning with mortification.

The experience, however, was soon eclipsed by a host of others still more ignominious. Journeying to the Transvaal in a railway train, the guard unceremoniously ordered him to quit the first-class compartment, though he had paid for it, and be take himself to the van. Refusing, he was brutally dragged out with his luggage. And the train at once steamed off. Ail this was on British soil! In the Transvaal itself things were even worse. As he was sitting on the box of a coach on the way to Pretoria, the guard asked him to dismount because he wanted to smoke there. A refusal brought two consecutive blows in quick succession. In Pretoria he was once kicked off a footpath by a sentry. The catalogue may be still further extended but it would be a weariness of the flesh.

The law suit which he had been engaged to conduct was at last over, and a social gathering was given in his honour on the eve of his departure for India. That evening Mr. Gandhi chanced to see a local newspaper which announced that a bill was about to be introduced into the colonial Parliament to disfranchise Indians and that other bills of a similar character were soon to follow. With true insight he immediately perceived the gravity of the situation, and explained to the assembled guests that if the Indian community in South Africa was to be saved from utter extinction immediate and resolute action should be taken. At his instance a message was at once sent to the colonial Parliament requesting delay of proceedings, which was soon followed up by a largely signed petition against the new measure. But all this was of no avail. The bill was passed in due course. Now another largely signed petition was sent to the Colonial Secretary in England, and in consequence the Royal Assent was withheld. But this again was of no avail for the same goal was reached by a new bill through a slightly different route.

Now it was that Mr. Gandhi seriously mooted the question of a central organisation in South Africa to keep vigilant watch over Indian interests. But it was represented to him that such an organisation would be impossible unless he himself consented to remain in South Africa. The prominent Indians guaranteed him a practice if he should choose to stay. In response to their wishes he enrolled himself in the Supreme Court of "Natal though not without some objection, at first, on the ground of his colour. Thus, began for him that long association with South Africa which was destined to have such memorable results.

Leading Native Community Across Seas

From a moral point of view the choice that he made to remain in South Africa, to which he had gone only on a temporary professional visit, was the first great act of Mr. Gandhi's public career. A young man with his life before him and every prospect of carving distinction for himself in his own native land is called upon to brush all that aside and devote himself to the uplift of his own countrymen in a far away land amidst circumstances of disgusting humiliation and struggle. How many in Mr. Gandhi's position would have made the same choice? How many would have had the same passivity to surrender themselves to the guiding hand of destiny? How many would have placed service above self? But to men born for great ends such crises of the soul come only to find them prepared. The South African Indian community were like a flock of sheep without a shepherd, surrounded by ravenous wolves, and Mr. Gandhi chose to be the shepherd. South Africa was the vineyard of the Lord in which he was called upon to dig and delve, and he chose to be the labourer. From the day that his resolve was taken he consecrated himself to his work as to a high and lofty mission.

His first step, was to make his countrymen in South Africa articulate. And with this object he organised them into various societies all over the land. He trained them in methods of constitutional agitation and for the purpose held meetings and conferences, and promoted petitions and memorials. He also sought out young men willing and capable and trained them for public work. And it was his character that imparted vitality to all his endeavours. By mixing with high and low on equal terms, by his readiness to succour the needy and console the afflicted, by the example he set of a simple, pure and austere life, by his transparent sincerity and perfect selflessness he made a profound impression upon them all and acquired an influence which deepened in the passage of the years into a boundless reverence. Nor should it be forgotten that, that amongst the European community itself there were some good men and true who saw and recognised in him a soul of transcendent goodness.

In the year 1896 Mr. Gandhi came to India to take his wife and children to South Africa. Before he left South Africa he wrote and published an 4 open letter' detailing the wrongs and grievances of his countrymen resident there.

News of the splendid work which he had done in South Africa had travelled before him to India, and Indians of all classes joined in according him an enthusiastic reception wherever he went. In these meetings Mr. Gandhi had of course to make some speeches. Our good friend, Reuter, sent highly garbled versions of his addresses to South Africa. He was represented as telling his Indian audiences that Indians in South Africa were uniformly treated like wild beasts. The blood of the Colonials was up and the feeling against Mr. Gandhi reached white heat. Meeting after meeting was held in which he was denounced in the most scathing terms. Meanwhile he was urgently requested to return to Natal without a moment's delay, and he embarked accordingly.

The steamer carrying Mr. Gandhi reached Durban on the same day as another steamer, which had left Bombay with 600 Indian passengers on board two days after Mr. Gandhi's own departure. The two ships were immediately quarantined indefinitely. Great things were transpiring at Durban meanwhile. The Colonials were determined not to land the Asiatics. Gigantic demonstrations were taking place, and the expediency of sending the Indians back was gravely discussed. It was plain that the Colonials would go any length to accomplish their purpose. The more boisterous spirits even proposed the sinking of the ship. Word was sent to Mr. Gandhi that if he and his compatriots should attempt to land they should do so at infinite peril; but threats were of no avail. On the day on which the new Indian arrivals were expected to land a huge concourse had assembled. There was no end of hissing, shouting, roaring and cursing. The Attorney-General of Natal addressed the infuriate gathering and promised them that the matter would receive the early attention of Parliament, commanding them at the same time in the name of the Queen to disperse. And the crowd dispersed. Mr. Gandhi came ashore sometime after the landing of his fellow-passengers, having previously sent his wife and children to the house of a friend. He was immediately recognised by some of the stragglers who at once began to set up a howl. A rickshaw was engaged, but the way was blocked.

Mr. Gandhi walked on foot with a European friend and when they reached one of the streets the pressure was so great that the two friends were separated. The crowd at once began to maul Mr. Gandhi till the Police, came and took him to the house of a friend. The Police Superintendent expressed his apprehensions that the mob in their frenzy would even set fire to the house. Mr. Gandhi was obliged to dress himself as a Police constable and take refuge in the Police Station. This ebullition of abnormal feeling subsided after some time and a momentous page in Mr. Gandhi's life was turned.

In October 1899 war broke out between the English and the Boers in South Africa. Mr. Gandhi, with the sagacity of a true leader at once perceived what a golden opportunity it was to the British Indians to vindicate their self-respect and readiness to suffer in the cause of the Empire. At his call hundreds of his countrymen in South Africa were glad to enlist themselves as Volunteers, but the offer was rejected with scorn by the powers that be. The offer was renewed a second time, only to meet with a similar fate. When however the British arms sustained some disasters, it was recognised that every man available should be put into the field and Mr. Gandhi's offer on behalf of his compatriots was accepted. A thousand Indians came forward, and were constituted into an Ambulance Corps, to assist in carrying the wounded to the hospitals. Of the service that was rendered in that direction, it is not necessary to speak as it has been recognised even in South Africa. At another time the British Indians were employed to receive the wounded out of the line of fire and carry them to a place more than twenty miles off. When the battle was raging, Major Bapte who was commanding came to Mr. Gandhi who of course was one of the Volunteers, and represented that if they worked from within the line of the fire they should be rendering inestimable service. At once all the Indian Volunteers responded to the request and dauntlessly exposed themselves to shot and shell. Many an Indian life was lost that day.

The war was over and the Transvaal became a part of the British Empire. Mr. Gandhi was under the impression that, since the wrongs of the British Indian subjects of the Queen were one of the declared causes of the war, under the new Government those wrongs would be a thing of the past. And accordingly he returned to India with no idea of going back, but he was reckoning without his host. The little finger of the new Government was thicker than the loins of the Boers. The Boers had indeed stung the Indian subjects of the Queen with whips but the new Government stung them with scorpions. A new Asiatic department was constituted to deal with Asiatics as a species apart. A most insidious policy of exclusion was maturing.

The prospect was dark and appalling and Mr. Gandhi had to return to the scene of his labours. He interviewed the authorities but he was assured that he had no business to interfere in the matter while they themselves were there to look after everything. Mr. Joseph Chamberlain was then in South Africa and a deputation led by Mr. Gandhi waited upon him in Natal. In Pretoria however a similar deputation was disallowed unless Mr. Gandhi was excluded. Evidently Mr. Gandhi's name was becoming gall and worm-wood to the authorities. But he was not the man to be frightened. He determined to fight out the battle in the Law Courts and enrolled himself on the Supreme Court of Pretoria.

He now felt more than ever the imperative need of an organ which should at once educate the South African Indian community on the one hand and be on the other the faithful mouthpiece of their views. In 1903 a press was bought and the paper "Indian Opinion" was ushered into existence. It was published in four languages, English, Tamil, Gujarati and Hindi. At first it didn't prove a success and entailed such heavy loss that during the first year alone Mr. Gandhi had to pay a sum of £2,000 out of his own pocket. Though in subsequent years the financial position of the paper has somewhat improved, it has never been a pecuniary success. Notwithstanding, it has grown to be a great force in South Africa and rendered invaluable service during the recent struggle.

In the year 1904 a virulent attack of plague broke out among the Indian Community in Johannesburg. The Municipal authorities were either ignorant or apathetic. Mr. Gandhi, however, was at once on the scene and sent word to the authorities that if immediate action were not taken an epidemic was in prospect. But no answer came. One day the plague carried off as many as twenty-one victims. Mr. Gandhi with three or four noble comrades at once broke open one of the Indian stores which was empty, and had the patients carried there and did what he could in the matter. The next morning the Municipal authorities bestirred themselves and took the necessary action. The plague lasted a month counting more than a hundred victims. We in India may shudder to think to what an appalling magnitude the outbreak may have grown but for the heroic endeavours of the subject of this sketch, and his devoted comrades. In such ways, indeed, had Mr. Gandhi's influence begun to bear fruit.

It was about this time also that Mr. Gandhi founded the famous "Phoenix Settlement". He had been reading Ruskin's "Unto This Last" and its influence sank deep into his mind.

He was at once on fire with the author's idea of country settlements and shortly after the plague subsided, Mr. Gandhi went to Natal and purchased a piece of land at Phoenix, a place situated "on the hill sides of a rich grassy country." Houses were built and a village sprang up on the mountain side. In this 'settlement' Mr. Gandhi sought to enshrine his ideal of the simple life. It was to be a retreat from the bustle of city life where men and women might by communion with nature seek to divest their life and mind of all artificial trappings and come nearer to the source of their own being. It was to be an ashram, a spot of sanctity and peace. Its members were to be a spiritual brotherhood and were to know no differences of rank. To all alike labour was to be a privilege and a joy. All had to dig, plough and cultivate the adjoining land with their own hands. Mr. Gandhi himself when he was in South Africa used to go to the village during his moments of leisure and take part in the work of cultivation like anybody else. But he had to fulfil this sublime idealistic impulse of his at immense pecuniary sacrifice, for the scheme, we are told "absolutely impoverished him."

Tough Discipline

It was here also that Mr. Gandhi practised a great tapasya. Here he laid upon himself and his family the yoke of an iron discipline in daily habit. He stripped himself of all luxury in externals. He wore the coarsest raiment and for food took only so much as would suffice to keep body and soul together. He slept upon a coarse blanket in the open air. He starved the flesh and reined in the mind. And his soul waxed in joy and strength. And to those that beheld it was a marvel and a wonder.

In 1906 the Zulus broke out in rebellion and a corps of twenty Indians with Mr. Gandhi as leader was formed to help to carry the wounded to the hospital. The corps subsequently acted as nurses and Mr. Gandhi ministered in person to the wounded Zulus. The founding of the Phoenix Ashram and the nursing of the Zulus with all their meaning in terms of the higher life were a fitting prelude to what was about to follow.

In the year 1906 the new Government of the Transvaal brought forward a new law affecting all Asiatics, which was sinister, retrograde and obnoxious in the last degree. One morning all the children of Asia in the Transvaal awoke and found themselves called upon to register themselves anew by giving thumb impressions. Thus, all Asiatics were placed on a level with convicts. And yet these light-hearted legislators and their compatriots were by profession the flock of an Asiatic whose injunction to his disciples was to go forth amongst the children of men as lambs amongst wolves! Who will dare to say that in the dealings of the western nations with 'coloured' races this spirit has ever been much in evidence? How else could these colonials have so merrily blackened a whole continent which has been the home of the oldest civilisations and has given to humanity its greatest prophets and saviours ? But in this case also the Asiatic lambs were destined to give a glorious object-lesson to the wolves.

The object of the new measure was apparently to prevent unlawful immigration from what they regarded as the pariah continent. Now the Indian Community throughout South Africa and their leaders were quite willing that reasonable restrictions should be placed on all future immigration though on abstract considerations of justice they could have insisted upon the right of the "open door". But what they had been agitating against all these years and what they could not reconcile themselves to was that this object should be compassed by laws which tended to differentiate them on any ground of colour or race. The principle of equality of all races before the law, however much its application may have to be tempered by considerations of circumstance, had been the very head and front of their demands. And now defiance arid contempt were hurled at them in the shape of this new law. It was at the same time a certainty that it was but the precursor in the Transvaal and in other parts of South Africa of more insidious and flagrant measures intended to drive out the Indian Community once and for ever. And it was hailed by the colonials as the beginning of the end, while the Indian Community was convulsed with indignation.

Meanwhile Mr. Gandhi and his co-workers were not idle. They proceeded to interview the member of the Government in charge of the new bill, but when they succeeded only in getting women excluded from its operation it was realised that there was now nothing left for persuasion to accomplish. The Legislative Council passed the new measure after the farce of a discussion. Infinitely more important to use are the proceedings of another meeting held in that very city and at the very time when the bill was being rushed through the council. It is an immense gathering, consisting of several thousands of Indians of all classes and creeds. A great spirit animates all. Impassioned speeches are made denouncing the new law. But now at the close the great throng rises up and shouts a solemn 'Amen.' It is the vow of passive resistance that he has thus been administered. Those thousands had decided not against the new bill but against the new Act. They had decided also that henceforth they were to be the masters of their own fate and not General Smuts or Botha or the Legislative Council. And the onlooker may well have whispered to himself, "Today we have been present at the lighting of a fire which will never go out."

It was a momentous step. But Mr. Gandhi on whom the burden of leadership now lay heavily was eager to take any step that promised an alternative solution-And accordingly a deputation under his leadership and that of Mr. Ali was sent to England to agitate if possible, against the Royal Assent being given to the new legislation. The Royal Assent was withheld in consequence till a constitutional Government should be installed in the Transvaal. As a result of its efforts a committee in London with Lord Ampthill, ex-governor of Madras, as President, Sir Mancherjee Bowanaggree as Executive Chairman, and Mr. Ritch as Secretary, was also formed to keep guard over Indian interests in South Africa. But the relief thus obtained was only temporary. A constitutional Government was soon formed in the Transvaal, the new measure was passed in hot haste, received the Royal Assent, and became law.

Legislative Council passed the new measure after the farce of a discussion. Infinitely more important to use are the proceedings of another meeting held in that very city and at the very time when the bill was being rushed through the council. It is an immense gathering, consisting of several thousands of Indians of all classes and creeds. A great spirit animates all. Impassioned speeches are made denouncing the new law. But now at the close the great throng rises up and shouts a solemn ' Amen.' It is the vow of passive resistance that has thus been administered. Those thousands had decided not against the new bill but against the new Act. They had decided also that henceforth they were to be the masters of their own fate and not General Smuts or Botha or the Legislative Council. And the onlooker may well have whispered to himself, "Today we have been present at the lighting of a fire which will never go out."

It was a momentous step. But Mr. Gandhi on whom the burden of leadership now lay heavily was eager to take any step that promised an alternative solution. And accordingly a deputation under his leadership and that of Mr. Ali was sent to England to agitate, if possible, against the Royal Assent being given to the new legislation. The Royal Assent was withheld in consequence till a constitutional Government should be installed in the Transvaal. As a result of its efforts a committee in London with Lord Ampthill, ex-Governor of Madras, as President, Sir Mancherjee Bowanaggree as Executive Chairman, and Mr. Ritch as Secretary, was also formed to keep guard over Indian interests in South Africa. But the relief thus obtained was only temporary. A constitutional Government was soon formed in the Transvaal, the new measure was passed in hot haste, received the Royal Assent, and became law.

Thus, was the Indian community in the Transvaal impelled upon the great destiny of 'passive resistance.' To register or not to register was now the question : to register and sell their honour and self-respect for a mess of pottage or not to register and take up arms against a sea of troubles.' Like the voice of God speaking to the inmost soul was Mr. Gandhi's appeal to his countrymen at this hour. There could be no question, he explained, of their submitting to this final and crowning challenge of colonial insolence to Indian manhood. There was nothing left but to bare the majesty of their own souls to the storm and defy it to do its utmost. The prison and the gaol were now to be the cells of their own self-discipline. All the forces of darkness in league were powerless to move them from the firm-set purpose of their own hearts. Was spirit greater than matter ? Was the body to be nailed to the cross or the soul? Was not Heaven itself beckoning them to the great Heights? In such wise did Mr. Gandhi adjure his countrymen.

The words of the leader awoke a responsive thrill in thousands of intrepid hearts. Like one man they vowed against the registration. Like one man they resolved to face prosecution and persecution, dungeon and death itself. Like one man they resolved to make atonement for the heaped-up humiliations of many years by a supreme and triumphant act of self-vindication which should rivet the eyes of the whole world. The hour of the spirit's rebound when individuals and communities alike cleave through every consideration save that of their own integrity, that hour had come.

The Passive Resistance Movement had commenced. The registering officers went about from place to place, but little business had they to do as ninety-five per cent, of the people remained true to their oath. The law took its course and a veritable saturnalia of imprisonments ensued. The gaols became literally crammed with the Indians who suffered for conscience's sake. High and low, rich and poor went to the gaol as to the bridal. Husband was separated from wife, child from parent, and yet the fervour and pertinacity of the sufferers abated not. Mr. Gandhi himself was sentenced to two months' simple imprisonment. During the trial he took full responsibility for the course adopted by the Indian community and asked for the maximum punishment for himself. The authorities were naturally perturbed to see the worm turning and for the first time displayed a chastened mood.

Negotiations were opened through the mediation of one, Mr. Cartwright, a journalist, and it was agreed that the new law should be suspended for three months, that in the meanwhile registration should be made voluntarily, and that at the end of the period it should be repealed.

In pursuance of this arrangement Mr. Gandhi himself, to set an example, went to the office to register. The position of a leader is fraught with peril, and a Pathan who had joined the Passive Resistance Movement imagined that Mr. Gandhi was playing the coward and betraying his trust. Under this impression he dealt him such severe blows on his way to the registration office that he instantly fell down senseless on the spot. As a result of the injuries received he hovered between life and death for some time, during which the wife of his good friend and admirer, the Eev. Mr. Doke, a baptist minister of Johannesburg, devotedly nursed him back to life. His friends afterwards asked him to take legal action against the Pathan but he replied that the Pathan had done only what he considered to be right!

This incident threw the situation into confusion for the moment but subsequently the process of voluntary registration was satisfactorily completed and the authorities were called upon to perform their part of the compact. But this they refused to do, and all efforts at compromise proving futile there was now no alternative but to resume the struggle.

Once more did the rapture of suffering come upon thousands and the prison-house become a holy of holies. And how glorious was the spirit which had come upon them! Gentle and meek and uncomplaining, it was the very spirit of that Cross which their persecutors professed to follow but honoured so little in practice. It was almost as if one heard these men exclaim, "Lord, forgive them, for they know not what they do." From every class and sect were the heroes drawn. Many among them were the poorest of the poor, living by the sweat of the brow and innocent of 'education.' Wealthy merchants went into voluntary insolvency rather than prove false to their vow. The ruin and misery caused, the dislocation of family life, the hunger and starvation of the women and children were indescribable. But the women amidst all the desolation of their hearts only cheered the men on! The passive resisters were subjected to cruel hardships and indignities in gaol that their spirit might be broken, but this served only to quicken and intensify it. They had tasted of an immortal cup and anguish itself had now become only the food of their souls.

To us in Southern India it is a matter for splendid pride that amongst them ail none displayed greater resolution or a more indomitable fibre than the children of the Tamil land. It has been calculated that out of a total population of nine thousand male Indians in the Transvaal two thousand seven hundred had in this way suffered 4 untold miseries in prison and many of them again and again. Needless to say, Mr. Gandhi himself was one of the victims this time also, being sentenced to a term of two months with hard labour. We have no space to refer to the hardships he endured with his brother sufferers in jail, to his many acts of self-denial, and to the sublime manner in which he bore up, believing as he did that suffering is the heaven-ordained path to perfection. That so many should have been consumed by the apostolic fire and should have so clearly realised the issues at stake is a tribute at once to the relentless fury of the persecutors, the spiritual force of Mr. Gandhi, and the greatness of common human nature.

After his release from his second term of imprisonment Mr. Gandhi organised two deputations, one to England and the other to India for the purpose of educating public opinion in both countries. Several of the delegates were arrested on the eve of their departure and sentenced to prison as passive resisters. But Mr. Gandhi and some others nevertheless went to England and were successful in awakening some interest in the matter. The Transvaal ministers were then in England and the Imperial authorities tried to bring about a settlement. But General Smuts was implacable and nothing worth mentioning came of it. Arrangements were however made for a body of volunteers who undertook to collect funds and keep public interest alive, and the deputation returned to South Africa.

The deputation to India consisted of but one individual, that doughty and indefatigable champion of the Indian cause in South Africa, and Editor of the paper 'Indian Opinion,' Mr. H. S. L. Polak. Feeling in India had reached a high pitch of resentment against the policy of the Transvaal Government even before his arrival. But when he under the direction of the late Mr. Gokhale toured the country and narrated in dozens of meetings the heartrending tale of the South African persecution that feeling easily reached boiling-point and the demand for reprisals came from every quarter of the land. Funds also came pouring in for the relief of the distressed children in a faraway land who had done so much to raise their motherland in the estimation of the world.

One great and immediate result of Mr. Polak's propaganda was that attention in India was concentrated upon the enormities of the Indenture system as never it had been concentrated before. And when in March 1912 the late Mr. Gokhale moved in the Imperial Legislative Council a resolution for its abolition in a speech of classic force and dignity, the Government of India had to bow to Indian public opinion and signify acceptance. It was the first great victory of the Passive Resistance Movement.

In South Africa itself the movement had a two-fold reaction. On the one hand, it made an indelible impression upon the better mind of the colonial and this found expression in the formation of a committee called the Hosken Committee, under the presidency of Sir William Hosken, a good, ardent and noble man, who in the face of obloquy from his own countrymen exposed the Indian cause with a zeal that was above all praise. On the other hand, it spurred the authorities to that increasing vindictiveness which imagines that the soul could be coerced by a more thoroughgoing application of brute force.

With the blindness that has characterised the persecutor in history the authorities in the Transvaal strengthened their hands by a new power, viz. that of deportation, hoping thereby to foil the Passive Resister. At first they deported the more prominent of them across the Natal border but these returned as fast as they were sent out. Not to be baulked the, authorities now went the length of deporting a good many of the passive resisters, about sixty-four in number, all the way to India. But these again were sent back with the sympathy and admiration of a whole nation. Utterly lost to all sense of shame the Transvaal authorities by hook and by crook did their level best to prevent them from landing. And one of the returning deportees, a lion-hearted youth Narayanaswamy, by name, hunted in this way from one British port to another died in Delgoa Bay in Portuguese territory. And his martyr-death threw a fresh halo of sanctity over the cause. The Government of India greatly impressed by the gravity of the situation in India consequent on the Transvaal occurrences moved the Imperial Government in England, who in their turn did their best to woo the Transvaalies to a more conciliatory mood. And the result was that the deportation process subsequently stopped.

After the various provinces of South Africa had been constituted into the South African Union the Imperial Government in England at the insistence of the Government of India strove once more to persuade the Union Government to effect a reasonable settlement of the problem, and for the purpose, addressed to the latter a despatch in October 1910, recommending the repeal of the law which had been the origin of the whole trouble, and the adoption of legislation on non-racial lines which, while prohibiting all future immigration in effect, will yet leave room for the entry into South Africa of a small and defined minimum of educated people. At the same time the Imperial Government pointed out that any such law should not have the effect of taking away any rights till then enjoyed by immigrants in the coast-lying provinces.

This time the Union Government were willing to consider the suggestion, and to give effect thereto brought forward the Union Immigration Bill in 1911, which while repealing the old law did not annul the racial distinction, and further took away several rights from the residents of the coast districts — the very thing deprecated by the Imperial Government. This bill was naturally unacceptable to the Indian Community and finally was not passed. An understanding however was arrived at by which the passive resistors agreed to suspend their movement, and the authorities agreed to introduce satisfactory legislation in 1912, meanwhile administering the law as though it had been already altered.

The measure of 1912 was however no better and the truce was extended for one more year. It was then that Mr. Gandhi invited the late Mr. Gokhale to South Africa to study the whole situation on the spot, and the latter with the full approval of the Indian and Imperial Governments sailed for that country and arrived at Capetown on 22nd October, 1912. He stayed for about three weeks and toured the whole country visiting every important city. Everywhere he was received with signal honour, not merely by the Indian community but also by the colonial authorities themselves, and succeeded in making a great impression by that sweet reasonableness for which he was so well-known. He interviewed the Union ministers and secured from them the promise of a satisfactory settlement, and amongst other things the repeal of the £3 tax which every ex-indentured Indian man and woman had to pay in Natal, and to which reference has been made already. Things seemed to augur well for the future and hope began to revive where despair had reigned before.

A fresh and extraordinary complication was now introduced into the situation in the shape of a judicial decision of the Union Court which declared all Indian marriages to be null and void under the law of the Union. The consternation into which it plunged the entire Indian Community is imagined than described. When the long-expected legislation was at last introduced into the Union Parliament in 1913, it was evident that it was merely tinkering with the whole problem without any attempt at solving it in a liberal or large hearted manner. Warnings were accordingly given and representations made to the authorities by the Indian leaders but to no purpose. A few amendments were made in the original bill but the Act as passed was absolutely inadequate to meet the requirements of the situation. At this juncture a deputation was sent to England to bring home to the Imperial authorities and the British public the profound danger of the whole position, and the certainty that if timely steps were not taken it would lead to the revival of passive resistance on a vastly enlarged scale. But it was in vain. It required still an appalling amount of suffering before the conscience of the Union could at all be moved.

The struggle accordingly recommenced with a grimness and determination which threw into the shade even the previous campaigns. The principal planks of the passive resistor this time were, the abolition of the £3 tax, the complete eradication of the racial bar as a principle of legislation, the recognition of the validity of Indian marriages, the right of entry into Cape Colony of all South Africa-born Indians, and the sympathetic and equitable administration of all laws affecting the British Indian immigrant.

Of the incidents of this final stage of the struggle one can speak only in terms of bated breath. For it had been decreed that the baptism of fire through which the Indian Community had been passing during these long years should now be bestowed on the only two classes which had hitherto remained outside it — the women and the indentured labourer. The Indian women in the Transvaal had indeed already played a memorable part, by the fine understanding they had displayed of the purposes of the whole movement, and by the whole-hearted sympathy and encouragement which they had given to their men-folk. But the time had now come for the women themselves to step into the flaming breach.

Like an arrow in the heart did they receive the judicial dictum which pronounced their marriages to be invalid. Or rather it was that the entrance of this arrow was but the occasion for the opening of the flood-gates of that idealism of which woman's heart is the chosen home. And in what a deluge did it thereafter pour! How many hundreds were the Indian women that sanctified the prison-houses of South Africa! And how superb was the intoxication that came upon the men-folk as they beheld their own mothers, wives and sisters mock at the crucifixion of the body! Never before in the history of the world had a more signal proof been given of the power of the human soul to defy the arrayed forces of wickedness and embrace suffering in the battle for honour and self-respect. The splendour and ecstasy of it all will last through the ages.

The account given by Mrs. Polak in the pages of ' Indian Opinion 'of the part played by women in the struggle is so interesting that it deserves to be quoted in full. She writes:

> "Ruskin has said: "A woman's duty is two-fold, her duty to her home and her duty to the State. Scarcely an Indian woman in South Africa has read Ruskin's words, probably never heard of them, but the spirit of truth manifests itself in many ways and places, and the Indian women of South Africa intuitively knew this as one of the true laws of life, and their work showed that they performed their greater duty accordingly. These women, without any training for public life, accustomed to the retirement of women of India, not versed or read in the science of sociology, just patient, dutiful wives, mothers, and daughters of a struggling class of workers, in an hour of need, moved by the spirit of a larger life, took up their duty to their country, and served it with that heroism of which such men alone are capable.

It is said so often that woman does not reason, and perhaps it is a charge largely true, but where the elementary laws of being are concerned, woman follows a surer path than any dictated by reason, and sooner or later gets to her goal. Every reform movement has shown that, from the moment women stand side by side with men in the maintenance of a principle, however dimly understood by them, the spirit of the movement grows, is crystallised, and success to the movement is assured.

The Western is so accustomed to think of the Indian woman as one living in retirement, without any broad thought and without any interest in public affairs, that it must have come with a shock of surprise to learn that many Indian women, some with babies in their arms, some expecting babies to be born to them, and some quite young girls, were leaving their homes and taking part in all the hardships of the Passive Resistance campaign.

The last phase of the fight, and the one through which today we rejoice in peace, was practically led in the early stages by a small band of women from Natal, who challenged prison to vindicate their right to the legal recognition of their wifehood, and a similar small band of women from Johannesburg.

The women from Natal, all of them wives of well-known members of the Indian community, travelled up to Volksrust, were arrested and sentenced to three months' hard labour, and were the first of hundreds to go to gaol. The women from the Transvaal travelled down the line, taking in the mines on their way, holding meetings and calling upon the men to refuse to work and to die rather than live as slaves, and at the call of these women, thousands laid down their tools and went on strike. I think it may safely be said that, but for the early work of these brave women, during the middle of last year, the wonderful response to the call of honour and country might never have taken place. About six weeks after, the Transvaal women left, they also were arrested, and a similar sentence to that passed upon the women of Natal, was passed upon them, and they were forcibly vaccinated. So these brave women were shut away from life, but the fight now so splendidly begun, went on.

A few days after the release of these last women, two gave birth to children, and another, a young girl of about twenty, passed away, and a third hovered between life and death for months, but the goal was won. Today, all these women are back in their homes and are busy in the usual routine of an Indian woman's life. There is absolutely none of the pride of heroism! about them. They are the same patient, dutiful women that India has produced for centuries; yet they endured the publicity, and no one who does not know India can understand how terrible to the Indian woman such publicity is. They endured the physical hardship, the mental sorrow, the heartache; for nearly all who did not take young children with them left young ones at home, endured hunger strikes, because they were deprived of fat to eat and sandals to put on — endured it all without harshness or bitterness. India has many things to be proud of, but of none more than the part the Indian women of South Africa took in the uplifting and recognition of a people here despised."

The foregoing account refers to a strike on the coal-mines. The organisation of a strike of the Indentured labourers was part and parcel of the scheme of the leaders for the final campaign. This strike and the famous march of the strikers to the Transvaal, we cannot better describe than in the words of an article entitled "That Wonderful March" in that self-same journal. It runs:

"The question of the repeal of the £3 tax had become argent already in 1908 and 1909, when an organisation had been formed for the purpose of securing it, and petitions widely signed had been sent to the then Natal Parliament, without other result than the passing of the ineffective Act of 1910, giving magistrates discretion — which some used, while others did not — to exempt certain classes of women in certain circumstances.

During his campaign in India, in 1909-10 and 1911-12, and his visit to England in 1911, Mr. Polak had pressed the question upon the attention of the people and Government of India and the British public, who had hitherto been ignorant as to the harsh incidence of the tax and grim misery that it entailed. Accordingly, when the Hon. Mr. Gokhale came to South Africa in 1912, and set himself to the task of examining Indian grievances on the spot, he immediately seized upon the tax as one that required and was capable of immediate remedy, and he, therefore, as he has told us, made special representations on the subject at the meeting of Ministers at Pretoria, when, he is positive, a definite undertaking was given him to repeal the tax. His efforts to that end had already been foreshadowed whilst he had travelled through the Union, and he had given assurances to vast crowds of those liable to the tax that he would not rest until he had secured its repeal, a resolve that had been much encouraged by the sympathetic speeches and conversations of prominent Natalians, both at the Durban banquet and at the subsequent Chamber of Commerce meeting. And these promises, fortified by the knowledge of what had transpired at Pretoria, Mr. Gandhi, upon his return from Zanzibar, whither he had accompanied Mr. Gokhale, repeated again and again in a responsible manner, to large numbers of those affected by the tax.

When, therefore, in 1913, a measure was introduced into the Union Parliament, at the end of the session, exempting women only from its operation, but requiring them to take out an annual licence, a message was sent to Mr. Gokhale in India requiring whether the promise of repeal had been limited to women. The reply was that it applied to all who were affected by the tax, and the Bill was promptly killed by Mr. Meyler and the late Sir David Hunter, who protested against its further progress, as they felt convinced that to pass it would be to delay total repeal indefinitely. Up to this time there had been no denial by the Government of the promise alleged.

At the rising of Parliament, Mr. Gandhi entered into fresh negotiations with the Union Government, reminding them of the promise, and asking for a definite undertaking of repeal of the tax in 1914. Meanwhile, in England, Mr. Polak, who had gone there at Mr. Gokhale's instance, had made it clear to the Imperial authorities and the British public that, whilst the repeal of the £3 tax had not previously formed part of the Passive Resistors' demands, the question had now become so acute, and Indian public feeling in South Africa had become so intense owing to what was regarded as the Union Government's breach of faith that, in the unfortunate event of the revival of the struggle, repeal of the tax would be made part and parcel of it. Lord Ampthill, too, after consulting with Mr. Gokhale, referred in explicit terms to the promise of repeal, in a portentous speech in the House of Lords. In the result, the Union Government declined to give an undertaking on the subject, though they still did not deny the promise, and the question therefore, formed one of the five points of Passive Resistance in Mr. A. M. Cachalia's letter of the 12th September, announcing the revival of the struggle. At the same time, Mr. Gokhale, in the face of the objections of his medical advisers, hurried back to India to rouse the Government and his fellow-country-men to action.

On September 28, and before any important activity had developed Mr. Gandhi addressed to the Secretary for the Interior a letter containing the following warning and appeal — "I know also what responsibility lies on my shoulders in advising such a momentous step, but I feel that it is not possible for me to refrain from advising a step which I consider to be necessary, to be of educational value, and, in the end, to be valuable both to the Indian community and to the State. This step consists in actively, persistently, and continuously asking those who are liable to pay the £3 tax to decline to do so and suffer the penalties for non-payment, and what is more important, in asking those who are now serving indenture and who will, therefore, be liable to pay the £3 tax upon the completion of their indenture, to strike work until the tax is withdrawn. I feel that in view of Lord Ampthill's declaration in the House of Lords, evidently with the approval of Mr. Gokhale, as to the definite promise made by the Government and repeated to Lord Gladstone, this advice to indentured Indians would be fully justified .... Can I not even now, whilst in the midst of the struggle, appeal to General Smuts and ask him to reconsider his decision .... on the question of the £3 tax?" The letter was shown to General Smuts who vouchsafed no reply, but who also did not even then repudiate the promise, nor did he warn the employers of the intentions of the Passive Resistance leaders. A fortnight later, in a statement circulated by Renter's Agency throughout the South African press, it was clearly stated that "the movement will also consist in advising indentured Indians to suspend work until the £3 Tax is removed. The indentured Indians will not be invited to join the general struggle." The public thus received ample warning of what was towards.

The Indian women who had joined the struggle as a protest against the refusal of the Government to legalise Indian marriages and who, as Passive Resisters, had unsuccessfully sought imprisonment at Vereeniging, Germiston and Volksrust, were allowed to pass into Natal unmolested, and the first steps taken to "call out" the Indians on the coal-mines in the northern part of the Province were due to the courage and devotion of these women, whose appearance there was almost in the nature of an accident. Under the guidance of Mr. C. K. T. Naidoo, they made Newcastle their headquarters, and, travelling from mine to mine, they made eloquent appeal to the Indian labourers and their families to cease work until an assurance of repeal of the tax was given by the Government. The response was immediate and general. Mine after mine was closed down, as the Indian labourers refused to work, and a state of panic ensued amongst the employers, who at first continued to give rations as an inducement to their employees to remain on the mines. A hurried conference of mine-owners was held at Durban, at which Mr. Gandhi was invited to be present, and he then explained the situation and referred to the promise made to Mr. Gokhale. He pointed out that the labourers were being asked to strike only so long as the £3 Tax was unrepealed, and because it had been alleged — an allegation that was subsequently discovered to be well-founded — that the employers were opposed to repeal.

The conference telegraphed to General Smuts enquiring about the promise, which was denied by him and by General Botha, for the first time; but it is significant that the late Mr. Fischer, who was also present at the meeting with the Ministers, did not repudiate it, though his physical condition did not preclude his doing so. Mr. Gokhale at once cabled, stating that a promise of repeal had undoubtedly been made to him, and, as a result of the hostile attitude now taken up by the Government and by the employers, the labourers were invited to leave the mines, where improper influences were being used to induce them to return to work. Mr. Gandhi placed himself at the head of a vast commissariat organisation, and, together with a small body of assistants, chief of whom was Mr. Albert Christopher, and with the cooperation of Mr. Kallenbach, the Indians — men, women and children — were fed and maintained at Newcastle, where they flocked by the hundred, coming by road and rail as fast as they could leave the mines, with the result that the latter, from Dundee and Ladysmith to Newcastle, were denuded of their labour supply. It was a pathetic and yet a cheering sight to watch these patient hundreds plodding slowly along muddy roads, in inclement weather, to the Newcastle centre, where they lived on a handful of rice, bread, and sugar a day, in the open, without shelter, without cooking accommodation beyond what they improvised on the bare veld, without comfort of any kind. But they were buoyed up with a great hope, and they had an inspiring leader. Mr. Kallenbach, too, fought their battles for them with the Newcastle municipality and magistracy, and later they saw how Mr. Gandhi shared their daily life and hardships, nursed the sick, and fed the hungry. They knew that the Indian women, who had urged them to strike, were cheerfully suffering imprisonment with hard labour, for their sake, and they felt in honour bound to struggle on until they had secured the repeal of the tax that weighed so heavily upon so many of them. And the women amongst them were no less heroic than the men. One mother, whose little child died of exposure on the road to Newcastle, was heard to say: "We must not pine for the dead; it is the living for which we must work." Such a spirit ensured ultimate success.

As their members swelled, it was felt that the only possible method of compelling the Union Government to realise their responsibilities and assume charge was to march the whole of the strikers into the Transvaal, there to court arrest and imprisonment, and it was accordingly decided to concentrate at Charles-town, the border village, where Messrs. Vallabhai and Mukhdoom rendered great service. At the head of a large "army," therefore, Mr. Gandhi marched there on October 30th, but just before the march commenced, a number of strikers were arrested and removed to the gaols after sentence of imprisonment. Day by day hundreds more marched to or entrained for Charlestown, where a vast camp was organised, under the sanitary control of the District Health Officer, Dr. Briscoe, and rations, that were pouring in from Durban and Johannesburg Indian merchants, to which were added supplies purchased with money that was being cabled in large sums from India, were daily distributed to a gathering of men, women and children that numbered finally over 3,000.

Meanwhile, Mr. Gandhi had telegraphed the intentions of the "invaders" to the Government, who apparently took no notice of the warning. Simultaneously, efforts were made, without success, by the Deputy Protector to induce the strikers to return to work, and large batches of them were arrested, and eventually imprisoned.

At last, a week after the notification, Mr. Gandhi commenced the now famous "invasion" of the Transvaal, with a following of over 2,000. The women and children were left behind at Charlestown, in charge of Miss Schlesin and Mr. Kallenbach, who worked day and night to make their lot somewhat easier. At the border, the "army" came to a stand, whilst Mr. Gandhi, who was near the rear, having remained behind to make final arrangements, came forward to interview the police officer who, with a small patrol, was on duty at the gate of entry.

Whilst these preliminaries were in train, the main body became impatient, and a mass of cheering, shouting Indians, clad in ragged clothes, and bearing their pitifully small belongings upon their heads, swarmed through the streets of Volksrust, determined to do or die, brushing the handful of police aside like so many helpless and insignificant atoms. They encamped on the farther side of the town, and the great march had commenced. The programme was to march, at the rate of some 25 miles a day, until the men were arrested, or Tolstoy Farm, at Lawley, near Johannesburg, was reached, and the Government were informed of each stopping-place. Eight days were set aside to reach their destination, unless they were earlier arrested, and, from the swing and energy of their marching, it was plain that a phenomenal feat was being performed by men, many of them heavily burdened, unused to conditions of "war" but accustomed to hard and simple life, and on a meagre and unusual diet. That night they reached Palmford, where special accommodation was offered to Mr. Gandhi, who, however, refused to accept hospitality which his humbler countrymen could not share.

Meanwhile, the Government were not altogether idle, but with that stupidity which almost invariably characterises governments in similar emergencies, they did the wrong thing, and issued a warrant for the arrest of Mr. Gandhi, hoping thus to demoralise the forces that he was leading. Mr. Gandhi surrendered to the warrant of Palmford, having, at the request of the authorities, pointed out some of his own followers to give evidence for him, as the Crown would not otherwise have been able to prove its case against him! He was motored swiftly to Volksrust, but the "army" silently and grimly pursued its march undeterred by the loss of its revered leader. At Voslksrust, Mr. Gandhi was charged with breach of the Immigration Act and applied for bail, as he was in charge of large numbers of men entirely dependent upon him, and his application was granted. Realising, however, the probable risks that would ensure if the people were left leader-less he addressed the following telegram to the Minister of the Interior:

> "Whilst I appreciate the fact of Government having at last arrested prime mover in passive resistance struggle, cannot help remarking that from point view humanity moment chosen most unfortunate. Government probably know that marchers include 122 women, 50 tender children, all voluntarily marching on starvation rations without provision for shelter during stages. Tearing me away under such circumstances from them is violation all considerations justice. When arrested last night, left men without informing them. They might become infuriated. I therefore, ask either that I may be allowed continue march with men, or Government send them by rail Tolstoy Farm and provide full rations for them. Leaving them without one in whom they have confidence, and without Government making provision for them, is, in my opinion, an act from which I hope on reconsideration Government will recoil. If untoward incidents happen during further progress march, or if deaths occur, especially amongst women with babies in arms, responsibility will be Government's."

No reply was returned to this humane appeal, but it was understood that the Government had no intention of assuming charge of this large body of men, women and children. Writing at the time of Mr. Gandhi's arrest, the special correspondent of the Natal Mercury sent his paper the following vivid description of the conditions prevailing both then and earlier at Charlestown:

> "We arrived at Palmford about 8:30 p.m. last night, and found them all sleeping in the veld, just below the station. Many of them were feeling the cold severely ... I visited Charlestown twice on the 5th (the day before the march commenced). The whole appearance of the town resembled nothing but an Indian bazar. The town was crowded with Indians... No sanitary arrangements were made at first, and the position from a health point of view was awful; but later Mr. Gandhi assisted the municipal officials, and the position was greatly improved. I found Mr. Gandhi at the back of an Indian store, in the yard, serving out curry and rice to his followers, who marched up and each man received his quota. One baker sold 5,000 loaves to the Indians in one day."

Mr. Gandhi, upon his release on bail, swiftly motored back to his followers, rejoining them on the march, which proceeded quietly as far as Paardeberg, where the remaining women and children were left behind in charge of a few of the men, who had become footsore. The main body reached Standerton on the morning of the 8th, where a number of strikers were arrested by their compound managers, assisted by a few police, and entrained for Natal. And here, too, Mr. Gandhi was re-arrested on the same charge as before. He again requested bail, and owing to the attitude of the strikers, who persistently refused to move from the Court precincts until their leader was restored to them, his request was granted, and the march was resumed immediately.

Sunday, the 9th, was an historic day. With a view to a final consultation with him before leaving for India, Mr. Polak had telegraphed to Mr. Gandhi, saying that he was joining him, and had received a wire suggesting Greylingstad as the meeting place, but with the warning that he (Mr. Polak) might be arrested if he came. He joined the column at a small place named Teakworth, a few miles on the Standerton side of Greylingstad. The "army, spread along the road for a distance of some three miles, was led by a small, limping, bent, but dogged man, coarsely dressed, and using a staff, with a serene and peaceful countenance, however, and a look of sureness and content. That was Gandhi, the principal Passive Resister. The two friends greeted each other, and eagerly exchanged news. Whilst thus engaged, and when about an hour distant from Greylingstad not far ahead was seen a Cape cart, and walking rapidly towards them were a couple of police officers, behind whom came Mr. M. Chamney, the Principal Immigration Officer of the Transvaal. Realising the pacific nature of the demonstration and of the Indian leader's intentions, Mr. Chamney had complimented Mr. Gandhi by undertaking his arrest upon a warrant issued under the Natal Indenture Law with no stronger support than this.

The Cape cart, with its precious freight, drove swiftly away, and the column resumed its march quietly, under the leadership of Mr. Polak, who had at once assumed the responsibility, preceded by the two mounted policemen. A few minutes later, Messrs. Cachalia and Bhyat, who, together with Mr. Badat of Volksrust, were in charge of the commissariat arrangements, of which Mr. Polak was in entire ignorance, joined the column, having accidentally missed it in, on another road, and they at once proceeded to Balfour, where it was due next morning and where food supplies were awaiting its arrival. The evening was fine and clear, and the cooking-fires that were lit from end to end of the veldt offered a bright and sparkling spectacle. Gradually, the buzz and throb of conversation sank, as sleep fell upon the camp. The night, however, was dismal and wretched, a cold wind howled mournfully down from the neighbouring hills, and a drizzle of rain added to the discomfort of the shelter-less throng.

But the night was portentous, for it was decreed that the march should end on the morrow, though of this the marchers were as yet unaware. At four in the morning it was resumed, and the moving mass of heroic men swung forward into their stride, covering the ground at a splendid pace, and, laden as they were, without waggons and without food, they travelled the distance between Greylingstad and Balfour, 13 miles in 3 ½ hours. Upon reaching the latter place without any police escort, just before 9 a.m., it became evident that the last stage had been reached, for three special trains were drawn up at the station to take back the strikers to Natal. Mr. Polak was approached by the Police Officer in charge of the arrangements, and by Mr. Chamney, to cooperate with them in effecting the arrest of the "army," and upon receiving their assurance that the men were really to be sent to Natal, where criminal proceedings were awaiting them, he replied that he would gladly do so as the whole object of the march had thus been fulfilled, and his own responsibility ceased. At the same time, he offered himself for arrest also, but he was informed that the Government did not desire this. He, however, warned the officials that, in Mr. Gandhi's enforced absence, it might be difficult for him to induce compliance with their desire, as but few of the men had ever seen him before. Mr. Gandhi, however, was passing through from Heideberg, *en route* for Dundee, where he was subsequently imprisoned, and sent a message urging the people quietly to surrender.

They were fed as rapidly as food could be supplied to them — a handful of rice and bread each — and then Mr. Chamney, having questioned them as to their proofs of rights of residence, proclaimed them prohibited immigrants. For the moment, chaos prevailed, as a number of stalwarts, who had set their hearts upon reaching Johannesburg, called upon the multitude to march forward, but instantly realising the danger of this movement, which, whilst it would have resulted in bloodshed, would have swept aside the small band of twenty-five policemen in the twinkling of an eye, and let loose an uncontrolled body of men to roam over the Transvaal, who would not afterwards probably have been located. Mr. Polak, followed by Messrs.

Cachalia and Bhyat, rushed to the head of the column and implored the people to remember that their object, as passive resisters, was not Johannesburg but gaol, and eventually peace was restored. Gradually, and in small groups, the men entrained, Mr. Polak accompanying the first train as far as Charlestown, where he was shortly afterwards arrested. Here, the strikers having been locked up without food or water for eight hours, the trains were not allowed to remain more than a couple of minutes, the platform being occupied by armed police, who kept back the women that had remained there and now urged their men-folk, with tears in their eyes and chocking voices, not to mind them but to remain true to their duty. And slowly the trains steamed south, bearing nearly two thousand humble heroes to a bitter fate and a shameful experience, but firm in the knowledge that they had done what they had set out to do, and that the repeal of the hated tax was now certain. The great and impressive march was over.

The Times has since declared that it must live in memory as one of the most remarkable manifestations in history of the spirit of Passive Resistance. It had achieved all that its organisers, in their fondest dreams, had hoped for it. It had proclaimed, as nothing else could have done, the stubborn endurance, the dogged persistency, the grim tenacity, the stern determination, the magnificent self-sacrifice of the Passive Resisters. And it assured success. It was not a defeat, as the shallow critics had at the time proclaimed it. Had the strikers not exercised, under the guidance of trusted leaders, immense self-control — there was no pillage, no disorder, no violence — all the forces that the Government had brought against them could not have prevented their swarming over the Transvaal. But it was the glorious ending of a peaceful demonstration of workers determined upon achieving freedom for themselves, their wives, their children. A splendid victory for Truth had been won. The honour of the Indian Motherland had been vindicated. Mr. Gokhale's word had been made good.

And the sign of this is to be found in the work of Messrs. Andrews and Pearson, the report of the Commission, its acceptance by the Government, the debates in Parliament, and the passing of Act 22 of 1914, repealing the £3 Tax for ever and granting freedom of residence in Natal to those who choose to remain unindentured. The real victory is that of the soul-force of the marchers, starving, weary, but buoyed up with unconquerable hope, over the brute-force of those who had declared their intention at all costs to maintain them in a condition of perpetual helot age."

Thus, ended the great march. The majesty of the law was once more vindicated by the arrest, trial and imprisonment of thousands.

Mr. Gandhi himself who as the account quoted above mentions, had been arrested at Volksrust and released on bail, was subsequently tried and sentenced to fifteen months. At the trial he delivered himself as follows: Addressing the Court at Volksrust, Mr. Gandhi said that he had given the Minister of the Interior due notice of his intention to cross the border with the prohibited immigrants and had informed the Immigration Officer at Volksrust of the date of crossing. He assured the Court that the present movement had nothing whatever to do with the unlawful entry of a single Indian for the purpose of residence in the Transvaal. He might fairly claim that during his whole career in the Transvaal he had been actuated by a desire to assist the Government in preventing surreptitious entry and unlawful settlement, but he pleaded guilty to knowingly committing an offence against the Section under which he was charged. He was aware that his action was fraught with the greatest risks and intense personal suffering to his followers. He was convinced that nothing short of much suffering would move the conscience of the Governor, or of the inhabitants of the Union, of which, in spite of this breach of the laws, he claimed to be a sane and law-abiding citizen.

The strike on the coal-mines had meanwhile spread to the sugar plantations in Natal. A savage attempt was made to suppress it and in the attempt some of the strikers were shot dead, and several injured.

The cup of suffering was now full to the brim. Resentment in India had reached white heat. The Government of India were alarmed at the situation. And Lord Hardinge then Viceroy of India, in his famous speech at Madras, placed himself at the head of Indian public opinion and asked for the appointment of a commission to institute a searching enquiry into the whole matter. The Imperial Authorities also bestirred themselves as they had never done before. And the authors of the policy which had led to such incalculable misery and bitterness now for the first time showed likewise unmistakable signs of relenting by acceding to the demand for the commission of enquiry.

But when it was actually constituted with Sir William Solomon as President, its composition rendered it so dubious that the Indian leaders resolved to ignore it altogether. It was at this crisis of affairs that the well-known missionary gentlemen, the Rev. Messrs. Andrews and Pearson, true children of the Man of Sorrows paid a visit to South Africa and by their persistent endeavours in influential circles were able to diffuse a healing spirit. All is well that ends well. The findings of the Solomon commission were favourable to the Indian community on all points referred to it for report. Its recommendations were endorsed without reservation by the Union Government and given effect to by the subsequent passing of the Indians Relief Act. This gave satisfaction to the Indian Community and Mr. Gandhi formally announced the closing of the struggle. It will be interesting at this stage to take stock of the results achieved by the concentrated suffering of eight long years. But we shall miss its significance if we do not grasp clearly at the outset that the battle was from first to last a moral and spiritual one, and was waged not for the compassing of material ends but for the vindication of manhood. And from this point of view it surely realised its purpose in a measure that the great protagonists of the movement themselves could not at first have dreamed of.

The struggle was the means, the struggle was the end. To those who have known the intensity of aspiration and elevation of character that made the fight possible the talk of material results must ever seem a pitiful meanness. Such have received the initiation of the highest self-knowledge. They have been face to face with that mood of the soul which sights nothing but endless horizons of spiritual endeavour and achievement. They have known that the life of the ordinary selfish man is not the real life but that deep within everyone high or low sleeps a heaven into which some day we shall all awake.

Furthermore they have created for their children and their children's children the priceless memory of a heroic past. And down to the remotest generations will linger the pride of how the forefathers braved the fury of the persecutor and staked their all for nothing but their own honour. Nay shall not the motherland herself treasure for ever the story of the deeds of the humblest of her children in a far away land as it has treasured the legend of Rama and Sita, or that of the Pandava brothers ? Will not humanity itself the world over feel a quickened sense of as it peruses the same golden record ? Has not another chapter been added to the world's Acts of the Apostles ?

Let us now reckon the tale of the martyrs to whom it was given to give their lives to the cause. There was that young girl, Valiamma of whom Mr. Gandhi has said: "Simpleminded in faith she had not the knowledge that he had, she did not know what passive resistance was, she did not know what it was the community would gain, but she was simply taken up with unbounded enthusiasm for her people — went to gaol, came out of it a wreck, and within a few days died." There were the two youths from the Tamil land, Nagappan and Narayanaswamy — the former died shortly after his release from prison, and the latter at Delgoa Bay after having vainly attempted to land in South Africa as already told. And lastly there was the old man Harbatsingh, a Hindustani stalwart who went to gaol as a passive resister when he was seventy-five, and who when questioned by Mr. Gandhi why he had come, had answered. "What does it matter ? I know what you are fighting for. You have not to pay the £3 tax but my fellow ex-indentured Indians have to pay that tax, and what more glorious death could I meet? And he met his death in the gaol at Durban.

Coming lower down the scale, the feeling of contempt for the 'coloured man' which had so long possessed the white settlers had yielded place to one of respect and admiration. The instinct of race-superiority has been knocked out of at least the better mind of the Union. The principle of differentiation on racial grounds has disappeared. The livery of manhood shines in place of the badge of servitude. Unfading lustre has been reflected upon the name of the mother-country, and an invaluable contribution made to the life of Indian Nationalism.

And last but not least, the struggle has removed the mask from the small emaciated figure known to the world as Mohandas Karamchand Gandhi, and set him before the world in his true lineaments — a moral giant, a spiritual hero, and a peerless soldier of God.

The material fruits of the struggle were in themselves by no means inconsiderable. The hated law which started the whole trouble was repealed. The £3 tax has been abolished. The recognition of Indian marriages has been secured. The system of indentured immigration has been put an end to. And most important of all, the passing of further laws intended to drive out the Indians from South Africa, which would certainly have followed, was nipped in the bud. But of none of these gains could it be said that it was wholly material.

There are still great disabilities under which the Indian resident of the Union has to labour. These we shall enumerate in the words of Mr. Gandhi himself: "There was still the gold law which had many a sting in it. There was still the Licensing laws throughout the Union which also contained many a sting. There was still a matter which the colonial born Indians could not understand or appreciate, namely, the water-tight compartments in which they had to live; whilst there was free inter-communication and inter-migration between the provinces for the Europeans, Indians had to be cooped up in their respective provinces. Then there was undue restraint on their trading activity. There was the prohibition as to their holding landed property in the Transvaal which was degrading and all these things took Indians into all sorts of undesirable channels." Further the Indians have yet to be admitted to the political franchise. The sympathy which takes an equal interest in all classes of the ruled is still far distant. And lastly the practical stoppage of immigration from India has deprived the South African Indians of that opportunity of living intercourse with the mother country which he cannot but value so highly. These and like wrongs will have to be set right in the future, God grant without the necessity of similar struggles!

The sense of triumph and rejoicing which marked the closing of the memorable struggle was mingled by the sadness of the thought that the great central figure, the genius and inspirer of the whole movement, the redeemer and Avatar of the Indian community in South Africa was soon to depart to the motherland for ever. Heightened a thousandfold was the pathos of farewell which in this case is best left to the imagination. His mission accomplished, the conquering hero returned to his native land in the faith, as he has said, that it is in India that the nearest approach to perfection is most possible."

Welcome Home

The welcome accorded to Mr. Gandhi on his return home, was characterised by all the warmth, affection, and delicate reverence which India alone of all lands knows to offer to the great soul. Since his return to this country he has been mainly devoting himself to a personal study and comprehension of the problems with which a great and ancient civilization in process of transition to a new order necessarily teems. For this purpose, he has been going about from place to place, making the acquaintance of people of all grades and conditions, and coming into contact with the leaders of thought and activity. A man's character is written in his slightest acts and when during the early days of his arrival in this countryi he was seen alighting from a third class compartment, at Howrah station, while the elite of Calcutta, assembled on the platform, were making a search for him in the first and second-class compartments, almost a sensation was caused. This was no vanity of humility on his part but proceeded from the firm resolve not to stain himself by any luxury which is not accessible to the poorest in the land. It was simply that passionate determination to one himself with the sorrows of the lowest and meanest of which his daily life — is so eloquent an expression. And recently, he has become the fiery champion of the woes of the third-class passenger! In his eyes there is no wrong so trivial as to be unworthy of his earnest attention and striving. Such is the spirit that he has brought to the task of nation-making in this land.

There was again that incident at the opening of the Hindu University, when the platform was crowded with Rajahs and Maharajahs, and Mr. Gandhi made a speech at which several people left the meeting construing his words to be disloyal. It was sheer misunderstanding, as it afterwards turned out, of the spirit of a man whose whole life is a consuming effort to throw out of himself the very seed of hatred and every slightest motion of mind or heart which could have the shadow of any reaction of evil.

The Champaran incident is still fresh in the mind of the public and requires no elaboration. He had gone there on invitation to undertake an enquiry as to the conditions of the labourers in the Indigo plantations and the treatment meted out to them by their employers. The District Magistrate of Champaran took it into his head that his presence was a serious danger to the district and would lead to a breach of the peace. And he had an order served upon Mr. Gandhi to the effect that the latter was to leave the district by the next available train.' Mr. Gandhi replied that he had come there out of a sense of duty and would stay and submit to the penalty of disobedience. At the trial that followed he simply pleaded guilty, and made a statement that he was faced by a conflict of duty, the duty of obeying the law and the duty of enquiry upon which he had come, and that under the circumstances he could only throw the responsibility of removing him on the administration. The Magistrate postponed judgement till some hours later in the day, and at the interview with the District Magistrate the same day he undertook not to go out to the village till instructions were received from the provincial administration. The case was adjourned to some days later, and the higher authorities subsequently issued instructions not to proceed with the prosecution. Some of the planters took the occasion to make a rabid attack upon Mr. Gandhi, but the recently published report of the Champaran commission of enquiry which was the immediate result of his visit has amply justified him.

The idea of a monster petition to the authorities from the people was not new in the modern political history of India. But when Mr. Gandhi revived the suggestion in connection with the Congress-Muslim-League scheme of reform, the moment was most opportune and the ideà caught like magic. He himself undertook the propaganda in his own province of Gujarat and carried it out with characteristic thoroughness. The true patriot can never be idle, neither can he ever rest on his oars.

Mr. Gandhi firmly believed that a common language is indispensable for India's unification, and ' Hindi is in his opinion best fitted to serve this purpose. And accordingly it is one of the objects of the Satyagrahasrama to promote and popularise the use of this vernacular as a medium of communication all over the country. And one of Mr. Gandhi's sons has recently settled at Madras and opened classes in Hindi. The life of the practical idealist is ever full of striking episodes and object-lessons. And when in April last Mr. Gandhi at the Delhi War Conference opened his address in English and closed it in Hindi, a thrill must have passed over that august assemblage, as of something sublimely audacious and unconventional.

Mr. Gandhi's now famous 4 fast' is too fresh in the minds of our countrymen to require more than a passing mention. The millhands in Ahmedabad struck work and demanded an increase of wages which their masters refused to give. Mr. Gandhi appeared on the scene and strove to bring about an amicable settlement, but all his efforts were in vain. He thereupon decided and declared his resolve, to abstain from all food, and fast to death, if need be, till the matter should be satisfactorily settled. And after he had fasted for some days (three days, we believe,) the millowners relented and acceded to the demands of the workers, and the strike and the fast came to an end.

Memorable Movement

The first great and memorable movement inspired by Mr. Gandhi in India was undeniably the Passive Resistance Movement in Kaira which came to an end but two months ago. To give anything like an adequate account of this movement would require a volume by itself. Here we can deal with it only in its barest outlines. There was serious and widespread failure of crops in the district of Kaira, in Gujarat, in the year 1916-17. It was a calamity of the first magnitude. Under the revenue rules the riots were entitled to suspension of the full revenue for one year if the yield was less than four annas in the rupee, and to half-suspension, if it was between four annas and six annas.

Now the authorities granted full suspension in the case of one village only out of a total of 600 villages, half-suspension with regard to 104 villages, and issued orders for the collection of the full revenue with regard to the rest. It was claimed on behalf of the riots that the Government was wrong in its estimate of the out-turn, and that the relief granted was utterly inadequate to meet the requirements of the situation. Mr. Gandhi, Mr. V. J. Patel and others conducted an enquiry with regard to the vast majority of villages and invited the Government to appoint a Committee or do something to ascertain the true extent and dimensions of the calamity. They interviewed the authorities major and minor, held meetings, passed resolutions. But petition, prayer and protest were of no avail.

The collection of revenue with the aid of coercive processes went merrily on. It was now that Mr. Gandhi sounded amidst the poor illiterate peasants of Kaira the trumpet of Satyagraha. His was now the same ringing call for the assertion of manhood which he had uttered to his compatriots in South Africa. What was the problem as it presented itself to the mind of Mr. Gandhi ? Was it simply a question of securing for the riots an year's respite from the payment of revenue ? By no means. To him the problem was far deeper, it was moral and spiritual.

The Government was in this case in the wrong, and the governed in the right; and the former had treated the representations of the latter with cool disdain. On the one side the Almighty Sircar, on the other the dumb riots cowering in abject terror. How long was this to go on ? The riots must learn to shake off their mortal dread of the Sircar and feel themselves to be entities. And how were they to do it ? Not by disorder, not by rebellion, but by wielding that most potent of all weapons — the weapon not of the weak but of the spiritually strong — the weapon of suffering. No power can deprive a man of his right and privilege of suffering. And by suffering, suffering and suffering to the uttermost, powers and principalities shall be overthrown. It is in this faith that Mr. Gandhi lives and works. It is this gospel that he now preached to the Kaira peasants. "Don't pay the revenue; submit to all penalties. Hold fast to truth. Enter ye the kingdom of Satyagraha "was his exhortation to them. And the response elicited showed that these peasants had the same stuff of heroism in them, the same perception of spiritual truths, the same instinct of idealism and the same readiness to sacrifice all for an idea that had distinguished the passive resisters in South Africa. About 2,500 of the riots, men and women, took the vow of Satyagraha and declined to pay the revenue.

The authorities on their part coaxed and threatened in turn. A relentless campaign of attachments was set on foot. Cattle, domestic utensils, ornaments, whatever chattels were available, were put under writ. But the spirit of the passive resisters continued unshaken. Wisdom dawned upon the authorities at last, and they issued orders that the collection of the revenue would be suspended for a year, and that at the same time the Government expected payment from such as were able to pay. The attachments were withdrawn and the struggle closed amidst scenes of pathos and rejoicing. England is proud of its Pyms and Hampdens, What cause for pride has India not got in the heroism of these humble peasants of Kaira who embraced suffering in a mood and spirit to which Pyms and Hampdens of English history were strangers!

But far the most pregnant act of his in India has been the establishment of the Satyagrahasrama. As its name signifies, it stands for truth, truth as the highest consideration of all, truth in thought, word and deed. Its members have likewise to take the vow of celibacy, the vow of control of the palate, the vow of non-thieving, the vow of Swadeshi, the vow of fearlessness, and the vow of redeeming the untouchables in India. That education should be imparted through the vernaculars is also one of its cardinal principles. The Ashram is thus the nucleus of a great new order for the perfecting of the individual and the uplifting of the nation.

It is as the embodiment of Saty a gratia, as a veritable lamp burning upon the altar, that Mohandas Karamchand Gandhi stands today before his countrymen. Truth-force or love-force, as he himself has translated the term into English, is to him the greatest of all powers. In proportion as individuals and nations alike fulfil the law of this power and fit themselves into it they live and grow: the rest is death.

The delicacy of insight and vision, the force of character, and all the virtues which have thrown a mantle of splendour over his name are but the fruit of this central realisation carried into action. It would be vain to speculate as to what he would have become had his life been cast in other places than South Africa. God sends his chosen servants to do the work appointed for them. It is ours to recognise them.

2

Mahatma's Journey

Mahatma Gandhi, Father of the Nation, Mohandas Karamchand Gandhi (2 October 1869 - 30 January 1948) was a major political and spiritual leader of India and the Indian Independence Movement. He was the pioneer of Satyagraha — resistance to tyranny through mass civil disobedience, firmly founded upon *ahimsa* or total non-violence — which led India to independence and inspired movements for civil rights and freedom across the world. He is commonly known in India and across the world as Mahatma Gandhi (Mahatma or "Great Soul", an epithet given by Rabindranath Tagore) and as Bapu (Bapu or "Father"). In India, he is officially accorded the honour of Father of the Nation. 2 October, his birthday, is commemorated each year as Gandhi Jayanti, a national holiday. On 15 June 2007, the United Nations General Assembly unanimously adopted a resolution declaring 2 October to be the "International Day of Non-Violence".

Gandhi first employed non-violent civil disobedience in South Africa, in the resident Indian community's struggle for civil rights. Upon his return to India, he organised poor farmers and labourers to protest oppressive taxation and widespread discrimination. Assuming leadership of the Indian National Congress, Gandhi led nationwide campaigns for the alleviation of poverty, for the liberation of women, for brotherhood amongst different religious and ethnic groups, for an end to untouchability and caste discrimination, and for the economic self-sufficiency of India, but above all for Swaraj — the independence of India from foreign domination. Gandhi famously led Indians first in the disobedience of the British-imposed salt tax with the 400 kilometres (249 miles) Dandi Salt March in 1930, and later in an open call for the British to Quit India in 1942. He was imprisoned for many years, on numerous occasions, in both South Africa and India.

Gandhi practised non-violence and truth in all situations, and advocated that others do the same. He lived simply, organising an ashram that was self-sufficient in its needs. Making his own clothes — the traditional Indian dhoti and shawl, woven with yarn he hand spun on a charkha — he lived on a simple vegetarian diet; he also undertook long fasts as forms of both self-purification and social protest.

In January 1948, before three pistol shots put an end to his life, Gandhi had been on the political stage for more than fifty years. He had inspired two generations of India, patriots, shaken an empire and sparked off a revolution which was to change the face of Africa and Asia. To millions of his own people, he was the Mahatma-the great soul-whose sacred glimpse was a reward in itself. By the end of 1947 he had lived down much of the suspicion, ridicule and opposition which he had to face, when he first raised the banner of revolt against racial exclusiveness and imperial domination. His ideas, once dismissed as quaint and utopian, had begun to strike answering chords in some of the finest minds in the world. "Generations to come, it may be", Einstein had said of Gandhi in July 1944, "will scarcely believe that such one as this ever in flesh and blood walked upon earth."

Though his life had been continual unfolding of an endless drama, Gandhi himself seemed to be the least dramatic of men. It would be difficult to imagine a man with fewer trappings of political eminence or with less of the popular image of a heroic figure. With his loin cloth, steel-rimmed glasses, rough sandals, a toothless smile and a voice which rarely rose above a whisper, he had a disarming humility. He used a stone instead of soap for his bath, wrote his letters on little bits of paper with little stumps of pencils which he could hardly hold between his fingers, shaved with a crude country razor and ate with a wooden spoon from a prisoner's bowl. He was, if one were to use the famous words of the Buddha, a man who had "by rousing himself, by earnestness, by restraint and control, made for himself an island which no flood could overwhelm."

Gandhi's, deepest strivings were spiritual, but he did not-as had been the custom in his country-retire to a cave in the Himalayas to seek his salvation. He carried his cave within him. He did not know, he said, any religion apart from human activity; the spiritual law did not work in a vacuum, but expressed itself through the ordinary activities of life. This aspiration to relate the spirit-not the forms-of religion to the problems of everyday life runs like a thread through Gandhi's career; his uneventful childhood, the slow unfolding and the near-failure of his youth, reluctant plunge into the politics of Natal, the long, unequal struggle in South Africa, and the vicissitudes of the Indian struggle for freedom, which under his leadership was to culminate in a triumph not untinged with tragedy.

Birth and Early Days

Mohandas Gandhi was born on October 2,1869, at Porbandar, on the western coast of India. His grandfather Uttamchand Gandhi and father Karamchand Gandhi occupied the high office of the diwan (Chief Minister) of Porbandar. To be Diwan of one of the princely states was a sinecure. Porbandar was one of some three hundred 'native' states in western India which were ruled by Princes whom the accident of birth and the support of the British kept on the throne. To steer one's course safely between wayward Indian Princes, the overbearing British 'Political Agent' of the suzerain power and the long-suffering subjects required a high degree of patience, diplomatic skill and commonsense. Both Uttamchand and Karamchand were good administrators. But they were also upright and honourable men. Loyal to their masters, they did not flinch from offering unpalatable advice. They paid the price for the courage of their convictions. Uttamchand Gandhi had his house besieged and shelled by the ruler's troops and had to flee the State; his son Karamchand also preferred to leave Porbandar, rather than compromise with his principles.

Karamchand Gandhi was, in the words of his son, "a lover of his clan, truthful, brave, generous." The strongest formative influence on young Mohandas, however, was that of his mother Putlibai. She was a capable woman who made herself felt in court circles through her friendship with the ladies of the palace, but her chief interest was in the home. When there was sickness in the family, she wore herself out in days and nights of nursing. She had little of the weaknesses, common to women of her age and class, for finery or jewellery. Her life was an endless chain of fasts and vows through which her frame seemed to be borne only by the strength of her faith.

The children clung to her as she divided her day between the home and the temple. Her fasts and vows puzzled and fascinated them. She was not versed in the scriptures; indeed except for a smattering of Gujarati, she was practically unlettered. But her abounding love, her endless austerities and her iron will, left a permanent impression upon Mohandas, her youngest son. The image of woman he imbibed from his mother was one of love and sacrifice. Something of her maternal love he came to possess himself, and as he grew, it flowed out in an ever-increasing measure, bursting the bonds of family and community, until it embraced the whole of humanity. To his mother, he owed not only a passion for nursing which later made him wash leper's sores in his ashram, but also an inspiration for his techniques of appealing to the heart through self-suffering — a technique which wives and mothers have practised from time immemorial.

Young Mohandas' school career was undistinguished. He did not shine in the classroom or in the playground. Quiet, shy and retiring, he was tongue-tied in company. He did not mind being rated as a mediocre student, but he was exceedingly jealous of his reputation. He was proud of the fact that he had never told a lie to his teachers or classmates; the slightest aspersion on his character drew his tears.

Like most growing children he passed through a rebellious phase, but contrary to the impression fostered by his autobiography, Gandhi's adolescence was no stormier than that of many of his contemporaries. Adventures into the forbidden land of meat-eating and smoking and petty pilfering were, and are not uncommon among boys of his age. What was extraordinary was the way his adventures ended. In every case when he had gone astray, he posed for himself a problem for which he sought a solution by framing a proposition in moral algebra. 'Never again' was his promise to himself after each escapade. And he kept the promise.

As said earlier, Mohandas Karamchand Gandhi was born in Porbandar, a coastal town in present-day Gujarat, Western India, on October 2, 1869. His father, Karamchand Gandhi, who belonged to the Hindu Modh community, was the diwan (Prime Minister) of the eponymous Porbandar state, a small princely state in the Kathiawar Agency of British India. His mother, Putlibai, who came from the Hindu Pranami Vaishnava community, was Karamchand's fourth wife, the first two wives having apparently died in childbirth. Growing up with a devout mother and the Jain traditions of the region, the young Mohandas absorbed early the influences that would play an important role in his adult life; these included, compassion to sentient beings, vegetarianism, fasting for self-purification, and mutual tolerance between individuals of different creeds.

In May 1883, at the age of 13, Gandhi was married through his parents' arrangements to Kasturba Makhanji (also spelled "Kasturbai" or known as "Ba"). They had five children, the first of whom died in infancy; Harilal Gandhi, born in 1888; Manilal Gandhi, born in 1892; Ramdas Gandhi, born in 1897; and Devdas Gandhi, born in 1900. Gandhi was a mediocre student in his youth at Porbandar and later Rajkot. He barely passed the matriculation exam for Samaldas College at Bhavnagar, Gujarat. He was also unhappy at the college, because his family wanted him to become a barrister.

At the age of 18 on 4 September 1888, Gandhi went to University College London to study law and train as a barrister. His time in London, the Imperial capital, was influenced by a vow he had made to his mother in the presence of the Jain monk Becharji, upon leaving India, to observe the Hindu precepts of abstinence from meat, alcohol, and promiscuity. Although, Gandhi experimented with adopting "English" customs — taking dancing lessons for example — he could not stomach his landlady's mutton and cabbage. She pointed him towards one of London's few vegetarian restaurants. Rather than simply go along with his mother's wishes, he read about, and intellectually embraced vegetarianism. He joined the Vegetarian Society, was elected to its executive committee, and founded a local chapter. He later credited this with giving him valuable experience in organising institutions. Some of the vegetarians he met were members of the Theosophical Society, which had been founded in 1875 to further universal brotherhood, and which was devoted to the study of Buddhist and Hindu literature. They encouraged Gandhi to read the Bhagavad Gita. Not having shown a particular interest in religion before, he read works of and about Hinduism, Christianity, Buddhism, Islam and other religions. He returned to India after being called to the bar of England and Wales by Inner Temple, but had limited success establishing a law practice in Bombay. Later, after applying and being turned down for a part-time job as a high school teacher, he ended up returning to Rajkot to make a modest living drafting petitions for litigants, but was forced to close down that business as well when he ran afoul of a British officer. In his autobiography, he describes this incident as a kind of unsuccessful lobbying attempt on behalf of his older brother. It was in this climate that (in 1893) he accepted a year-long contract from an Indian firm to a post in Natal, South Africa, then part of the British Empire.

Truthful and Religious Parents

'Gandhi' is a family name. The Gandhi's had been merchants for many years. They lived in a town called Porbandar. It now belongs to Gujarat State. The town had stone walls around it. As the stones shone in the sun, the town was known as 'Shwetapuri' (the White City).

Uttamchand Gandhi was the grandfather of Gandhiji. He was the Diwan or the Prime Minister or the Rana (ruler) of Porbandar. His son Karamchand Gandhi was Gandhiji's father. Gandhiji's full name was Mohandas Karamchand Gandhi. He was born on October 2, 1869.

Karamchand Gandhi was the Diwan of Porbandar State for some time, and later became the Diwan of Raikot State. Like his father, he too was an honest and a courageous man. His wife's name was Putlibai. Mohandas Karamchand Gandhi was their youngest son.

Karamchand Gandhi was a very practical man. Gandhiji describes his father in his autobiography as follows: 'My father was a lover of his clan, truthful, brave and generous.' Often there used to be readings from the Ramayana and the Mahabharata in his house. There used to be religious discussions also among Jain, Parsi and Muslim scholars. Young Gandhi listened to all this with attention.

Putlibai was in the habit of visiting temples every day. She used to take Gandhi also with her. She used to keep stern vows and fasts. Religious practices were her very life breath. Her influence on the son was great. Many years later, Gandhiji, recollecting his early years, said, 'If there is any purity in me, it is all due to my mother.' The son imbibed from his mother the qualities of service, sacrifice and affection for others.

Gandhi, as a Student

Young Gandhi had his primary education up to the seventh year at Porbandar. Then his education continued at Rajkot. Gandhi was a very shy boy. He never found fault with elders. He was very obedient.

Once an Inspector of Schools visited the school. The teacher dictated some English words. Gandhi had miss-spelt the word 'Kettle'. The teacher noticed this, and made signs to the boy to correct it by copying from his neighbour. But Gandhi did not do so. He also felt that the same teacher, who had taught him that copying was bad, was not right in prompting him to do so. Still, the respect he had for his teacher did not grow less.

At that time, Gandhi had occasion to see two plays. They were 'Shravana Pitribhakti' and 'Harishchandra'. These two plays left a deep impression on his mind. The devotion of Shravana to his aged parents was a model in itself. Harishchandra suffered great misery for the sake of truth. Gandhi began to consider if he could not also live like them.

On the plastic mind of the young, example and company act as powerful forces. When Gandhi joined the High school in his thirteenth year, he fell into evil company. But he soon realised his folly and returned to the right path.

Sheik Mehtab, a classmate of Gandhi, was a strong boy. He always excelled all the boys in games and sports. Gandhi came to believe that, in order to expel the English rulers from our country, it was necessary that one should become strong like Sheik by eating meat. This false belief took deep root in his mind. He tried to eat meat in secret. He found it distasteful. In the same way, he smoked cigarettes. He also stole a piece of gold to pay his brother's debts. He felt sad because he had not the freedom to act as he wished. In a moment of despair, he tried to kill himself, by swallowing Matura seeds (an effective poison). But he lost courage and could not do so. At last he felt sorry for his conduct. He confessed his guilt in a letter and, with trembling hands, handed it to his father. The father did not say even a word, and simply shed tears of sorrow. This melted Gandhi's heart. He touchingly refers to this incident in his autobiography: 'Those pearl-drops of love cleansed my heart, and washed my sin away.'

Gandhi was only an ordinary boy both in the Primary School and in the High School. No special qualities were seen in him. At school he never took part in any games. He would not even freely mix with his companions. The fear that somebody would make fun of him always filled his mind.

Great Force of Religion

Gandhi was married to Kastur Ba in his thirteenth year. Kastur Ba was also a girl of the same age. It was a case of childmarriage, and child marriage was accustom of those days. It was a marriage of two persons, who did not understand anything about it. The immediate result of this was that a year's studies were spoiled. By the time Gandhi's High School education ended, a child was born, and died, and another was born. A boy of fifteen or sixteen years had already become a father. By that time Gandhi's father also had passed away.

A Gujarati poem, by Shyamlal Bhat, that Gandhi read in deep impression on his mind. The lines were:

> For a bowl of water give a goodly meal;
> For a kindly greeting bow thou down with zeal;
> For simple penny pay thou back with gold;
> If thy life were rescued, life does not withhold.
>
> Thus, the words and actions of the wise regard;
> Every little service tenfold they reward.

But the truly noble know all men as one,
And return with gladness good for evil done.

This became the ideal of Gandhi's life. He understood that revenge was not true religion. He understood what the 'Religion of Humanity' was. He understood the great force of religion.

Off to England

Mohan passed the matriculation examination of Bombay University in 1887. His father's death a year earlier had strained the means of the family. Being the only boy in the family who had persevered in his studies, its hopes rested on him and he was sent to Bhavnagar, the nearest town with a college. Unfortunately for Mohan the teaching was in English. He was unable to follow the lectures and despaired of making any progress. Meanwhile, Mavji Dave, a friend of the family, suggested that Mohan should go to English to qualify at the bar. Mohan jumped at the idea of going abroad. His elder brother had no doubt that the proposal was attractive but wondered how they could afford it. His mother was reluctant to let her youngest boy sail to an alien land to face unknown temptations and dangers. The Modh Bania caste to which the Gandhis belonged, threatened to excommunicate the whole family if its injunction against foreign travel was infringed. All these hurdles were, however, successfully overcome by Mohan's determination to go abroad, and in September 1888, at the age of 18, he sailed for England.

From the rural surroundings of Rajkot to the cosmopolitan atmosphere of a steamship was a tremendous change for Mohan. Adaptation to Western food, dress and etiquette was a painful process. Both on board the ship and in London in the first few weeks, Mohan could not help feeling that he was making a fool of himself. He had promised his mother before leaving India that he would not "touch wine, woman or meat". The vegetarian vow became a continual source of embarrassment to him. His friends feared that his food fads would ruin his health, and make of him, socially, a square peg. To disarm his critics and to prove that, vegetarianism apart, he was not impervious to the new environment, he decided to put on a thick veneer of 'English culture'. Having made up his mind to become an 'English Gentleman', he spared neither time nor money. Whatever the cost, the veneer had to be the best in the market. New suits were ordered from the most fashionable tailors in London; the watch was adorned with a double gold chain from India; under expert tuition, lessons began in elocution, dancing and music.

Gandhi could not, however, throw himself into this experiment with complete self-abandon. The habit of introspection had never deserted him. English dancing and music did nit come easy to him. He began to see that drapers and dance halls could turn him into an English gentleman, but only an English gentleman about town. After a brief three months' excursion, the introvert returned to his shell. There was a rebound from extreme extravagance to meticulous economy. He began to keep an account of every farthing he spent. He changed his rooms, cooked his own breakfast and, to save bus fares, walked eight to ten miles daily. He was able to pare down his expenses to £2 a month. He began to feel keenly the obligations to his family and was glad that he had reduced the calls on his brother for funds. Simplicity harmonised his inward and outward life; the dandyism of the first three months had been only a defensive armour against those who considered him a misfit in English society.

Vegetarianism, which had been a source of embarrassment to him, soon became an asset. He came across a book entitled Plea for Vegetarianism by Henry S. Salt, whose arguments went home. A meatless diet had been hitherto a matter of sentiment to him; henceforth, it was one of reasoned conviction. Vegetarianism was no longer an inconvenient obligation to his parents; it became a mission, the starting point of a discipline of body and mind which was to transform his life. With the zeal of a new convert, Gandhi devoured books on developed an interest in cooking, outgrew the taste for condiments, and came to the sensible conclusion that the seat of taste is not in the tongue but in the mind. The control of the palate was one of the first steps in that discipline which was to culminate many years later in total sublimation.

The immediate effect of vegetarianism was to give a new poise to young Gandhi, and to draw him out of his shell. He made his first venture into journalism by contributing nine articles to the Vegetarian. These articles, largely descriptive, and had occasional flashes of humour. That he should have sent these articles for publication at all is a notable achievement, if we recall that back home in Bhavnagar College he had been unable to follow lectures in English. He became a member of the Executive committee of the London Vegetarian Society. In Bays water where he stayed for a short time, he formed a vegetarian club. He came into contact with at least one eminent vegetarian, Sir Edwin Arnold, the author of the Light of Asia and The song Celestial, the two books which moved him deeply. He was stirred by the life if the Buddha and the message of the Gita. In the vegetarian restaurants and boarding houses of London he came across not only food faddists but also a few devout men of religion. He owed his introduction to the Bible to one such contact.

The New Testament, particularly the Sermon on the Mount went straight to his heart. The verses, "But I say unto you that ye resist not evil; but whosoever shall thee at the law and take away thy coat, let him have thy cloak also" reminded him of the lines of the Gujarati poet, Shamal Bhatt, which he used to hum as a child:

For a bowl of water give a goodly meal;
For a kindly greeting bow thou down with zeal;
For a single penny pay thou back with gold;
If the life be rescued, life do not withhold.

Thus, the words and actions of the wise regard;
Every little service tenfold they reward.

But the truly noble know all men as one,
And return with gladness good for evil done.

The teachings of the Bible, the Buddha and Bhatt fused in his mind. The idea of returning love for hatred, and good for evil, captivated him; he did not yet comprehend it full, but it continued to ferment in his impressionable mind.

In England

After completing his High School studies, Gandhi joined the Samaldas College, Bhavnagar and continued his studies for some time. One day, a Swamiji who came to Gandhi's house remarked: "Why don't you send this boy to England for studies? The family can regain its honour." This appealed to Gandhi. He had a great desire to study medical science; but his brother was not in favour of it. Further, in those days it was supposed to be, against religion to cross the sea. His mother too did not consent. Her fear was that her son might take to liquor and meat eating. At last, Gandhi gave his word to his mother that he would not do anything immoral, and got her consent. His brother agreed to bear the burden of the expenses, though he was not a rich man. It was finally decided that Gandhi should go to England and study Law to become a Barrister.

Gandhi was only nineteen years old then. He was to leave for England on September 4, 1888. The elders of his caste learnt this. They opposed his journey. But Gandhi disobeyed them and left. The elders declared that Gandhi was an outcaste.

Gandhi had learnt from some elders about life in London as also about manners to be observed in English society. Friends had told him that it was difficult to live without drinking wine and eating meat, in a cold country like England. But Gandhi tried hard to keep his promise to his mother. He went in search of vegetarian hotels, and was content to eat whatever food he got there. Every day he had to walk a long distance from his residence to the hotel. But he never felt it a hardship. In the end, he decided to cook his food himself.

Gandhi also tried to practice English gentlemen's ways and manners and to learn to speak French, dancing and the art of public speaking. His expenses increased. Neither could he learn any of them. And then the realisation came to him that his brother was struggling hard to send him money. Then he gave up all needless expenses, and began to live a simple life. His studies became his sole aim.

Gandhi developed great intimacy with an English family. He pretended to be an unmarried man. He used to be quite free with the two-grownup daughters of the family. It looked as if the friendship would go beyond the proper limits. It was a testing time for Gandhiji. At that hour, he remembered the promise he had made to his mother. It saved him from a moral fall. He felt repentant, and wrote a letter of apology to the lady of the house, confessing that he was a married man and the father of a child.

Gandhi stayed in England for two years and eight months. He obtained the degree of Barrister-at-Law. Without staying even for a day more, he started on the return journey to India, on June 12, 1891.

During his stay in England, Gandhi tried some experiments in vegetarian diet. He came to the conclusion that a human being should not eat non-vegetarian food for any reason. He got acquainted with some great persons of the day, like Dadabhai Naoroji and Dr. Beasant. But there was no indication at all that some day Gandhi would become a great man. For the first time Gandhi read the Bhagavad Gita, in the company of two English Theosophist friends. Together they studied 'The Song Celestial' (the English translation of the Gita) by Sir Edwin Arnold. This roused Gandhi's interest in the Holy Books of the Hindu religion; and his interest grew with time. The teaching of the Gita was a source of spiritual strength to Gandhi.

What Next?

A great sorrow awaited Gandhi on his return to India. His mother had passed away while he was in England. But his brother had not informed him of this. In England, Gandhiji had dreamed of telling his mother how he had struggled hard to keep his promise to her and of her joy when she listened to his story. But Gandhi was denied this pleasure.

Now, Gandhi was an young man of twenty-two. His son Harilal was a boy of four. Gandhi began the practice of law with great zeal in Bombay. But he lacked the courage to plead a case in the court. He could not conduct the very first case. He was deeply disappointed in the profession. He could not get any suitable work. At last he returned to Rajkot. His brother too was disappointed.

At this time, there arose a hope that the eldest brother Lakshmi Das might become the Diwan of Porbandar State. But he had incurred the anger of the British Political Agent. Gandhi had met that Political Agent when he was in London. Lakshmi Das naturally expected that his brother would recommend his case. Though, Gandhi was unwilling he called on the Political Agent and pleaded the case. He was warned that it was improper to make such a plea. Still Gandhi continued to plead for his brother. This put out the Agent, and he ordered his servant to show Gandhi the door. Gandhi felt greatly ashamed. But he was helpless. He felt distressed at his pitiable condition. This bitter event led to a total change in his way of life.

Briefless Barrister

In 1891 Gandhi passed the law examination successfully, but was assailed by doubts and anxieties. He had read the law, but could he practise it? He found it hard enough to speak to strangers in a small party. How would he be able to cross swords with his rivals in the courtroom? He had heard of legal luminaries like Sir Ferozeshah Mehta of Bombay and could well imagine the sorry figure he would cut in comparison. It was thus "with just a little leaven of hope mixed with despair" that he sailed for India.

A great shock lay in store for him when he landed at Bombay, as his mother had died while he was in England. It was only natural that he should have been anxious to justify the hopes of his family which had invested so much on his foreign education. His elder brother frankly expected rich dividends in the form of "wealth, and name and fame". The barrister's degree, however, was not an open sesame to the top of the bar. Gandhi noticed that the home-bred Vakils of Rajkot knew more of Indian law and charged lower fees than England sure ridicule; Gandhi, therefore, accepted the advice of friends to go to Bombay to study India law and to secure what briefs he could.

His experience in Bombay was no happier than in Rajkot. After waiting unconscionably, he got his first brief for the modest fee of thirty rupees. As he rose to cross-examine a witness, he was unable to collect his thoughts, collapsed into his chair and refunded the fee to his client. This was a disgraceful debut, which filled the young barrister with black despair as to his future in a profession he had entered at such a heavy cost.

The straits to which he had been reduced may be surmised from the fact that he applied and was turned down for a part time job as a teacher in a Bombay high school with the modest salary of seventy rupees (£5 1/2) a month. It was with some relief that he discovered that he had a flair for drafting memorials and petitions. He wound up his little establishment in Bombay and returned to Rajkot where petition-writing brought him an income of three hundred rupees a month. He might have settled down as a barrister scribe if he had not incurred the displeasure of the British Political Agent in Rajkot in whose court most of his work lay. So, when an offer of a job came to him from South Africa, he gladly accepted it. The contract was for a year in connection with a civil suit; the remuneration was £105, a first-class return fare and actual expenses. The fee was modest and it was not quite clear whether he was engaged as counsel or as a clerk, but he was in no position to pick and choose. He could hardly have imagined the new vistas of maturity and public service which the South African adventure was to open to him.

The Africa Days

In the 'Dark Continent'

Gandhi landed at Durban in May 1893. His employer Dada Abdullah, one of the wealthiest Indian merchants in Natal, took him to see the Durban court. When the European magistrate ordered Gandhi to take off his turban, he refused, left the courtroom and wrote a letter of protest in the local press in which he was mentioned "as an unwelcome visitor". The experience in Durban, however, was nothing compared with what befell him in the course of his journey from Durban to Pretoria. When his train reached Maritzburg late in the evening, he was ordered to leave the first class compartment and shift to the van compartment. He refused, but was unceremoniously turned out of the carriage.

It was a bitterly cold night as he crept into the unlit waitingroom of Maritzburg station and brooded over what had happened. His client had given him no warning of the humiliating conditions under which Indians lived in South Africa. Should he not call off the contract and return to India? Should he accept these affronts as part of the bargain? So far Gandhi had not been conspicuous for assertiveness; on the contrary he had been pathologically shy and retiring. But something happened to him in that wind-swept waitingroom of Maritzburg railway station as he smarted under the insult inflicted on him.

The iron entered his soul. In retrospect, this incident seemed to him as one of the most creative experiences of his life. From that hour, he refused to accept injustice as a part of the natural-or unnatural-order in South Africa. He would reason, he would plead; he would appeal to the better judgement and the latent humanity of the ruling race; he would resist, but he would never be a willing victim of racial arrogance. It was not so much a question of redeeming his own self-respect as that of his community, his country, even of humanity.

The helpless resignation of the mass of Indian settlers, the fact that they were illiterate, had few rights and did not know how to assert the rights they had. All this had the miraculous effect of dissipating young Gandhi's own diffidence. The feeling of inferiority which had dogged him as a student in England and as a budding lawyer in India vanished. In Bombay he had been unable to face a small cause court but one of the first things he did on arrival at Pretoria was to convene a meeting of the Indian residents "to present to them a picture of their condition in Transvaal".

During the next twelve months, Gandhi was busy with the civil suit which had brought him to Pretoria. In June 1894, he returned to Durban to sail for India. At the farewell party which his grateful client Dada Abdullah gave him at Sydenham, a pleasant suburb of Durban, Gandhi happened to glance through the pages of the Natal Mercury, and learnt that a bill was being introduced into the Natal Legislature to disfranchise India settlers. Gandhi's host and other Indian merchants present at the party were unable to throw any light on this measure. They knew enough English to be able to converse with their white customers, but few of them could read newspapers, much less follow the proceedings of the Natal Legislature. They had come to Natal for trade, and politics did not interest them. They had not yet realised that politics could affect their trade. "This is the first nail into our coffin", was Gandhi's comment. The Indian merchants pleaded with him to stay on in Natal to take up the fight on their behalf. Gandhi agreed to defer his stay for a month.

Gandhi lost no time in settling down to work; the farewell party converted itself into a political committee to plan Indian opposition to the bill. A sound instinct seems to have guided the young barrister in organising his first political campaign. He infused a spirit of solidarity into the heterogeneous elements composing the Indian community, and brought home the implications of the disfranchising measures not only to his own people, but to the saner section of the European public opinion and the Natal Government Most important of all, he gave the widest publicity to his campaign to quicken the conscience of the peoples and Governments of India and Great Britain; through petitions to the legislatures, statements in newspapers, letters to prominent persons in Natal, Britain and India, and through public meeting, Gandhi stressed the justice of the Indians, case. All this created a great stir but the disfranchising bill was nevertheless passed by the Natal Legislature. On the insistence of his Indian friends in Durban, Gandhi agreed to prolong his stay in Natal, and was enrolled as an advocate to the Supreme Court. Since he retaining fees to produce a minimum 300 a year which he reckoned enough to pay his way in Durban.

The Call from South Africa

Some Gujarati merchants had trade relations with South Africa. One of them, a relative of a merchant called Dada Abdullah.

Sheth, was a friend of Gandhi's brother, He asked Gandhi's brother if Gandhi would be willing to go to South Africa to assist his relative's English Lawyer in a lawsuit pending before a court. The work would take a year. All expenses would be borne by the merchant and, in addition, Gandhi would get one hundred and five pounds as fees. This seemed a good opportunity to Gandhi, as he was not only disappointed in the profession, but had also been put to shame by the English Political Agent. He obtained his brother's consent and set sail to South Africa in April 1893. He was only twenty-four years old.

'Do you have Self Respect?'

Two or three days had passed after Gandhi's arrival in Durban, in Natal State. Gandhi was wearing a turban on his head when he went to the court. The judge, noticing it, ordered him to remove it. All Indians, except the Muslims, who habitually wore a turban, had to remove it as a mark of respect to the court. Gandhi refused to remove it and went out of the court. This was the first insult that he had to suffer in South Africa.

After a week Gandhi had to make a journey by train. He had bought a first class ticket.

The train reached Maritzburg station. It was a bitter cold night. An officer of the railway came to Gandhi and asked him to vacate his seat for a white man, and to move to the van on the train. Gandhi refused. The railway officials, with the help of the police, had his things, thrown out. He was also removed from the carriage by force. The train left. Gandhi sat alone on the platform in the dark station and brooded over the insult he had suffered. In India a white officer put him to shame; should such a thing happen here too! The cup of sorrow was full. The next day, he continued the journey. It had to be done partly by horse coach and partly by train. Only Europeans were permitted to sit inside the carriage. Gandhi could not sit with them. He sat outside by the side of the coachman. Some time later, he was ordered to sit on the footboard. Gandhi could not bear it. He refused to carry out the order. The supervisor of the carriage, a European, attacked Gandhi and began to thrash him. Gandhi suffered the blows but did not at all move from where he sat. At last, the passengers intervened and checked the supervisor.

Thus; Gandhi was subject to untold shame. But when he learnt that such a shame was the fate of all Indian settlers, he was a transformed man.

Indians had begun to settle in South Africa in 1860. Many of them were labourers in the sugarcane, tea and coffee plantation's belonging to Englishmen.

In the eyes of the white Europeans all Indians were 'coolies'; the merchants were 'coolie merchants'; Barrister Gandhi was a 'coolie Barrister'. All were put to shame by being called 'Girmitias' and 'Samy'. (Girmitia is an ugly form of 'permit', and 'Samy' the ugly form of 'Swamy'). In Natal no Indian was allowed to move about after 9 at night. In Orange Free State, no Indian could acquire property; he could neither be an agriculturist or a tradesman. In Transvaal, he had no right to own land; in addition to this, he had to pay a settlement tax of three pounds. All Indians had to live in dirty areas. Once Gandhi himself was knocked down by police patrol-guards, for being out after 9 at night. In short, Indians were not considered as human beings. The South African Indian problem was thus a problem of life and death for a hundred thousand people. It was a problem of life and death for a hundred thousand people. It was a problem of life and death for a hundred thousand people. It was a problem of self-respect. All Indians suffered the shame mutely.

Barrister Gandhi, Leader of the Fight for Self-respect

Gandhi was successful in bringing about a compromise in the lawsuit of Abdullah Sheth. His work in South Africa was over.

The time to return to India had come. A meeting was arranged to bid him farewell. Those who had assembled discussed a news item, which had appeared in the papers that day, under the title

'The Indian Franchise'. Finally they decided to request Gandhi to stay in South Africa for some time more, to help them. Gandhi agreed. The assembly to bid farewell to Gandhi was converted into an action committee to fight for citizenship rights of the Indian settlers of South Africa. This laid the foundation for Gandhi's stay in South Africa. Thus, the seed of the fight for the rights of Indian brethren was sown.

Gandhi started an organisation and called it 'The Natal Indian Congress'. It was to carry on the struggle of the Indians. He also started a newspaper. It was called 'The Indian Opinion'. The paper became an organ to give information about the struggle.

It created unity and a sense of self-respect among the Indian settlers. Gandhi once visited India and attended the session of the Indian National Congress; he spoke about the hardships of the South African Indians, and got the Congress to pass a resolution supporting the struggle.

While in India, Gandhi made some speeches about the South African question. They were misreported in the press. The white men of South Africa who read the report became angry with Gandhi. They were waiting for Gandhi's return. As soon as he left the ship, they attacked him. His life was in danger. They kept shouting 'Hang Gandhi'. They also threw brickbats and rotten eggs at him. At that critical time, the wife of a European police officer courageously entered the fray, and led Gandhi to a place of safety.

Gandhi was determined in his struggle. He united the Indian settlers and carried on the struggle. At that time, the Zulus, the natives of South Africa, rose in rebellion against the British. Gandhi suspended the struggle, formed a Red Cross Corps, and served the wounded soldiers. This was a great service. The British Government appreciated it, and awarded him the 'Kaiser-e-Hind' medal.

Birth of 'Satyagraha'

Towards the end of 1907, the Government of South Africa tightened its laws against the Asian settlers in South Africa. It was called the 'Asiatic Act'. It lay down that all men and women of Asian origin above the age of eight years should get their names registered. In addition to this, the Government recognised only

Christian marriages as legal. The result of this was that a Hindu couple or a Muslim couple who were married according to Hindu and Muslim religious rites were no longer considered as legally wedded husband and wife. Further, there was restriction on movement from one province to another.

Gandhi advised his men not to honour and obey the Registration Law. This led to a fierce struggle. Gandhi called it 'Satyagraha'; it was the use of 'Soul-Force' or 'Love-Force' against 'Brute-Force' or violence. He trained men, women and children as volunteers to offer Satyagraha. He called his band a 'Peace Brigade'. It had to enter Transval from Natal. This was the civil disobedience that he planned. It continued for six months. All the Satyagrahis including Gandhi were arrested and put into prison. At last, the Government of South Africa came to an honourable settlement with Gandhi. The citizenship rights of Indians were recognised. Thus, Gandhi was the champion of the self-respect of the Indians in South Africa.

Satyagraha, this new way of struggle in South Africa, began a new chapter in the political history of the world, Politics is generally understood to permit cheating, killing and violence. Its policy is that the end justifies the means. But Gandhi taught the principle that both the end and the means must be equally pure and moral. He himself put that principle into practice. He showed that if this is to be possible, love or non-violence alone is the way to it.

The Young Politician

The first experience of political agitation into which Gandhi had been pitch forked cured him of what once had seemed an incorrigible self-consciousness. Not that he had a sudden attack of egotism; he was conscious of his limitations, and in a letter dated July 5, 1894 to Dadabhai Naoroji, the eminent leader of the Indian National Congress, wrote: "A word for myself and I have done. I am inexperienced and young and, therefore, quite liable to make mistakes. The responsibility undertaken is quite out of proportion to my ability. So, you will see that I have not taken the matter up, which is beyond my ability, in order to enrich myself at the expense of the Indians. I am the only available person who can handle the question." The concept of inferiority is a relative one; in a community looking to him for leadership, Gandhi forgot his own limitations. As the only available person, he undertook a task from which elsewhere he would have shrunk.

Gandhi had come to South Africa in 1893 for a year. He could hardly have imagined that he would have to stay on for the best part of two decades. The struggle of the Indian immigrants for elementary civic rights was to be long and hard The disfranchising of the Indians which had been the immediate cause of Gandhi's intervention in the politics of Natal was only a symptom of the racial malaise that had begun to afflict the Dark Continent.

"The Asiatics", wrote Lord Milner, "are strangers forcing themselves upon a community reluctant to receive them." In fact, the Indian emigration to South Africa in the 1860s started at the instance of the European settlers who were in possession of vast virgin lands ideal for tea, coffee and sugar plantations, but lacked manpower. The Negro could not be compelled to work after the abolition of slavery. Recruiting agents of the European planters toured some of the poorest and most congested districts of India and painted rosy prospects of work in Natal. Free passage, board and lodging; a wage of ten shillings a month for the first year rising by one shilling every year; and the right to a free return passage to India after five years' 'indenture' (or alternatively, the option to settle in the land of their adoption) drew thousands of poor and illiterate Indians to distant Natal.

The European planters and merchants did not relish the idea of Indian Labourers settling down as free citizens at the end of the five year' 'indenture'. A tax of £3 was therefore levied on every member of the family of an ex-indentured labourer even though he was merely exercising his right to settle in Natal in terms of the agreement which had governed his emigration from India. It was a crippling tax for the poor wretches whose wages ranged between ten and twelve shillings month.

The Indian merchant who had followed the Indian labourer to Natal had disabilities of his own. No one could trade without a licence, which a European could have for the asking and Indian only after much effort and expense, if at all. And since an educational test in a European language was made a *sine qua non* for an immigrant from India, except of course the semi-slave indentured labourers who continued to be imported.

The legal disabilities on Indians were bad enough, but the daily humiliations they suffered were worse. They were commonly described as "Asian dirt to be heartily curse, chokeful of vice, that live upon rice and the black vermin". They were not allowed to walk on footpaths. First and second class tickets were not issued to them. If a white passenger objected, they could be unceremoniously bundled out of a railway compartment; they had sometimes to travel on footboards of trains. European hotels would not admit them.

Gandhi realised that what the India urgently needed was a permanent organisation to look after their interests. Out of deference to Dadabhai Naoroji, Who had presided over the Indian National Congress in 1893, he called the new organisation Natal Indian Congress. He was not conversant with the Constitution and functions of the Indian National Congress. This ignórance proved an asset, as he fashioned the Natal Congress in his own way to suit the needs of the Natal Indians, as a live body functioning throughout the year and dedicated not only to politics but to the moral and social uplift of its members. Though it served a community which had very little political experience, it was not a one-man show. An indefatigable secretary though he was, Gandhi enlisted popular interest and enthusiasm at every step. He made the enrolment of members and the collection of subscriptions into something more than a routine. He employed a gently but irresistible technique for exerting moral pressure on halfhearted supporters. Once in a small village, he sat through the night and refused to take his dinner until at dawn his host, an Indian merchant, agreed to raise his subscription for the Natal Indian Congress from three to six pounds.

In these early years of his politics apprenticeship, Gandhi formulated his own code of conduct for a politician. He did not accept the popular view that in politics one must fight for one's; arty, right or wrong. He avoided exaggeration and discouraged it in his colleagues. The Natal Indian Congress was not merely an instrument for the defence of political and economic rights for the Indian minority, but also a lever for its internal reform and unity. He did not spare his own people and roundly criticised them for their shortcomings. He was not only the stoutest champion of the Natal Indians, but also their severest critic.

Under his leadership, the Indian community in Natal endeavoured to secure the repeal of discriminatory laws and vexatious regulations and stave off further oppressive measures. Gandhi was in touch with Naoroji and other members of the British committee of the Indian National Congress in London. He sought their advice and support in representing the South African Indian Indian's case to the Secretary of State for India, and British Colonial Secretary.

He was an indefatigable correspondent, bombarding his friends, opponents, newspaper editors and men in authority in three continents, with telegrams, letters and memoranda on the grievances of the India in South Africa. It is a measure of Gandhi's success as a publicist that the Indian National Congress Recorded its protest against the disabilities imposed upon the Indian settlers in South Africa, and the London Times devoted several leading articles to this problem. In 1896 he paid a brief visit to India to canvass public support for the cause he had made his own. On return to Natal from this trip on January 10,1897, he was nearly lynched in the streets Durban by a mob of Europeans who had been infuriated by Press reports of Gandhi's advocacy of the Indian cause in his native land.

On the outbreak of the Boer War in 1899, Gandhi organised an Indian Ambulance Corps of 1100 men. Vere Stent, the editor of the Pretoria News, has left a fascinating pen-portrait of Gandhi in the battlefield: "After a night's work which had shattered men with much bigger frames, I came across Gandhi in the early morning sitting by the roadside-eating a regulation biscuit. Every man in (General) Buller's force was dull and depressed, and damnation was heartily invoked on everything. But Gandhi was stoic in his bearing, cheerful and confident in his conversation and had a kindly eye."

It must be recognised that Gandhi's ideas on non-violence had not yet fully matured. His argument at this time was that Indian settlers in British colonies, while demanding all the privileges of citizenship must also accept all its obligations, which included participation in the defence of the country of adoption. Gandhi's gesture in raising an ambulance corps on behalf of a minority which was denied elementary rights was a fine one, but it was wasted. The end of the Boer War brought no relief to the

Indians. Their grievances remained unredressed. Indeed, new chains were forged for them in the former Boer Colonies.

Gandhi's Work in South Africa

Gandhi's work in South Africa dramatically changed him, as he faced the discrimination commonly directed at blacks and Indians. One day in court at Durban, the magistrate asked him to remove his turban. Gandhi refused and stormed out of the courtroom. He was thrown off a train at Pietermaritzburg, after refusing to move from the first class to a third class coach while holding a valid first class ticket.

Travelling further on by stagecoach, he suffered other hardships on the journey as well, including being barred from many hotels. These incidents have been acknowledged by several biographers as a turning point in his life, explaining his later social activism. It was through witnessing first-hand the racism, prejudice and injustice against Indians in South Africa that Gandhi started to question his people's status, and his own place in society. However, these events by no means explain why he inculcated non-violence instead of aggressive revolution.

At the end of his contract, Gandhi prepared to return to India. However, at a farewell party in his honour in Durban, he happened to glance at a newspaper and learned that a bill to deny the right to vote to Indians was being considered by the Natal Legislative Assembly. When he brought this up with his hosts, they lamented that they did not have the expertise necessary to oppose the bill, and implored Gandhi to stay and help them. He circulated several petitions to both the Natal Legislature and the British Government in opposition to the bill. Though unable to halt the bill's passage, his campaign was successful in drawing attention to the grievances of Indians in South Africa.

Supporters convinced him to remain in Durban to continue fighting against the injustices levied against Indians in South Africa. He founded the Natal Indian Congress in 1894, with himself as the Secretary. Through this organisation, he moulded the Indian community of South Africa into a homogeneous political force, publishing documents detailing Indian grievances and evidence of British discrimination in South Africa. Gandhi returned briefly to India in 1896 to bring his wife and children to live with him in South Africa. When he returned in January 1897, a white mob attacked and tried to lynch him. In an early indication of the personal values that would shape his later campaigns, he refused to press charges against any member of the mob, stating it was one of his principles not to seek redress for a personal wrong in a court of law.

At the onset of the South African War, Gandhi argued that Indians must support the war effort in order to legitimise their claims to full citizenship, organising a volunteer ambulance corps of 300 free Indians and 800 indentured labourers called the Indian Ambulance Corps, one of the few medical units to serve wounded black South Africans. He himself was a stretcher-bearer at the Battle of Spion Kop, and was decorated. At the conclusion of the war, however, the situation for the Indians did not improve, but continued to deteriorate.

In 1906, the Transvaal government promulgated a new Act compelling registration of the colony's Indian population. At a mass protest meeting held in Johannesburg on September 11th that year, Gandhi adopted his methodology of satyagraha (devotion to the truth), or non-violent protest, for the first time, calling on his fellow Indians to defy the new law and suffer the punishments for doing so, rather than resist through violent means. This plan was adopted, leading to a seven-year struggle in which thousands of Indians were jailed (including Gandhi himself on many occasions), flogged, or even shot, for striking, refusing to register, burning their registration cards, or engaging in other forms of non-violent resistance. While the government was successful in repressing the Indian protesters, the public outcry stemming from the harsh methods employed by the South African government in the face of peaceful Indian protesters finally forced South African General Jan Christiaan Smuts to negotiate a compromise with Gandhi.

Gandhi left South-Africa in 1914, and went back to India after a visit to England

Role in Zulu War

In 1906, after the British introduced a new poll-tax, Zulus in South Africa killed two British officers. The British declared a war against the Zulus, in retaliation. Gandhi actively encouraged the

British to recruit Indians. He argued that Indians should support the war efforts in order to legitimise their claims to full citizenship. The British, however, refused to offer Indians positions of rank in their military. However, they accepted Gandhi's offer to let a detachment of Indians volunteer as a stretcher bearer corps to treat wounded British soldiers. On July 21, 1906, Gandhi wrote in Indian Opinion — "The corps had been formed at the instance of the Natal Government by way of experiment, in connection with the operations against the Natives consists of twenty three Indians". Gandhi urged the Indian population in South Africa to join the war through his columns in Indian Opinion — "If the Government only realised what reserve force is being wasted, they would make use of it and give Indians the opportunity of a thorough training for actual warfare."

In Gandhi's opinion, the Draft Ordinance of 1906 brought the status of Indians below the level of Natives. He therefore urged Indians to resist the Ordinance along the lines of Satyagraha, by taking the example of "Kaffirs". In his words, "Even the half-castes and kaffirs, who are less advanced than we, have resisted the government. The pass law applies to them as well, but they do not take out passes".

Satyagraha Struggle in South Africa

It was the passage of the Asiatic Registration Act in Transvaal in 1907 which convinced Gandhi that the method of protest, petition and prayer which he had sedulously pursued for nearly fourteen years had failed. It was at this juncture that he evolved a new technique, which came to be known as Passive Resistance; but as it ruled out both verbal and physical violence, it differed in important respects from the campaign waged on behalf of the suffragettes in England. The principles and techniques of Gandhi's movement were to evolve gradually in the ensuing months ant years; its author was a man for whom theory was the handmade of action.

It is not possible here to give a detailed account of the Satyagraha struggle which Gandhi led in South Africa for seven years. It required great courage, patience and organising ability to persuade the small Indian community to pit itself against the government. Gandhi had to reckon with the immense political and economic power wielded by the dominant European community, the stubbornness of the local government in South Africa, the reluctance of the British Colonial Office to antagonise the Union Government in Pretoria, the apathy of the Government of India and the limited resources of the small India minority fighting for its survival on an alien soil.

Gandhi himself worked under terrific pressure. In January 1908, he was arrested for breach of the registration law and clapped into prison. The following month he was released after an understanding seemed to have been reached with the government. A few days later, he was beaten up and severely injured by a compatriot, who accused him of betraying the Indian cause.

The truce with the Transvaal Government did not last long. The Satyagraha campaign had to be renewed. There were acts of defiance by the Indians and punitive measures by the authorities. Gandhi set up a small colony — Tolstoy Farm — at an 1100 acre site, 21 miles from Johannesburg where his colleagues in the Satyagraha struggle and their families could support a frugal and hard existence — which was in fact harder than life in jail-by-running a cooperative farm. "We had all become labourers," Gandhi recalled later, "put on labourer's dress, but in the European style, viz. Workman's trousers and shirts which were imitated from prisoner's uniform".

Those who went to Johannesburg on private errands had to walk. Gandhi himself, though past forty and living only on fruits, did not think much of walking forty miles a day; he once did 55 miles without feeling any the worse for it. All residents of Tolstoy Farm including children had their quota of manual labour. Those who had known this austere discipline could have little fear of goal.

In 1912, Gokhale, one of the most eminent Indian politicians of the day, paid a visit to South Africa and discussed the problems of the Indian community with General Smuts and other members of the South African Government. He returned to India with the impression that the Asiatic Registration Act and the hated £3 tax on the ex-indentured labourers would be abolished. When this did not happen, and an additional provocation was given by

Supreme Court Judgement invalidating marriages of non-Christians in South Africa, Gandhi launched what turned out to be the final phase of his struggle in South Africa.

A party of eleven Indian women, including Gandhi's wife Kasturba, courted imprisonment by crossing from Natal into Transvaal without a permit. The Indian labourers in the coal mines at New Castle went on a sympathetic strike. The mine-owners retaliated by cutting off water and electric connection to the areas where the labourers lived. Gandhi had no option but to take charge of the miners and their families, 2037 men, 127 women and 57 children. He decided to walk them from New Castle to Tolstoy Farm, but was arrested on the way.

In Volksrust jail he was make to dig stones and sweep the compound. Later he was transferred to Pretoria jail and lodged in a dark cell ten feet long and seven feet wine, which was lit up at night only to check up on the prisoner. He was denied a bench, refused permission to walk in the cell and subjected to numberless pinpricks. Summoned for evidence in a case, he was marched to the court with hand-cuffs on his hands and manacles on his feet. Meanwhile, the Indian labourers had been put into special trains, and taken back to New Castle mines where they were forced to go underground by mounted military police.

The 'blood and iron' policy of the South African Government stirred India deeply. Gokhale sent two earnest Christian young men, C. F. Andrews and Pearson, to assist Gandhi. Lord Hardinge, the viceroy of India, courageously denounced the high-handed policies of the South African Government. Negotiations began between Gandhi and the South African Government under pressure from Delhi and London.

Eventually an agreement was reached. Some of the major points on which the Satyagraha struggle had been waged were conceded to the Indians. The tax on the ex-indentured labourers was abolished; marriages performed according to Indian rites were legalised, and a domicile certificate bearing the holder's thumb-imprint was too a sufficient evidence of the right to enter South Africa.

In 1939, a quarter of a century after the conclusion of the Satyagraha campaign, General Smuts, Gandhi's chief antagonist in South Africa, recalled: ' 'Gandhi himself received what no doubt he desired a short period of rest and quiet in goal. For him everything went according to plan. For me the defender of law and order — there was the usual trying situation, the odium of carrying out a law which had no strong public support, and finally the discomfiture when the law had to be repealed. For him it was a successful coup."

In goal Gandhi had prepared a pair of sandals for General Smuts, who wrote that there was no hatred and personal ill-feeling, and when the fight was over, "there was the atmosphere in which decent peace would be concluded".

3

The Making of Mahatma

In 1914 Gandhi left South Africa. He had gone there as a junior counsel of a commercial firm for £105 a year; he had stayed on to command, and then voluntarily to give up a peak practice of £5000 a year. In Bombay as a young lawyer he had a nervous breakdown while cross-examining witnesses in a petty civil suit. In South Africa, he had founded a new political organisation with the sure touch of a seasoned politician. The hostility of the European politicians and officials and the helplessness of the Indian merchants and labourers had put him on his mettle. No glittering rewards for him; the perils ranged from professional pinpricks to lynching. Nevertheless, it was a piece of good fortune that he began his professional and political career in South Africa. Dwarfed as he had felt by the great lawyers and leader of India, it is unlikely that he would have developed much initiative in his homeland. When he founded the Natal Indian Congress at the age of twenty-five, he was writing on a tabula rasa: he could try out ideas which in an established political organisation would have been laughed out court.

What had truth and vows to do with politics? It was a question which often recurred in Indian politics, and if Gandhi was not confounded by it, it was because, far back in South Africa, he had observed and confirmed the connection. For a man who was no doctrinaire, and whose theory often lagged behind practice, it was a decided advantage that the scene of his early activities should have been one where he was unfettered by political precedents or professionals. Natal and Transvaal were no bigger than some of the smallest provinces of India. The struggle for Indian independence was conducted Gandhi on much larger scale and on much bigger issues, but there were not a few occasions when he derived inspiration from his experience in South Africa.

Not only his politics, but his personality took shape in South Africa. The most formative years of his life had been spent there. His interest in moral and religious questions dated back to his early childhood. But it was only in South Africa that he had an opportunity of studying them systematically. His Quaker friends in Pretoria failed to convert him to Christianity, but they whetted his innate appetite for religious studies. He delved deep into Christianity and other religions, including his own.

In his first year in South Africa he read 'quite eighty books', most of them on religion. One of these was Tolstoy's Kingdom of God is Within You. Tolstoy became his favourite author and in the coming years he read the Gospels in Brief, What to do? The Slavery of Our Times, How Shall We Escape? Letters to a Hindu and The First Step. Tolstoy's bold idealism and fearless candour gripped him, his Christian anarchism dissipated the spell of institutional religion. Tolstoy's emphasis on the necessity of an accord between moral principles and daily life confirmed his own strivings for self-improvement.

Few men read so little to so much profit as Gandhi did. A book was for Gandhi not a mere diversion for the hour, it was embodied experience, which had to be accepted or rejected. Ruskin's "Unto This Last" drove him with compelling urgency from the capital of Natal to the wilderness of Zululand to practise a life of voluntary poverty, and literally to live by the sweat of his brow. It was in Tolstoy's books that we may seek one of the strongest influences on Gandhi. He was, of course, not given to indiscriminate imitation. But in Tolstoy he found a writer whose views elaborated his own inchoate beliefs. It was not only on the organised or covert violence of the modern state and the right of the citizen to civil disobedience that Gandhi found support in Tolstoy.

There were innumerable subjects, ranging from modern civilization and industrialism to sex and schools, on which he tended to agree with Tolstoy's analysis. There was an exchange of letters between the two which gives an impression of gratitude and reverence by the young Indian on the threshold of his career, and of delightful surprise by the aged Tolstoy. "And so your activity in Transvaal," wrote Tolstoy to Gandhi, "as it seems to us, at the end of the world, is the most essential work, the most important of all the work now being done in the world, and in which not only the nations of the Christian, but of all the world will undoubtedly take part."

While books on Christianity and Islam were easily available in South Africa, Gandhi had to send for books on Hinduism from India. He corresponded with his friend Raychandbhai, whose influence in favour of Hinduism was decisive at a time when Gandhi's Quaker friends believed him to be on the way to baptism. The study of comparative religion, the browsing on theological works, the conversations and correspondence with the learned, brought Gandhi to the conclusion that true religion was more a matter of the heart than of the intellect, and that genuine beliefs were those which were literally lived.

Gandhi's style of life was also transformed during these years. From the Gita which he described as his "spiritual dictionary", he had imbibed the ideal of "non-possession" which set him on the road to voluntary poverty, and of "selfless action "which equipped him with an extraordinary stamina for his public life. He trained himself as a dispenser in a charitable hospital in order to be able to attend on the 'indentured' labourers, the poorest Indians in South Africa. At Phoenix near Durban, and at Tolstoy Farm near Johannesburg, he set up little colonies, where he and those who shared his ideals, could find a haven from the heat and dust of towns, and men's greed and hatred, A pen-portrait of Gandhi as he was in his late-30s has been left by his first biographer Rev. Joseph J. Doke of Johannesburg: "A small, lithe, spare figure stood before me, and a refined earnest face looked into mine. The skin was dark, the eyes dark, but the smile which lighted up the face, and that direct fearless glance simply took one's heart by storm. I judged him to be some thirty-eight years of age, which proved correct. He spoke English perfectly and was evidently a man of culture...There was a quite assured strength about him, a greatness of heart, a transparent honesty that attracted me at once to the Indian leader. Our Indian friend lives on a higher plane than most men do. His actions, like the actions of Mary of Bethany, are often counted eccentric, and not infrequently misunderstood. Those who do not know him think there is some unworthy motive behind, some Oriental 'slimness' to account for such profound unworldliness. But those who know him well are ashamed of themselves in his presence. Money, I think has no charm for him. His compatriots...wonder at him, grow angry at his strange unselfishness, and love him with the love of pride and trust. He is one of those outstanding characters with whom to walk is a liberal education...whom to know is to love."

Return to India

A hero's welcome awaited Gandhi when he landed on January 9, 1915, at the Apollo Bunder in Bombay. Three days later he was honoured by the people of Bombay at a magnificent reception in the palatial house of a Bombay magnate Jehangir Petit. The Government of India joined with the people of India in showering honours on Gandhi. He received a "Kaiser-I-Hind" gold medal in the King's birthday honours list of 1915. His association with Gokhale was guarantee enough of his being a safe politician. Of course, he had led an extra-constitutional movement in South Africa, defied laws and filled goals, but the cause for which he had fought appeared as much humanitarian as political, dear to all Indian as and all Englishmen whose sense of humanity had not been blunted by racial arrogance or political expediency. Lord Hardinge's open support of the Satyagraha Movement had in any case removed the stigma of rebellion from South Africa's Indian movement.

Gandhi was in no hurry to plunge into politics. His political mentor on the Indian scene was Gokhale. One of the first things Gokhale did was to extract a promise from Gandhi that he would not express himself upon public questions for a year, which was to be a "year of probation". Gokhale was very keen that Gandhi should join the Servants of India Society in Poona. Gandhi was only too willing to fall in with the wishes of Gokhale, but several members of the Society feared that there was too great a gap between the ideals and methods of the Society and those of Gandhi.

While the question of his admission as a 'Servant of India' was being debated, Gandhi visited his home towns of Porbandar and Rajkot and went on to Shantiniketan in West Bengal, the cosmopolitan University of the Poet Rabindranath Tagore.

The trip to Shantiniketan ended abruptly with a telegram from Poona that Gokhale was dead. Gandhi was stunned. He mourned Gokhale by going barefoot for a year, and out of respect for the memory of his mentor, made another effort to seek admission to the Servants of India Society. Finding a sharp division of opinion in the Society on this point, he withdrew his application for admission.

During 1915—the year of probation—Gandhi eschewed politics severely. In his speeches and writings he confined himself to the reform of the individual and the society and avoided the issues which dominated Indian politics. His restraint was partly due to self-imposed silence and partly to the fact that he was still studying conditions in India and making up his mind.

Struggle for India's Independence

In 1915, Gandhi returned from South Africa to live in India. He spoke at the conventions of the Indian National Congress, but was primarily introduced to Indian issues, politics and the Indian people by Gopal Krishna Gokhale, a respected leader of the Congress Party at the time.

The Backdrop of Independence Movement

The term "Indian Independence Movement" is diffused, incorporating various national and regional campaigns, agitations and efforts of both Non-violent and Militant philosophy and involved a wide spectrum of Indian political organisations, philosophies, and movements which had the common aim of ending the British Colonial Authority as well as other colonial administrations in the Indian subcontinent. The initial resistance to the movement can be traced back to the very beginnings of Colonial Expansion in Karnataka by the Portuguese in the 16th century and by the British East India Company in Northern India, in the middle and late-1700s. The mainstream movement from the latter part of the 1800s was increasingly led by the Indian National

Congress with prominent moderate leaders seeking only Dominion status within the commonwealth. Beginning of early-1900s saw a more radical approach towards political independence proposed by leaders as the Lal Bal Pal and Sri Aurobindo. Militant nationalism also emerged in the first decades, culminating in the failed Indo-German Pact and Ghadar Conspiracy during the World War I. The end of the war saw the Congress adopt the policies of non-violent agitation and civil disobedience led by Mahatma Gandhi. Other leaders, such as Netaji Subhash Chandra Bose, later came to adopt a military approach to the movement. The World War II period saw the peak of the movements like INA movement led by Netaji Subhas Chandra Bose from East Asia and Quit India Movement.

India remained a Dominion of The Crown till 26 January 1950, when it adopted its Constitution to proclaim itself a Republic. Pakistan proclaimed itself a Republic in 1956 but faced a number of internal power struggles that has seen suspensions of democracy. In 1971, the Pakistani Civil War culminating in the 1971 War saw the splintering-off of East Pakistan into the nation of Bangladesh.

The Independence Movement also served as a major catalyst for similar movements in other parts of the world, leading to the eventual disintegration and dismantling of the British Empire and its replacement with the Commonwealth of Nations. Gandhi's philosophy of non-violent resistance inspired the American Civil Rights Movement (1955-68) led by Martin Luther King, Jr., the quest for democracy in Myanmar led by Aung San Suu Kyi and the African National Congress's struggle against apartheid in South Africa led by Nelson Mandela. However, not all these leaders adhered to Gandhi's strict principle of non-violence and non-resistance.

European Rule

European traders came to Indian shores with the arrival of the Portuguese explorer Vasco da Gama in 1498 at the port of Calicut in search of the lucrative spice trade. After the 1757 Battle of Plassey, during which the British army under Robert Clive defeated the Nawab of Bengal, the British East India Company established itself. This is widely seen as the beginning of the British Raj in India. The Company gained administrative rights over Bengal, Bihar, and Orissa in 1765 after the Battle of Buxar. They then annexed Punjab in 1849 after the death of Maharaja Ranjit Singh in 1839 and the First Anglo-Sikh War (1845–1846) and then the Second Anglo-Sikh War (1848–49).

The British Parliament enacted a series of laws to handle the administration of the newly-conquered provinces, including the Regulating Act of 1773, the India Act of 1784, and the Charter Act of 1813; all enhanced the British government's rule. In 1835 English was made the medium of instruction. Western-educated Hindu elites sought to rid Hinduism of controversial social practices, including the varna (caste) system, child marriage, and sati. Literary and debating societies initiated in Bombay and Madras became fora for open political discourse. The educational attainment and skillful use of the press by these earlv reformers created the growing possibility for effecting broad reforms within colonial India, all without compromising larger Indian social values and religious practices.

Even while these modernising trends influenced Indian society, Indians increasingly despised British rule. The memoirs of Henry Ouvry of the 9th Lancers record many "a good thrashing" to careless servants. A spice merchant, Frank Brown, wrote to his nephew that stories of maltreatment of servants had not been exaggerated and that he knew people who kept orderlies "purposely to thrash them". As the British increasingly dominated the continent, they grew increasingly abusive of local customs by, for example, staging parties in mosques, dancing to the music of regimental bands on the terrace of the Taj Mahal, using whips to force their way through crowded bazaars (as recounted by General Henry Blake), and mistreating sepoys. In the years after the annexation of Punjab in 1849, several mutinies among sepoys broke out; these were put down by force.

Regional Movements Prior to 1857

Several regional movements against foreign rule were staged in various parts of pre-1857 India. However, they were not united and were easily controlled by the foreign rulers. Examples include the rebellion of Abbakka Rani in Karnataka from 1555 to 1570 against the Portuguese, Sannyasi Rebellion in Bengal in the 1770s, the 1787 ethnic revolt against Portuguese control of Goa known as the Conspiracy Of The Pintos, the revolt of Titumir in Bengal in 1830s and uprisings by South Indian local chieftains like Veerapandya Kattabomman against British rule. Other movements included the Santal Rebellion and the resistance offered to the British by Titumir in Bengal, the Kittur Rebellion led by Rani Chennamma in Karnataka, Polygar Wars in Tamil Nadu, Kutch Rebellion in Saurashtra.

Indian Revolt of 1857

The Indian Rebellion of 1857 was a period of uprising in the northern and central India against British rule in 1857-58. The rebellion was the result of decades of ethnic and cultural differences between Indian soldiers and their British officers. The indifference of the British towards Indian rulers like the Mughals and ex-Peshwas and the annexation of Oudh were political factors triggering dissent amongst Indians. Dalhousie's policy of annexation, the doctrine of lapse or escheat, and the projected removal of the descendants of the Great Mughal from their ancestral palace to the Qutab, near Delhi also angered some people.

The specific reason that triggered the rebellion was the rumoured use of cow and pig fat in .557 calibre Pattern 1853 Enfield (P/53) rifle cartridges. Soldiers had to break the cartridges with their teeth before loading them into their rifles. So if there was cow and pig fat, it would be offensive to Hindu and Muslim soldiers, respectively. In February 1857, sepoys (Indian soldiers in the British army) refused to use their new cartridges. The British claimed to have replaced the cartridges with new ones and tried to make sepoys make their own grease from beeswax and vegetable oils, but the rumour persisted.

In March 1857, Mangal Pandey, a soldier of the 34th Native Infantry in Barrackpore, attacked his British sergeant and wounded an adjutant. General Hearsay, who said Pandey was in some kind of "religious frenzy," ordered a *jemadar* to arrest him but the jemadar refused. Mangal Pandey was hanged on 7 April along with the jemadar. The whole regiment was dismissed as a collective punishment. On May 10, when the 11th and 20th Cavalry assembled, they broke rank and turned on their commanding officers. They then liberated the 3rd Regiment, and on 11 May the sepoys reached Delhi and were joined by other Indians. The Red

Fort, the residence of the last Mughal Emperor Bahadur Shah Zafar, was attacked and captured by the sepoys. They demanded that he reclaim his throne. He was reluctant at first, but eventually agreed to the demands and became the leader of the rebellion.

Soon, the revolt spread throughout northern India. Revolts broke out in places like Meerut, Jhansi, Kanpur, Lucknow, etc. The British were slow to respond, but eventually responded with brute force. British moved regiments from the Crimean War and diverted European regiments headed for China to India.

The British fought the main army of the rebels near Delhi in Badl-ke-Serai and drove them back to Delhi before laying siege on the city. The siege of Delhi lasted roughly from 1 July to 31 August. After a week of street fighting, the British retook the city. The last significant battle was fought in Gwalior on 20 June 1858. It was during this battle that Rani Lakshmi Bai was killed. Sporadic fighting continued until 1859 but most of the rebels were subdued. Some notable leaders were Ahmed Ullah, an advisor of the ex-King of Oudh; Nana Sahib; his nephew Rao Sahib and his retainers, Tantia Topi and Azimullah Khan; the Rani of Jhansi; Kunwar Singh; the Rajput chief of Jagadishpur in Bihar; Firuz Saha, a relative of the Mughal Emperor, Bahadur Shah Zafar and Pran Sukh adav who along with Rao Tula Ram of Rewari fought with Britishers at Nasibpur, Haryana.

The Aftermath

The war of 1857 was a major turning point in the history of modern India. The British abolished the British East India Company and replaced it with direct rule under the British crown. A Viceroy was appointed to represent the Crown. In proclaiming the new direct-rule policy to "the Princes, Chiefs, and Peoples of India," Queen Victoria promised equal treatment under British law, but Indian mistrust of British rule had become a legacy of the 1857 rebellion.

The British embarked on a programme in India of reform and political restructuring, trying to integrate Indian higher castes and rulers into the government. They stopped land grabs, decreed religious tolerance and admitted Indians into the civil service, albeit mainly as subordinates. They also increased the number of British soldiers in relation to native ones and allowed only British soldiers to handle artillery. Bahadur Shah was exiled to Rangoon,

Burma where he died in 1862, finally bringing the Mughal dynasty to an end. In 1877, Queen Victoria took the title of Empress of India.

Rise of Organised Movements

The decades following the Sepoy Rebellion were a period of growing political awareness, manifestation of Indian public opinion and emergence of Indian leadership at national and provincial levels. Dadabhai Naoroji formed East India Association in 1867, and Surendranath Banerjee founded Indian National Association in 1876. Inspired by a suggestion made by A.O. Hume, a retired British civil servant, seventy-three Indian delegates met in Bombay in 1885 and founded the Indian National Congress. They were mostly members of the upwardly mobile and successful western-educated provincial elites, engaged in professions such as law, teaching, and journalism. At its inception, the Congress had no well-defined ideology and commanded few of the resources essential to a political organisation.

It functioned more as a debating society that met annually to express its loyalty to the British Raj and passed numerous resolutions on less controversial issues such as civil rights or opportunities in government, especially the civil service. These resolutions were submitted to the Viceroy's government and occasionally to the British Parliament, but the Congress's early gains were meagre. Despite its claim to represent all India, the Congress voiced the interests of urban elites; the number of participants from other economic backgrounds remained negligible.

The influences of socio-religious groups such as Arya Samaj (started by Swami Dayanand Saraswati) and Brahmo Samaj (founded, among others, by Raja Ram Mohan Roy) became evident in pioneering reform of Indian society. The inculcation of religious reform and social pride was fundamental to the rise of a public movement for complete nationhood. The work of men like Swami Vivekananda, Ramakrishna Paramhansa, Sri Aurobindo, Subramanya Bharathy, Bankim Chandra Chatterjee, Sir Syed Ahmed Khan, Rabindranath Tagore and Dadabhai Naoroji spread the passion for rejuvenation and freedom.

By 1900, although the Congress had emerged as an all-India political organisation, its achievement was undermined by its singular failure to attract Muslims, who felt that their representation in government service was inadequate. Attacks by Hindu reformers against religious conversion, cow slaughter, and the preservation of Urdu in Arabic script deepened their concerns of minority status and denial of rights if the Congress alone were to represent the people of India. Sir Syed Ahmed Khan launched a movement for Muslim regeneration that culminated in the founding in 1875 of the Mohammedan Anglo-Oriental College at Aligarh, Uttar Pradesh (renamed Aligarh Muslim University in 1921). Its objective was to educate wealthy students by emphasising the compatibility of Islam with modern western knowledge. The diversity among India's Muslims, however, made it impossible to bring about uniform cultural and intellectual regeneration.

Rise of Indian Nationalism

The first spurts of nationalistic sentiment that rose amongst Congress members were when the desire to be represented in the bodies of government, to have a say, a vote in the lawmaking and issues of administration of India. Congressmen saw themselves as loyalists, but wanted an active role in governing their own country, albeit as part of the Empire. This trend was personified by Dadabhai Naoroji, who went as far as contesting, successfully, an election to the British House of Commons, becoming its first Indian member.

Bal Gangadhar Tilak was the first Indian nationalist to embrace Swaraj as the destiny of the nation. Tilak deeply opposed the British education system that ignored and defamed India's culture, history and values. He resented the denial of freedom of expression for nationalists, and the lack of any voice or role for ordinary Indians in the affairs of their nation. For these reasons, he considered Swaraj as the natural and only solution. His popular sentence "Swaraj is my birthright, and I shall have it" became the source of inspiration for Indians.

In 1907, the Congress was split into two. Tilak advocated what was deemed as extremism. He wanted a direct assault by the people upon the British Raj, and the abandonment of all things British. He was backed by rising public leaders like Bipin Chandra Pal and Lala Lajpat Rai, who held the same point of view. Under them, India's three great states - Maharashtra, Bengal and Punjab shaped the demand of the people and India's nationalism. Gokhale criticised Tilak for encouraging acts of violence and disorder. But the Congress of 1906 did not have public membership, and thus Tilak and his supporters were forced to leave the party.

But with Tilak's arrest, all hopes for an Indian offensive were stalled. The Congress lost credit with the people, A Muslim deputation met with the Viceroy, Minto (1905–10), seeking concessions from the impending constitutional reforms, including special considerations in government service and electorates. The British recognised some of Muslim League's petitions by increasing the number of elective offices reserved for Muslims in the Government of India Act 1909. The Muslim League insisted on its separateness from the Hindu-dominated Congress, as the voice of a "nation within a nation."

Partition of Bengal

In 1905, Curzon, the Viceroy and Governor-General (1899–1905), ordered the partition of the province of Bengal for improvements in administrative efficiency in that huge and populous region, where the Bengali Hindu intelligentsia exerted considerable influence on local and national politics. The partition outraged Bengalis. Not only had the government failed to consult Indian public opinion, but the action appeared to reflect the British resolve to divide and rule. Widespread agitation ensued in the streets and in the press, and the Congress advocated boycotting British products under the banner of swadeshi. People showed unity by tying Rakhi on each other's wrists and observing Arandhan (not cooking any food).

During the partition of Bengal new methods of struggle were adopted. These led to swadeshi and boycott movements. The Congress-led boycott of British goods was so successful that it unleashed anti-British forces to an extent unknown since the Sepoy Rebellion. A cycle of violence and repression ensued in some parts of the country. The British tried to mitigate the situation by announcing a series of constitutional reforms in 1909 and by appointing a few moderates to the imperial and provincial councils. In what the British saw as an additional goodwill gesture, in 1911 King-Emperor George V visited India for a durbar (a traditional court held for subjects to express fealty to their ruler), during which he announced the reversal of the partition of Bengal and the transfer of the capital from Calcutta to a newly planned city to be built immediately south of Delhi, which later became New Delhi. However, ceremony of transfer on 23 December 1912 was marked by the attempt to assassinate the then Viceroy, Lord Hardinge, in what came to be known as the Delhi-Lahore conspiracy.

World War I

World War I began with an unprecedented outpouring of loyalty and goodwill towards the United Kingdom from within the mainstream political leadership, contrary to initial British fears of an Indian revolt. India contributed massively to the British war effort by providing men and resources. About 1.3 million Indian soldiers and labourers served in Europe, Africa, and the Middle East, while both the Indian government and the Princes sent large supplies of food, money, and ammunition. However, Bengal and Punjab remained hotbeds of anti-colonial activities.

Terrorism in Bengal, increasingly closely linked with the unrests in Punjab, was significant enough to nearly paralyse the regional administration. Also from the beginning of the war, expatriate Indian population, notably from United States, Canada, and Germany, headed by the Berlin Committee and the Ghadar Party, attempted to trigger insurrections in India on the lines of the 1857 uprising with Irish Republican, German and Turkish help in a massive conspiracy that has since come to be called the Hindu German conspiracy. This conspiracy also attempted to rally Afghanistan against British India. A number of failed attempts were made at mutiny, of which the February mutiny plan and the Singapore mutiny remains most notable. This movement was suppressed by means of a massive international counter-intelligence operation and draconian political acts (including the Defence of India act 1915) that lasted nearly ten years.

In the aftermath of the WW I, high casualty rates, soaring inflation compounded by heavy taxation, a widespread influenza epidemic, and the disruption of trade during the war escalated, human suffering in India. The Indian soldiers smuggled arms into India to overthrow the British rule. The pre-war nationalist movement revived as moderate and extremist groups within the Congress submerged their differences in order to stand as a unified front. In 1916, the Congress succeeded in forging the Lucknow Pact, a temporary alliance with the Muslim League over the issues of devolution of political power and the future of Islam in the region.

The British themselves adopted a "carrot and stick" approach in recognition of India's support during the war and in response to renewed nationalist demands. In August 1917, Edwin Montagu, the secretary of state for India, made the historic announcement in Parliament that the British policy for India was "increasing association of Indians in every branch of the administration and the gradual development of self-governing institutions with a view to the progressive realisation of responsible government in India as an integral part of the British Empire."

The means of achieving the proposed measure were later enshrined in the Government of India Act 1919, which introduced the principle of a dual mode of administration, or diarchy, in which both elected Indian legislators and appointed British officials shared power. The act also expanded the central and provincial legislatures and widened the franchise considerably. Diarchy set in motion certain real changes at the provincial level: a number of non-controversial or "transferred" portfolios, such as agriculture, local government, health, education, and public works, were handed over to Indians, while more sensitive matters such as finance, taxation, and maintaining law and order were retained by the provincial British administrators.

Impact of Gandhi's Arrival in India

Mahatma Gandhi had been a prominent leader of the anti-Apartheid Movement in South Africa, and had been a vocal opponent of basic discrimination and abusive labour treatment as well as suppressive police control such as the Rowlatt Acts. During these protests, Gandhi had perfected the concept of satyagraha, which had been inspired by the philosophy of Baba Ram Singh (famous for leading the Kuka Movement in the Punjab in 1872). The end of the protests in South Africa saw oppressive legislation repealed and the release of political prisoners by General Jan Smuts, head of the South African Government of the time.

Gandhi, a stranger to India and its politics after twenty years, had initially entered the fray not with calls for a nation-state, but in support of the unified commerce-oriented territory that the

Congress Party had been asking for. Gandhi believed that the industrial development and educational development that the Europeans had brought with them were required to alleviate many of India's problems.

Gopal Krishna Gokhale, a veteran Congressman and Indian leader, became Gandhi's mentor. Gandhi's ideas and strategies of non-violent civil disobedience initially appeared impractical to some Indians and Congressmen. In Gandhi's own words, "civil disobedience is civil breach of unmoral statutory enactments." It had to be carried out non-violently by withdrawing cooperation with the corrupt state. Gandhi's ability to inspire millions of common people became clear when he used satyagraha during the anti-Rowlatt Act protests in Punjab.

Gandhi's vision would soon bring millions of regular Indians into the movement, transforming it from an elitist struggle to a national one. The nationalist cause was expanded to include the interests and industries that formed the economy of common Indians. For example, in Champaran, Bihar, the Congress Party championed the plight of desperately poor sharecroppers and landless farmers who were being forced to pay oppressive taxes and grow cash crops at the expense of the subsistence crops which formed their food supply. The profits from the crops they grew were insufficient to provide for their sustenance.

Beginning of the Movement

Rowlatt Bills

The Government of India rushed the Rowlatt Bills, through the Imperial Legislative Council in March 1919 in the teeth of the opposition of all the elected Indian members. Gandhi heard the debate in the Imperial Legislative Council and saw how the eloquent logic of Indian councilors had been wasted on the official benches. "You can wake a man," he wrote later, "only if he is really asleep; no effort that you may make will produce any effect upon him if he is merely pretending sleep". The conviction grew upon him that the Government of India was impervious to popular feeling. A Government which really cared for public opinion would not have enacted a measure — whatever its merits — which had been opposed by every shade of public opinion.

The constitutional opposition to Rowlatt Bills having proved fruitless, Gandhi felt that recourse must be had to Satyagraha to secure the repeal of the Rowlatt Bills. Already in February 1919, he had drafted and circulated a pledge of resistance to Rowlatt Bills: "In the event of those bills becoming law and until they are withdrawn, we shall refuse civilly to obey these laws and such other laws as a committee to be hereafter appointed may think fit, and further affirm that in this struggle we shall faithfully follow truth and refrain from violence to life, person and property."

Now that the Government had put the first Rowlatt Bill on the statute-book, Gandhi — though he had not yet fully recovered from his illness — picked up the gauntlet. He toured the country to educate the people in the implications of the Satyagraha pledge and founded a new organisation, the Satyagraha Sabha. He called for a day of "hartal", when all business was to be suspended and people were to fast and pray as a protest against the hated legislation.

The idea of a "hartal" as a measure of mourning or protest was not a novel one in India, but as a one-day national strike, it was a masterly stroke. The hartal in Delhi was observed owing to a misunderstanding on March 30 instead of April 6, and it was also marred by some rioting. Gandhi promptly condemned the excesses of the mob as well as those of the local officials who, he said, had used a hammer to crush a fly. Tension mounted in Punjab where the local leaders felt that Gandhi's presence would assist in maintaining peace. But the Government did not let Gandhi reach Punjab; while he was on his way to Delhi, he was taken out of his compartment at a small station and put in another train bound for Bombay, where he was released,. He would have again left for Delhi, had he not discovered that in his absence disturbances had broken out in the city of Bombay, Ahmedabad, Nadiad and other places in his own province which was the least expected to forget his doctrine of non-violence. He came to the conclusion that he had underrated the latent forces of violence. He decided to retrace his steps, to give up the idea of seeking re-arrest, restrict and finally suspend Satyagraha. He observed a three-day fast to atone for his "Himalayan miscalculation" in launching a mass movement without making sure that the people were ready for it.

Meanwhile, events in Punjab had moved to a tragic climax. At Amritsar, two local leaders were arrested on April 10. A crowd which had gathered to demand their release ran amuck, attacked two banks and murdered five Europeans. On the day of the Baisakhi festival, Amritsar's Jallianwala Bagh, where a public meeting was held, became the scene of a holocaust. Under the orders of General Dyer, 1,650 rounds were fired in ten minutes; nearly 400 persons were killed, and 1,200 injured. The Governor, Sir Michael O'Dwyer and his advisers made themselves believe that British rule was in danger.

Martial Law was imposed on several districts in the Punjab. A draconian regime followed. The Government appointed a committee of Enquiry headed by Lord Hunter to enquire into the genesis of the Punjab disturbances. The Indian National Congress decided to boycott the Hunter Committee and appointed a non-official committee consisting of eminent lawyers, such as C.R. Das, M. R. Jayakar, Abbas Tyabji and Gandhi. It was as a member of this non-official committee that Gandhi learnt the truth about he martial law regime in the Punjab. He discovered shocking instances of high-handedness based on incontrovertible evidence which he himself scrupulously sifted. The fanciful image of the British Empire as a merciful dispensation of providence that he had cherished seemed to crumble to the ground.

Gandhi's alienation from the Raj was not yet complete. He argued that the Punjab had been wronged by a few erratic officers and hoped that the Government would, when it knew the truth, make amends. In this hope he was disappointed. The British officers responsible for misrule in he Punjab were not recalled immediately; indeed they were lionised by the European community. The report of the Hunter Committee, when it came out, struck Gandhi as little better than "thinly disguised whitewash". After hearing the debate on the Punjab tragedy in the British Parliament, one Indian correspondent wrote to Gandhi: "Our friends revealed their ignorance; our enemies their insolence."

Reluctantly and almost painfully, Gandhi was driven to the conclusion that the system of government which he had been trying to mend needed to be ended.

Gandhi's links with the British Empire would not have snapped so dramatically were it not for another strand in Indian politics, represented by the "Khilafat" Movement. Indian Muslims were agitated over the terms Turkey was likely to get from the victorious

Allied Powers and over the fate of Muslim holy places in the Middle East. Gandhi feared that the pent-up Muslim frustration might burst the dykes and turn into violent channels. Hence, he offered to lead the Muslim community on the Khilafat issue, if it accepted his technique. It is significant that Gandhi's programme of non-violent non-cooperation with the British Government was endorsed by he leaders of the "Khilafat" Movement even before it was approved by the Indian National Congress in September 1920.

Rowlatt Act and its Aftermath

The positive impact of reform was seriously undermined in 1919 by the Rowlatt Act, named after the recommendations made the previous year to the Imperial Legislative Council by the Rowlatt Commission, which had been appointed to investigate what was termed the "seditious conspiracy" and the German and Bolshevik involvement in the millitant movements in India. The Rowlatt Act, also known as the Black Act, vested the Viceroy's government with extraordinary powers to quell sedition by silencing the press, detaining the political activists without trial, and arresting any individuals suspected of sedition or treason without a warrant. In protest, a nationwide cessation of work (hartal) was called, marking the beginning of widespread, although not nationwide, popular discontent. The agitation unleashed by the acts culminated on 13 April 1919, in the Jallianwala Bagh massacre (also known as the Amritsar Massacre) in Amritsar, Punjab. The British military commander, Brigadier-General Reginald Dyer, blocked the main entrance, and ordered his soldiers to fire into an unarmed and unsuspecting crowd of some 5,000 men, women and children. They had assembled at Jallianwala Bagh, a walled in courtyard in defiance of the ban. A total of 1,651 rounds were fired, killing 379 people (as according to an official British commission; Indian estimates ranged as high as 1,499) and wounding 1,137 in the episode, which dispelled wartime hopes of home rule and goodwill in a frenzy of post-war reaction.

Champaran and Kheda Satyagraha

The first Satyagraha revolutions inspired by Mahatma Gandhi in the Indian Independence Movement occurred in Kheda district of Gujarat and the Champaran district of Bihar between the years of 1918 and 1919.

Champaran, Bihar: In Champaran, a district in state of [Bihar], tens of thousands of landless serfs, indentured labourers and poor farmers were forced to grow [indigo] and other cash crops instead of the food crops necessary for their survival. These goods were bought from them at a very low price. Suppressed by the ruthless militias of the landlords (mostly British), they were given measly compensation, leaving them mired in extreme poverty. The villages were kept extremely dirty and unhygienic, and [alcoholism], [untouchability] and [purdah] were rampant. Now in the throes of a devastating famine, the British levied an oppressive tax which they insisted on increasing in rate. The situation was desperate. Desperate of this situation people began rebellions.

Kheda, Gujarat: In Kheda, a district of villages and small towns in Gujarat, the peasants mostly owned their own lands, and were economically better-off than their compatriots in Bihar, although on the whole, the district was plagued by poverty, scant resources, the social evils of alcoholism and untouchability, and overall British indifference and hegemony.

However, a terrible famine had struck the district and a large part of Gujarat, and virtually destroyed the agrarian economy. The poor peasants had barely enough to feed themselves, but the British government of the Bombay Presidency insisted that the farmers not only pay full taxes, but also pay the 23 per cent increase stated to take effect that very year.

Gandhi's Solution: While many civic groups sent petitions and published editorials, Gandhi proposed satyagraha-non-violence, mass civil disobedience. While it was strictly non-violent, Gandhi was proposing real action, a real revolt that the oppressed peoples of India were dying to undertake.

Gandhi also insisted that neither the protestors in Bihar nor in Gujarat allude to or try to propagate the concept of Swaraj, or Independence. This was not about political freedom, but a revolt against abject tyranny amidst a terrible humanitarian disaster. While accepting participants and help from other parts of India, Gandhi insisted that no other district or province revolt against the Government, and that the Indian National Congress not get involved apart from issuing resolutions of support, to prevent the British from giving it cause to use extensive suppressive measures and brand the revolts as treason.

In Champaran: Gandhi established an ashram in Champaran, organising scores of his veteran supporters and fresh volunteers from the region. He organised a detailed study and survey of the villages, accounting the atrocities and terrible episodes of suffering, including the general state of degenerate living. Building on the confidence of villagers, he began leading the clean-up of villages, building of schools and hospitals and encouraging the village leadership to undo purdah, untouchability and the suppression of women. He was joined by many young nationalists from all over India, including Ramarshi Deo Trivedi "Rishi Ji", Brajkishore Prasad, Dr. Rajendra Prasad, Dr. Anugrah Narayan Sinha and Jawaharlal Nehru.

But his main assault came as he was arrested by police on the charge of creating unrest and was ordered to leave the province. Hundreds of thousands of people protested and rallied outside the jail, police stations and courts demanding his release, which the court unwillingly did. Gandhi led organised protests and strike against the landlords, who with the guidance of the British government, signed an agreement granting more compensation and control over farming for the poor farmers of the region, and cancellation of revenue hikes and collection until the famine ended. It was during this agitation, that Gandhi was addressed by the people as Bapu (Father) and Mahatma (Great Soul).

In Kheda: In Gujarat, Gandhi was only the spiritual head of the struggle. His chief lieutenant, Sardar Vallabhbhai Patel and a close coterie of devoted Gandhians, namely Narhari Parikh, Mohanlal Pandya and Ravi Shankar Vyas toured the countryside, organised the villagers and gave them political leadership and direction. Many aroused Gujaratis from the cities of Ahmedabad and Vadodara joined the organisers of the revolt, but Gandhi and Patel resisted the involvement of Indians from other provinces, seeking to keep it a purely Gujarati struggle.

Patel and his colleagues organised a major tax revolt, and all the different ethnic and caste communities of Kheda rallied around it. The peasants of Kheda signed a petition calling for the tax for this year to be scrapped in wake of the famine. The government in Bombay rejected the charter. They warned that if the peasants did not pay, the lands and property would be confiscated and many arrested. And once confiscated, they would not be returned even if most complied. None of the villages flinched.

The tax withheld, the government's collectors and inspectors sent in thugs to seize property and cattle, while the police forfeited the lands and all agrarian property. The farmers did not resist arrest, nor retaliate to the force employed with violence. Instead, they used their cash and valuables to donate to the Gujarat Sabha which was officially organising the protest.

The revolt was astounding in terms of discipline and unity. Even when all their personal property, land and livelihood were seized, a vast majority of Kheda's farmers remained firmly united in the support of Patel. Gujaratis sympathetic to the revolt in other parts resisted the government machinery, and helped the shelter the relatives and property of the protesting peasants. Those Indians who sought to buy the confiscated lands were ostracised from society. Although nationalists like Sardul Singh Caveeshar called for sympathetic revolts in other parts, Gandhi and Patel firmly rejected the idea.

The Government finally sought to foster an honourable agreement for both parties. The tax for the year in question, and the next would be suspended, and the increase in rate reduced, while all confiscated property would be returned.

Gujaratis also worked in cohesion to return the confiscated lands to their rightful owners. The ones who had bought the lands seized were influenced to return them, even though the British had officially said it would stand by the buyers. It was the first place from where Ghandhiji started satyagrah.

Success and Legacy: Gandhi's resulting fame spread like fire all over the nation. He had become a defining influence on Indian Nationalism. People in Gujarat still revere Gandhi and Sardar Patel, and their role in the freedom struggle. Gujarat is the most industrialised and progressive state in India today. In Bihar, poverty and social conflict pervades what was the founding of the Satyagraha Movement. The Naxalite insurgency is centered around the same age-old problem of class struggle between poor farmers and rich landlords, now involving terrorism.

Gandhi's Ashram

While his political views were yet unformed, Gandhi's immediate problem was to settle the small band of relatives and associates in the South African struggle who had cast their lot in with him. He decided to found an ashram and locate it at Kochrab, a village near Ahmedabad. Later the ashram was shifted to a more permanent site on the bank of the river Sabarmati.

Gandhi once defined an ashram as "group life lived in a religious spirit". The word "religious" was used here in the widest sense. The ashram did not enforce on its inmates any theology or ritual, but only a few simple rules of personal conduct. Some of the vows administered in the ashram, such as those to truth, non-violence and chastity, were of universal application; others, such as those to eradicate untouchability, to do physical labour and to practise fearlessness were intended to meet the peculiar conditions of the Indian society, which was caste-ridden, discounted dignity of labour and was dominated by an alien government.

All these vows were to be observed in an intelligent and creative way. They were not intended to be mechanical formulae, but as practical aids to moral and spiritual growth. They may appear to be platitudes, but nevertheless they embodied ancient truths which were none the less valid for not having been realised by the common run of mankind in workaday life.

A mere enumeration of the vows is enough to indicate that life in the ashram was austere. It was also busy. Everyone had to put in some manual work. There was a spinning and weaving department, a cowshed and a large farm. Every inmate of the ashram cleaned his own plates and washed his own clothes. There were no servants.

The atmosphere was, however, not so much of a monastery but that of a large family under a kindly but exacting patriarch. Gandhi was Bapu, the father of the household, Kasturba was Ba, the mother. It was a motley group including little children and octogenarians, graduates of American and European universities and Sanskrit scholars, devout whole-hoggers, and thinly disguised sceptics. It was a human laboratory where Gandhi tested his moral and spiritual hypotheses.

It was also to him what the family is to most people, a haven from the dust and din of the world. It was a family linked not by blood or property, but by allegiance to common ideals. Gandhi ruled the ashram but his authority in the ashram, as well as in the rest of the country, was moral. When things went wrong or a member of the ashram was guilty of a serious lapse, Gandhi would take the blame upon himself and atone for it by undertaking a fast.

World War I

When World War I broke out, Gandhi was on the high seas, he was homeward bound, though he hoped to spend a few weeks in England. On August 6, 1914, he landed on English soil and lost no time in calling a meeting of his Indian friends to raise an ambulance unit. The argument that the Empire's crisis was India's chance did not impress him: "I knew the difference of status between an Indian and an Englishman," he wrote later, "but I did not believe that we had been quite reduced to slavery. I felt then that it was more the fault of individual officials than of the British system, and that we could convert them by love. If we would improve our status through the help and cooperation of the British, it was our duty to win their help by standing by them in their hour of need."

Were it not for an attack of pleurisy, Gandhi may have continued to serve in the ambulance unit he had raised, and his return to India may have been indefinitely delayed.

When he arrived in India he found that nationalist opinion was opposed to unconditional support for the war effort. Only those who were politically backward or flourished on official patronage were for loyalty at all costs. Gandhi did not favour a bargain with the government by offering cooperation at a price and said: "That we have been loyal at a time of stress is no test of fitness for swaraj (self-government). Loyalty is no merit. It is a necessity of citizenship all the world over."

During the years 1916-18, Gandhi did not take active part in politics. His ideals and methods did not quite fit in with those of the two dominant groups in the Indian National Congress. The Moderates did not like his extra-constitutional methods of Satyagraha, the Extremists did not like his studied tenderness to the British Government during the war. He did not participate in the Home Rule agitation nor in the negotiations which led to the Lucknow pact between the Indian National Congress and the All India Muslim League. He seemed to be isolated from the main currents of Indian politics. It was not Gandhi, but the Annie

Besant-Tilak combination which dominated the national scene and impressed the Government. Edwin Montague, a member of the British Cabinet, who visited India in 1917, recorded in his diary that Tilak was "at the moment probably the most powerful man in India." Gandhi seemed to Montague "a social reformer with a real desire to find grievances and to cure them not for any reasons of self advertisement, but to improve the conditions of his fellowmen. He dresses like a coolie, forswears all personal advancement, lives practically on the air and is a pure visionary."

The fact that he was committed to abstention from political agitation during the war did not prevent Gandhi from championing just grievances which could not brook delay. In the summer of 1917, he went to the indigo-growing district of Champaran and took up the cause of the tenants against the European planters. The same year he led the textile workers of Ahmedabad in a strike against the mill-owners.

The following year, he agitated for reduction of land tax in Kaira district where crops had suffered from the failure of rains. The local officers were perturbed by Gandhi's activities but the Government was anxious not to precipi9tate a show-down. Gandhi himself took care to localise these conflicts and sought solutions which secured a modicum of rustice to the workers and peasants without creating a national crisis.

Early in 1918, the war seemed to be going badly for the Allies; a German thrust was expected on the western front, and the Viceroy summoned prominent leaders of Indian opinion to a War Conference in Delhi. Gandhi supported the resolution on recruitment with a single sentence in Hindi: "With a full sense of my responsibility, I beg to support the resolution."

After the War Conference, Gandhi threw himself heart and soul into a recruiting campaign There was something comic in this votary of non-violence touring the villages of his home province of Gujarat to secure recruits for the British Indian army to fight in the battle fronts of Europe. Not infrequently, unable to get bullock-carts for their journeys in the interior of the Gujarat countryside, Gandhi and his colleagues had to march on foot twenty miles a day. The strain was too much for him and at last a severe attack of dysentery laid him low.

Meanwhile the war came to end, and Gandhi learnt that the Sedition Committee Report had been published and the Government of India proposed to introduce legislation to curb civil liberties. He had been almost alone among Indian leaders who had argued for unconditional support to Britain in her hour of need in the hope of a worthy gesture at the end of the war. He felt that he had received stone for bread. He had done his best to keep out of political agitation during the war. Now he felt an irresistible call to fight a wrong perpetrated in peace.

4

Non-cooperation Movement

The Non-cooperation Movement, was the first-ever series of nationwide people's movements of non-violent resistance and Civil Disobedience, led by Mahatma Gandhi and the Indian National Congress. The movement opened the Gandhi Era in the Indian Independence Movement and took place from September 1920 until February 1922.

The Rowlatt Acts were legislation that imposed authoritarian restrictions upon Indian people. The notion of habeas corpus was discarded, and the police and army were empowered to search and seize property, detain and arrest any Indian without the slightest need for evidence. Promulgated by the British Parliament, the Viceroy and the Imperial Legislative Council, they were to be enforced on April 6, 1919.

Furthermore, many Indians were already infuriated by the British authorities' decision to send Indian soldiers to World War I without the slightest desire to consult the Indian people in any manner or form. The calls of liberal and moderate political leaders like Muhammad Ali Jinnah, Annie Besant, Gopal Krishna Gokhale and Bal Gangadhar Tilak for Home Rule were accompanied only by petitions and major public meetings, and not disorder or obstruction of government services.

Champaran, Kheda, Khilafat and Amritsar

Mahatma Gandhi had shown in South Africa and in 1918 in Champaran, Bihar and Kheda, Gujarat that the only way to earn the respect and attention of British officials was to actively resist government activities through civil disobedience.

Now in Champaran and Kheda in 1918 he led impoverished farmers, mired in social evils like unhygienic conditions, domestic violence, discrimination, oppression of women and untouchability. On top of their miseries, these people were forced to grow cash crops like indigo, tobacco and cotton, instead of food, and virtually not compensated. In addition, they would have to pay taxes despite a famine. The Governments of the affected regions signed agreements suspending taxation in face of the famine, allowing the farmers to grow their own crops, releasing all political prisoners and returning all property and lands seized. It was the biggest victory against the British Empire since the American Revolution.

Mahatma Gandhi was assisted by a new generation of Indian revolutionaries like Rajendra Prasad and Jawaharlal Nehru. In Kheda, the entire revolt had been led by Sardar Vallabhbhai Patel, who was to become Gandhi's lieutenant. Millions of India's Muslims were also antagonised by the Government's support of Mustafa Kemal of Turkey, who had overthrown the Sultan of Turkey, also the Caliph of Islam. Muslim leaders formed the Khilafat committee to protest the actions and find a way to effectively stop the British authorities from neglecting their concerns.

A public meeting of unarmed civilians at Jallianwala Bagh in Amritsar was fired upon by troops under the command of Reginald Dyer. Hundreds of people died and perhaps thousands were injured. Women, children and the elderly were not spared. The outcry in Punjab led to thousands of arrests, beatings and more deaths at the hands of police and some violent protesters. The Amritsar Massacre became the most infamous event of British rule in India. To Gandhi and many others, it became clear that a reckoning with the British was not far off.

Satyagraha

Gandhi's idea was a nationwide protest against the Rowlatt Acts. All offices and factories would be closed. Indians would be encouraged to withdraw from Raj-sponsored schools, police services, the military and the civil services, and lawyers to leave the Raj's courts. Public transportation, English-manufactured goods, especially clothes would be boycotted.

Veterans like Bal Gangadhar Tilak, Bipin Chandra Pal, Muhammad Ali Jinnah, Annie Besant opposed the idea outright. The All India Muslim League also criticised the ideas. But the younger generation of Indian nationalists were thrilled and backed Gandhi. The Congress Party adopted his plans, and he received extensive support from Muslim leaders like Maulana Azad, Mukhtar Ahmed Ansari, Hakim Ajmal Khan, Abbas Tyabji, Maulana Muhammad Ali and Maulana Shaukat Ali. Gandhi was elected President of the Indian National Congress in 1919 and 1920, as well as the All India Home Rule League — the latter erstwhile dominated by Gandhi's critics like Jinnah, Besant and Tilak.

Success and Suspension

The success of the revolt launched was a total shock to British authorities and a massive encouragement to millions of Indians. Then on February 4, 1922, in the Chauri Chaura, after violent clashed between the local police and the protestors in which three protestors were killed due the police firing, Gandhi felt that the revolt was veering off-course. He did not want the movement to degenerate into an orgy of violence where police and angry mobs attacked each other back and forth, victimising civilians in between.

Gandhi went on a fast lasting 3 days, appealing to the Indian public for all resistance to end, and called off the mass Civil Disobedience Movement.

The Aftermath

Non-cooperation Movement was withdrawn because of the Chauri-Chaura incident. Despite stopping a national revolt single-handedly, on March 10, 1922, Gandhi was arrested, and on March 18, 1922, he was imprisoned for two years for publishing seditious materials. The British judge who passed the sentence was shaking with emotion of admiration, and said he would himself be the happiest if the government released Gandhi.

Although most Congress leaders remained firmly behind Gandhi, the disillusioned broke away. The Ali brothers would soon become fierce critics, and Motilal Nehru and Chittaranjan Das formed the Swaraj Party, rejecting Gandhi's leadership. Many nationalists had felt that the Non-cooperation Movement should not have been stopped due to isolated incidents of violence, and most nationalists, while retaining confidence in Gandhi, were depressed.

Contemporary historians and critics suggest that the movement was successful enough to break the back of British rule, and possibly even result in the independence most Indians strove for till 1947.

But many historians and Indian leaders of the time also defend Gandhi's judgement. If he had not stopped the revolts, India would probably have descended into an anarchy-style rebellion which would alienate common Indians and impress only violent revolutionaries.

The Redemption

Gandhi's commitment to non-violence was redeemed when between 1930 and 1934, India committed itself to full independence and tens of millions again revolted in the Salt Satyagraha which made India's cause famous worldwide for its unerring adherence to non-violence. The Satyagraha ended in glorious success — the demands of Indians were met, and the Congress Party was recognised as the real representative of Indian people. The Government of India Act 1935 also gave India its first taste in democratic, self-governance.

First Non-cooperation Movement

The first Satyagraha Movement urged the use of Khadi and Indian material as alternatives to those shipped from Britain. It also urged people to eat British educational institutions and law courts; resign from government employment; refuse to pay taxes; and forsake British titles and honours. Although this came too late to influence the framing of the new Government of India Act of 1919, the movement enjoyed widespread popular support, and the resulting unparalleled magnitude of disorder presented a serious challenges to foreign rule. However, Gandhi called off the movement following the Chauri Chaura incident, which saw the death of twenty-two policemen at the hands of an angry mob.

In 1920, the Congress was reorganised and given a new Constitution, whose goal was Swaraj (independence). Membership in the party was opened to anyone prepared to pay a token fee, and a hierarchy of committees was established and made responsible for discipline and control over a hitherto amorphous and diffuse movement. The party was transformed from an elite organisation to one of mass national appeal and participation.

Gandhi was imprisoned in 1922 for six years, but was released after serving two. On his release from prison, he set up the Sabarmati Ashram in Ahmedabad, on the banks of river Sabarmati, established the newspaper Young India, and inaugurated a series of reforms aimed at the socially disadvantaged within Hindu society — the rural poor, and the untouchables.

This era saw the emergence of new generation of Indians from within the Congress Party, including C. Rajagopalachari, Jawaharlal Nehru, Vallabhbhai Patel, Subhash Chandra Bose and others — who would later on come to form the prominent voices of the Indian Independence Movement, whether keeping with Gandhian Values, or diverging from it.

The Indian political spectrum was further broadened in the mid-1920s by the emergence of both moderate and militant parties, such as the Swaraj Party, Hindu Mahasabha, Communist Party of India and the Rashtriya Swayamsevak Sangh. Regional political organisations also continued to represent the interests of non-Brahmins in Madras, Mahars in Maharashtra, and Sikhs in Punjab. However, Brahmin like Mahakavi Subramanya Bharathi, Vanchinathan and Neelakanda Brahmachari played a major role from Tamil Nadu in both freedom struggle and fighting for equality for all castes and communities.

Purna Swaraj

Following the rejection of the recommendations of the Simon Commission by Indians, an all-party conference was held at Bombay in May 1928. This was meant to instil a sense of resistance among people. The conference appointed a drafting committee under Motilal Nehru to draw up a Constitution for India. The Calcutta session of the Indian National Congress asked the British government to accord dominion status to India by December 1929, or a countrywide Civil Disobedience Movement would be launched. By 1929, however, in the midst rising political discontent and increasingly violent regional movements, the call for complete independence from Britain began to find increasing grounds within the Congress leadership. Under the presidency of Jawaharlal Nehru at its historic Lahore session in December 1929, The Indian National Congress adopted a resolution calling for complete independence from the British. It authorised the Working Committee to launch a Civil Disobedience Movement throughout the country. It was decided that 26 January 1930 should be observed all over India as the Purna Swaraj (complete independence) Day. Many Indian political parties and Indian revolutionaries of a wide spectrum united to observe the day with honour and pride. Purna Swaraj has been asked by Bhagat Singh while the hearing of "Bomb blast in Parliament to oppose Simon Commission" in supreme court in year 1928, till that time Congress of India was asking for Dominion independence.

Non-Violence and Non-cooperation

The programme of "non-violent non-cooperation" included the boycott of councils, courts and schools, set up by the British and of all foreign cloth. With some naivete Gandhi claimed that his movement was not unconstitutional: In his dictionary, constitutional and moral were synonymous terms. The British saw that the success of "non-cooperation" would paralyse their administration. Lord Chelmsford, the Viceroy, tried to kill with ridicule "the most foolish of all foolish schemes", which would "bring ruin to those who had any stake in the country". A number of eminent "moderate" politicians joined official critics in underlining the risks of mass non-cooperation as proposed by Gandhi.

That a political programme had no chance of success without an adequate organisation to implement it, Gandhi had realised at the age of twenty-five, when he had founded the Natal Indian Congress to fight for the rights of Indians in Natal. The Indian National Congress, had, therefore, to be refashioned, if it was to prove an efficient instrument of non-violent non-cooperation. Gandhi saw that what the country needed was not a forum for an annual pageant and feast of oratory, but a militant organisation in touch with the masses. Under the new Constitution, the Congress was given a broad-based pyramidal structure by formation of village, taluka, district and provincial committees, with the All

India Congress Committee and the Working Committee at the apex. The Congress was thus reorganised not only on a more representative basis, but in such a way that it could function efficiently between its annual sessions. It ceased to be a preserve of the upper and middle classes; its doors were opened to the masses in the small towns and villages whose political consciousness Gandhi himself was quickening.

Gandhi was swept to the top of Indian politics in 1919-20 because he had caught the imagination of the people. He was loved and respected as the Mahatma, the great soul; with voluntary poverty, simplicity, humility and saintliness, he seemed a rishi (sage) of old who had stepped from the pages of an ancient epic to bring about the liberation of his country. Nay, to millions he was the incarnation of God. It was not only for his message that people came to him, but for the merit of seeing him. The sacred sight of the Mahatma — his darshan — was almost equivalent to a pilgrimage to holy Banaras. The unthinking adoration of the multitude sometimes made Gandhi feel sick. "The woes of the Mahatma", he wrote, "are known only to the Mahatma". But this adoration was the mainspring from which was drawn the immense influence he exercised over Indian public life.

Gandhi had struck some of the inner chords of Indian humanity; his appeal for courage and sacrifice evoked a ready response because he was himself the epitome of these qualities. It was because he was, to use Churchill's epithet, a "naked fakir", because his life was one of austerity and self-sacrifice that a great emotional bond grew between him and the Indian people. The number of such "fakirs" was to multiply fast. Among those who gave up their lucrative careers and queued up for prison under Gandhi's leadership were Motilal Nehru, Rajendra Prasad, C.R. Das, Vallabhbhai Patel, and C. Rajagopalachari. Life acquired a new meaning for them. Abbas Tyabji, a former Chief Justice of Baroda, wrote from a village that he was feeling twenty years younger. "God?" he exclaimed, "what an experience! I have so much love and affection for the common folk to whom it is now an honour to belong. It is the fakir's dress that has broken down all barriers." It is of this period that Jawaharlal Nehru has written in his autobiography that the movement absorbed him so wholly that he "gave up all other associations and contacts, old friends, books, even newspapers except in so far as they dealt with the work in hand.... I almost forgot my family, my wife, my daughter."

From the autumn of 1920, the Non-cooperation Movement gathered momentum. The attitude of the Government at first was one of caution. It was reluctant to launch a drastic repression, as it did not want to alienate moderate Indian opinion. Soon after his arrival in India in April, 1921, Lord Reading, the new Viceroy, met Gandhi. In a private letter to his son, the Viceroy confessed to a feeling of excitement, almost a thrill, in meeting his unusual visitor and described his religious and moral views as admirable, though he found it difficult to understand his practice of them in politics.

Throughout 1921, the tension between the Congress and the Government was steadily mounting. There was no meeting of minds between Gandhi and Reading. The Ali Brothers, the principal leaders of the Khilafat, were arrested in September 1921 on a charge of inciting the army to disloyalty; their offence was repeated by a number of Indian leaders including Gandhi. This was a challenge which was difficult for the Government not to accept. The official optimism that the movement would melt away by internal differences or popular apathy proved to be misplaced. Nearly thirty thousand non-cooperators were arrested.

The Government was reluctant to touch Gandhi until a favourable opportunity came. Indeed as late as December 1921, Lord Reading seemed willing to hold a Round Table Conference with Gandhi and other Indian leaders to reach an understanding and to avoid unseemly scenes during the visit to India of the Prince of Wales. Lord Reading was, however, hardly in a position to make any substantial political concessions. Meanwhile, Gandhi was under increasing pressure from his adherents to launch a civil disobedience campaign.

The Ahmedabad Congress in December 1921 invested him with authority to launch a mass movement. Mass civil disobedience was, in the words of Gandhi, "an earthquake, a sort of general upheaval on the political plane — the Government ceases to function... the police stations, the courts, offices, etc. all cease to be Government property and shall be taken charge of by the people." He proposed to proceed cautiously. His plan was to launch civil disobedience in one district; if it succeeded he proposed to extend it to the adjacent districts, and so on, until the whole of India was liberated. But he gave a clear warning that if violence broke out in any form in any part of the country, the movement would lose its character as a movement of peace, "even as a lute would begin to emit notes of discord the moment a single string snaps."

A riot which disfigured Bombay during the visit of Prince of Wales in November 1921 had led Gandhi to postpone civil disobedience. Nevertheless, two months later, under growing pressure from his colleagues, he decided to launch a no-tax campaign in Bardoli taluka in Gujarat. He communicated the step he contemplated, with his reasons for it, in a letter to the Viceroy. This was taken by the Government of India as an ultimatum. A head-on collision between the Government on the one hand and the nationalist forces on the other seemed imminent. Gandhi's letter to the Viceroy was dated February 1, 1922. Three days later, there was a clash between a procession and the police at Chauri Chaura, a small village in the United Province, in which the police station was set on fire and 22 policemen were killed.

Gandhi viewed the Chauri Chaura tragedy as a red signal, a warning that the atmosphere in the country was too explosive for a mass movement. He decided to retrace his steps, to cancel the plans for civil disobedience in Bardoli, to suspend the aggressive part of the non-cooperation campaign, and to shift the emphasis to the 'constructive' programme of hand-spinning, communal unity, abolition of untouchability, etc. His action shocked and bewildered his closest colleagues. Their reaction is best expressed in Romain Rolland's words: "It was dangerous to assemble all the forces of a nation and to hold the nation panting before a prescribed movement, to lift one's arm to give the final command, then at the last moment, let one's arm drop and thrice call a halt just as the formidable machinery has been set in motion. One risks ruining the brakes and paralysing the impetus." The Viceroy, Lord Reading, cheerfully confided to his son that Gandhi "had pretty well run himself to the last ditch as a politician by extraordinary manifestation in the last month or six weeks before his arrest".

Swaraj and Salt March

Gandhi stayed out of the limelight for most of the 1920s, preferring to resolve the wedge between the Swaraj Party and the Indian National Congress, and expanding initiatives against untouchability, alcoholism, ignorance and poverty. He returned to the fore in 1928. The year before, the British government had appointed a new constitutional reform commission under Sir John Simon, with not a single Indian in its ranks. The result was a boycott of the commission by Indian political parties. Gandhi pushed through a resolution at the Calcutta Congress in December 1928 calling on the British government to grant India dominion status or face a new campaign of non-violence with complete independence for the country as its goal. Gandhi had not only moderated the views of younger men like Subhas Chandra Bose and Jawaharlal Nehru, who sought a demand for immediate independence, but also modified his own call to a one year wait, instead of two.

The British did not respond. On 31 December 1929, the flag of India was unfurled in Lahore. 26 January 1930 was celebrated by the Indian National Congress, meeting in Lahore, as India's Independence Day. This day was commemorated by almost every other Indian organisation. Making good on his word, Gandhi launched a new satyagraha against the tax on salt in March 1930, highlighted by the famous Salt March to Dandi from March 12 to April 6, marching 400 kilometres (248 miles) from Ahmedabad to Dandi, Gujarat to make salt himself. Thousands of Indians joined him on this march to the sea. This campaign was one of his most successful at upsetting British rule; Britain responded by imprisoning over 60,000 people.

The government, represented by Lord Edward Irwin, decided to negotiate with Gandhi. The Gandhi-Irwin Pact was signed in March 1931. The British Government agreed to set all political prisoners free in return for the suspension of the Civil Disobedience Movement. Furthermore, Gandhi was invited to attend the Round Table Conference in London as the sole representative of the Indian National Congress.

The conference was a disappointment to Gandhi and the nationalists, as it focused on the Indian Princes and Indian minorities rather than the transfer of power. Furthermore, Lord Irwin's successor, Lord Willingdon, embarked on a new campaign of repression against the nationalists. Gandhi was again arrested, and the government attempted to destroy his influence by completely isolating him from his followers. This tactic was not successful. In 1932, through the campaigning of the Dalit leader B. R. Ambedkar, the government granted untouchables separate electorates under the new Constitution. In protest, Gandhi embarked on a six-day fast in September 1932, successfully forcing the government to adopt a more equitable arrangement via negotiations mediated by the Dalit cricketer turned political leader Palwankar Baloo. This was the start of a new campaign by Gandhi to improve the lives of the untouchables, whom he named Harijans, the children of God.

On 8 May 1933 Gandhi began a 21-day fast of self-purification to help the Harijan Movement. This new campaign was not universally embraced within the Dalit community, however, as prominent leader B. R. Ambedkar condemned Gandhi's use of the term Harijans as saying that Dalits were socially immature, and that privileged caste Indians played a paternalistic role. Ambedkar and his allies also felt Gandhi was undermining Dalit political rights. Gandhi, although born into the Vaishya caste, insisted that he was able to speak on behalf of Dalits, despite the availability of Dalit activists such as Ambedkar.

In the summer of 1934, three unsuccessful attempts were made on his life.

When the Congress Party chose to contest elections and accept power under the Federation scheme, Gandhi decided to resign from party membership. He did not disagree with the party's move, but felt that if he resigned, his popularity with Indians would cease to stifle the party's membership, that actually varied from communists, socialists, trade unionists, students, religious conservatives, to those with pro-business convictions and that these various voices would get a chance to make themselves heard. Gandhi also did not want to prove a target for Raj propaganda by leading a party that had temporarily accepted political accommodation with the Raj.

Gandhi returned to the head in 1936, with the Nehru presidency and the Lucknow session of the Congress. Although Gandhi desired a total focus on the task of winning independence and not speculation about India's future, he did not restrain the Congress from adopting socialism as its goal. Gandhi had a clash with Subhas Bose, who had been elected to the presidency in 1938. Gandhi's main points of contention with Bose were his lack of commitment to democracy, and lack of faith in non-violence. Bose won his second term despite Gandhi's criticism, but left the

Congress when the All-India leaders resigned *en masse* in protest against his abandonment of the principles introduced by Gandhi.

Salt Satyagraha

The Salt Satyagraha was a campaign of non-violent protest against the British salt tax in colonial India which began with the Salt March to Dandi on March 12, 1930. It was the first act of organised opposition to British rule after Purna Swaraj, the declaration of independence by the Indian National Congress. Mahatma Gandhi led the Dandi march from his Sabarmati, Ashram to Dandi, Gujarat to make salt, with growing numbers of Indians joining him along the way. When Gandhi broke the salt laws in Dandi at the conclusion of the march on April 6, 1930, it sparked large scale acts of civil disobedience against the British Raj salt laws by millions of Indians.

Gandhi was arrested by Mr. Kinsella on May 5, 1930, just days before his planned raid on the Dharasana Salt Works. The Dandi March and the ensuing Dharasana Satyagraha drew worldwide attention to the Indian Independence Movement through extensive newspaper and newsreel coverage. The satyagraha against the salt tax continued for almost a year, ending with Gandhi's release from jail and negotiations with Viceroy Lord Irwin at the Second Round Table Conference. Over 80,000 Indians were jailed as a result of the Salt Satyagraha. The campaign had a significant effect on changing world and British attitudes towards Indian independence, and caused large numbers of Indians to actively join the fight for the first time, but failed to win major concessions from the British.

The Salt Satyagraha campaign was based upon Gandhi's principles of non-violent protest called satyagraha, which he loosely translated as "truth-force." In early-1930 the Indian National Congress chose satyagraha as their main tactic for winning Indian independence from British rule and appointed Gandhi to organise the campaign. Gandhi chose the 1882 British Salt Act as the first target of satyagraha. The Salt March to Dandi, and the beating of hundreds of non-violent protesters in Dharasana, demonstrated the effective use of civil disobedience as a technique for fighting social and political injustice. The satyagraha teachings of Gandhi and the March to Dandi had a significant influence on American civil rights activist Martin Luther King, Jr., and his fight for civil rights for blacks and other minority groups in the 1960s.

Declaration of Independence

At midnight on December 31, 1929, the Indian National Congress raised the tricolour flag of India on the banks of the Ravi at Lahore. The Indian National Congress, led by Gandhi and Jawaharlal Nehru, publicly issued the Declaration of Independence, or Purna Swaraj, on January 26, 1930. The declaration included the readiness to withhold taxes, and the statement: We believe that it is the inalienable right of the Indian people, as of any other people, to have freedom and to enjoy the fruits of their toil and have the necessities of life, so that they may have full opportunities of growth. We believe also that if any government deprives a people of these rights and oppresses them the people have a further right to alter it or abolish it. The British government in India has not only deprived the Indian people of their freedom but has based itself on the exploitation of the masses, and has ruined India economically, politically, culturally and spiritually. We believe therefore, that India must sever the British connection and attain Purna Swaraj or complete independence.

The Congress Working Committee gave Gandhi the responsibility for organising the first act of civil disobedience, with Congress itself ready to take charge after Gandhi's expected arrest. Gandhi's plan was to begin civil disobedience with a satyagraha aimed at the British salt tax. The 1882 Salt Act gave the British a monopoly on the collection and manufacture of salt, limiting its handling to government salt depots and levying a salt tax. Violation of the Salt Act was a criminal offence. Even though salt was freely available to those living on the coast, Indians were forced to purchase it from the colonial government.

Gandhi's choice of the salt tax was met with incredulity by the Working Committee of the Congress, though Gandhi had his reasons for choosing the salt tax. The salt tax was a deeply symbolic choice, since salt was used by nearly everyone in India. It represented 8.2 per cent of the British Raj tax revenue, and most significantly hurt the poorest Indians the most. Gandhi felt that this protest would dramatise Purna Swaraj in a way that was meaningful to the lowliest Indians. He also reasoned that it would build unity between Hindus and Muslims by fighting a wrong that touched them equally.

Satyagraha

Mahatma Gandhi, along with many members of the Congress Party, had a long-standing commitment to non-violent civil disobedience, which he termed satyagraha, as the basis for achieving Indian independence. Referring to the relationship between satyagraha and Purna Swaraj, Gandhi saw "an inviolable connection between the means and the end as there is between the seed and the tree." He wrote, "If the means employed are impure, the change will not be in the direction of progress but very likely in the opposite. Only a change brought about in our political condition by pure means can lead to real progress."

Satyagraha is a synthesis of the Sanskrit words Satya (truth) and Agraha (holding firmly to). For Gandhi, satyagraha went far beyond mere "passive resistance" and became strength in practicing non-violent methods. In his words:

Truth (satya) implies love, and firmness (agraha) engenders and therefore serves as a synonym for force. I thus began to call the Indian movement Satyagraha, that is to say, the Force which is born of Truth and Love or non-violence, and gave up the use of the phrase "passive resistance", in connection with it, so much so that even in English writing we often avoided it and used instead the word "satyagraha"....

His first significant attempt in India at leading mass satyagraha was the Non-cooperation Movement from 1920-22. Even though it succeeded in raising millions of Indians in protest against the British created Rowlatt Acts, violence broke out at Chauri Chaura, where a mob killed 22 unarmed policemen. Gandhi suspended the protest, against the opposition of other Congress members. He decided that Indians were not yet ready for successful non-violent resistance. The Bardoli Satyagraha in 1928 was much more successful. It succeeded in paralysing the British government and winning significant concessions. More importantly, due to extensive press coverage, it scored a propaganda victory out of all proportion to its size. Gandhi later claimed that success at Bardoli confirmed his belief in Satyagraha and Swaraj: "It is only gradually that we shall come to know the importance of the victory gained at Bardoli...Bardoli has shown the way and cleared it. Swaraj lies on that route, and that alone is the cure..." Gandhi recruited heavily from the Bardoli Satyagraha participants for the Dandi march, which passed through many of the same villages that took part in the Bardoli protests.

Preparing for the March

On February 5, newspapers reported that Gandhi would begin civil disobedience by defying the salt laws. The salt satyagraha would begin on March 12 and end in Dandi with Gandhi breaking the salt act on April 6. Gandhi chose April 6 to launch the mass breaking of the salt laws for a symbolic reason — it was the first day of "National Week", begun in 1919 when Gandhi conceived of the national hartal (strike) against the Rowlatt Act.

Gandhi prepared the worldwide media for the march by issuing regular statements from Sabarmati, at his regular prayer meetings and through direct contact with the press. Expectations were heightened by his repeated statements anticipating arrest, and his increasingly dramatic language as the hour approached: "We are entering upon a life and death struggle, a holy war; we are performing an all-embracing sacrifice in which we wish to offer ourselves as oblation." Correspondents from dozens of Indian, European, and American newspapers, along with film companies, responded to the drama and began actively covering the event.

For the march itself, Gandhi wanted the strictest discipline and adherence to satyagraha and ahimsa. For that reason, he recruited the marchers not from Congress Party members, but from the residents of his own ashram, who were trained in Gandhi's strict standards of discipline. The 23 day march would pass through 4 districts and 48 villages. The route of the march, along with each evening's stopping place, was planned ahead of time based on recruitment potential, past contacts, and timing. Gandhi sent scouts to each village ahead of the march so he could plan his talks at each resting place, based on the needs of the local residents. Events at each village were scheduled and publicised in Indian and foreign press.

On March 2, 1930 Gandhi wrote to the Viceroy, Lord Irwin, offering to stop the march if Irwin met eleven demands, including reduction of land revenue assessments, cutting military spending, imposing a tariff on foreign cloth, and abolishing the salt tax. His strongest appeal to Irwin regarded the salt tax:

> If my letter makes no appeal to your heart, on the eleventh day of this month I shall proceed with such co-workers of the Ashram as I can take, to disregard the provisions of the Salt Laws. I regard this tax to be the most iniquitous of all from the poor man's standpoint. As the Independence Movement is essentially for the poorest in the land, the beginning will be made with this evil.

Irwin did not take the threat of a salt protest seriously, writing to London, "At present the prospect of a salt campaign does not keep me awake at night." After the Viceroy ignored the letter and refused to meet with Gandhi, the march was set in motion. The eve of the march brought thousands of Indians to Sabarmati to hear Gandhi speak at the regular evening prayer. An American academic writing for The Nation reported that "60,000 persons gathered on the bank of the river to hear Gandhi's call to arms. This call to arms was perhaps the most remarkable call to war that has ever been made."

March to Dandi

On March 12, 1930, Gandhi and 78 male satyagrahis set out on foot for the coastal village of.Dandi, Gujarat, 390 kilometres from their starting point at Sabarmati Ashram. According to The Statesman, the official government newspaper which usually played down the size of crowds at Gandhi's functions, 100,000 people crowded the road that separated Sabarmati from Ahmedabad. The first day's march of 21 kilometres (13 mi) ended in the village of Aslali, where Gandhi spoke to a crowd of about 4,000. At Aslali, and the other villages that the march passed through, volunteers collected donations, registered new satyagrahis, and received resignations from village officials who chose to end cooperation with British rule.

As they entered each village, crowds greeted the marchers, beating drums and cymbals. Gandhi gave speeches attacking the salt tax as inhuman, and the salt satyagraha as a "poor man's battle." Each night they slept in the open, asking of the villagers nothing more than simple food and a place to rest and wash. Gandhi felt that this would bring the poor into the battle for independence, necessary for eventual victory.

Thousands of satyagrahis and leaders like Sarojini Naidu joined him. Every day, more and more people joined the march. At Surat, they were greeted by 30,000 people. When they reached the railhead at Dandi, more than 50,000 were gathered. Gandhi gave interviews and wrote articles along the way. Foreign journalists made him a household name in Europe and America. The New York Times wrote almost daily about the Salt March, including two front page articles on April 6 and April 7. Near the end of the march, Gandhi declared, "I want world sympathy in this battle of Right against Might."

Upon arriving at the seashore on April 5, Gandhi was interviewed by an Associated Press reporter. He stated:

> I cannot withhold my compliments from the government for the policy of complete non-interference adopted by them throughout the march .... I wish I could believe this non-interference was due to any real change of heart or policy. The wanton disregard shown by them to popular feeling in the Legislative Assembly and their high-handed action leave no room for doubt that the policy of heartless exploitation of India is to be persisted in at any cost, and so the only interpretation I can put upon this non-interference is that the British Government, powerful though it is, is sensitive to world opinion which will not tolerate repression of extreme political agitation which civil disobedience undoubtedly is, so long as disobedience remains civil and therefore necessarily non-violent .... It remains to be seen whether the Government will tolerate as they have tolerated the march, the actual breach of the salt laws by countless people from tomorrow.

The following morning, after a prayer, Gandhi raised a lump of salty mud and declared, "With this, I am shaking the foundations of the British Empire." He then boiled it in sea water, producing illegal salt. He implored his thousands of followers to likewise begin making salt along the seashore, "wherever it is convenient" and to instruct villagers in making illegal salt.

Mass Civil Disobedience

Mass civil disobedience spread throughout India as millions broke the salt laws by making salt or buying illegal salt. Salt was sold illegally all over the coast of India. A pinch of salt made by Gandhi himself sold for 1,600 rupees (equivalent to $750 dollars at the time). In reaction, the British government incarcerated over sixty thousand people by the end of the month.

What had begun as a Salt Satyagraha quickly grew into a mass Satyagraha. British cloth and goods were boycotted. Unpopular forest laws were defied in Maharashtra, Karnataka, and Central Provinces. Gujarati peasants refused to pay tax, under threat of losing their crops and land. In Midnapore, Bengalis took part by refusing to pay the chowkidar tax. The British responded with more laws, including censorship of correspondence and declaring the Congress and its associate organisations illegal. None of those measures slowed the Civil Disobedience Movement.

In Peshawar, satyagraha was led by a Muslim Pashto disciple of Gandhi, Ghaffar Khan, who had trained a 50,000 member army of non-violent activists called *Khudai Khidmatgar*. On April 23, 1930, Ghaffar Khan was arrested. A crowd of Khudai Khidmatgar gathered in Peshawar's Kissa Khani (Storytellers) Bazaar. The British ordered troops to open fire with machine guns on the unarmed crowd, killing an estimated 200-250. The Pashtun satyagrahis acted in accord with their training in non-violence, willingly facing bullets as the troops fired on them. One British Indian Army regiment, troops of the renowned Royal Garhwal Rifles, refused to fire at the crowds. The entire platoon was arrested and many received heavy penalties, including life imprisonment.

The civil disobedience in 1930 marked the first time women became mass participants in the struggle for freedom. Thousands of women, from large cities to small villages, became active participants in satyagraha. Gandhi had asked that only men take part in the salt march, but eventually women began manufacturing and selling salt throughout India. Usha Mehta, an early Gandhian activist, remarked that "Even our old aunts and great-aunts and grandmothers used to bring pitchers of salt water to their houses and manufacture illegal salt. And then they would shout at the top of their voices: 'We have broken the salt law!'" The growing number of women in the fight for independence was a "new and serious feature" according to Lord Irwin. A government report on the involvement of women stated "thousands of them emerged....from the seclusion of their homes...in order to join Congress demonstrations and assist in picketing: and their presence on these occasions made the work the police was required to perform particularly unpleasant."

There were outbreaks of violence in Kolkata, Karachi, and Gujarat. Unlike his suspension of satyagraha after violence broke out during the Non-cooperation Movement, this time Gandhi was "unmoved". Appealing for violence to end, at the same time Gandhi honoured those killed in Chittagong and congratulated their parents "for the finished sacrifices of their sons.... A warrior's death is never a matter for sorrow."

British documents show that the British government was shaken by satyagraha. non-violent protest left the British confused about whether or not to jail Gandhi. John Court Curry, a British police officer stationed in India, wrote in his memoirs that he felt nausea every time he dealt with Congress demonstrations in 1930. Curry and others in British government, including Wedgwood Benn, Secretary of State for India, preferred fighting violent rather than non-violent opponents.

The Aftermath

Gandhi himself avoided further active involvement after the march, though he stayed in close contact with the developments throughout India. He created a temporary ashram near Dandi. From there, he urged women followers in Mumbai to picket liquor shops and foreign cloth. He said that "a bonfire should be made of foreign cloth. Schools and colleges should become empty."

For his next major action, Gandhi decided on a raid of the Dharasana Salt Works in Gujarat. He wrote to Lord Irwin, again telling him of his plans. Around midnight of May 4, as Gandhi was sleeping on a cot in a mango grove, the District Magistrate of Surat drove up with two Indian officers and thirty heavily-armed constables. He was arrested under an 1827 regulation calling for the jailing of people engaged in unlawful activities, and held without trial near Pune.

The Dharasana Satyagraha went ahead as planned, with Abbas Tyabji, a seventy-six year old retired judge, leading the march with Gandhi's wife Kasturba at his side. Both were arrested before reaching Dharasana and sentenced to three months in prison. After their arrests, the march continued under the leadership of Sarojini Naidu, a woman poet and freedom fighter, who warned the satyagrahis, "You must not use any violence under any circumstances. You will be beaten, but you must not resist: you must not even raise a hand to ward off blows." Soldiers began clubbing the satyagrahis with steel tipped lathis in an incident that attracted international attention. United Press correspondent Webb Miller reported that:

> Not one of the marchers even raised an arm to fend off the blows. They went down like ten-pins. From where I stood I heard the sickening whacks of the clubs on unprotected skulls. The waiting crowd of watchers groaned and sucked in their breaths in sympathetic pain at every blow. Those struck down fell sprawling, unconscious or writhing in pain with fractured skulls or broken shoulders. In two or three minutes the ground was quilted with bodies. Great patches of blood widened on their white clothes. The survivors without breaking ranks silently and doggedly marched on until struck down.

Vithalbhai Patel, former Speaker of the Assembly, watched the beatings and remarked, "All hope of reconciling India with the British Empire is lost forever." Following attempts by the British to censor Miller's story, it eventually appeared in 1,350 newspapers throughout the world, and was read into the official record of the United States Senate. Salt Satyagraha succeeded in drawing the attention of the world. Millions saw the newsreels showing the march. Time magazine declared Gandhi its 1930 Man of the Year, comparing Gandhi's march to the sea "to defy Britain's salt tax as some New Englanders once defied a British tea tax." Civil disobedience continued until early-1931, when Gandhi was finally released from prison to hold talks with Irwin. It was the first time the two held talks on equal terms. The talks would lead to the Second Round Table Conference at the end of 1931.

Long Term Impact

Salt Satyagraha produced scant progress towards dominion status or independence for India, and did not win any major concessions from the British. It also failed to attract Muslim support — many Muslims actively boycotted the satyagraha. Congress leaders decided to end satyagraha as official policy in 1934. Nehru and other Congress members drifted further apart from Gandhi, who withdrew from Congress to concentrate on his Constructive Programme, which included his efforts to end untouchability. Even though British authorities were again in control by the mid-1930s, Indian, British, and world opinion increasingly began to recognise the legitimacy of claims by Gandhi and the Congress Party for independence. The Satyagraha campaign of the 1930s also forced the British to recognise that their control of India depended entirely on the consent of Indians — Salt Satyagraha was a significant step in the British losing that consent.

Nehru considered Salt Satyagraha the high water mark of his association with Gandhi, and felt that its lasting importance was in changing the attitudes of Indians:

Of course these movements exercised tremendous pressure on the British Government and shook the government machinery. But the real importance, to my mind, lay in the effect they had on our own people, and especially the village masses....Non-cooperation dragged them out of the mire and gave them self-respect and self-reliance....They acted courageously and did not submit so easily to unjust oppression; their outlook widened and they began to think a little in terms of India as a whole....It was a remarkable transformation and the Congress, under Gandhi's leadership, must have the credit for it.

More than thirty years later, Satyagraha and the March to Dandi exercised a strong influence on American civil rights activist Martin Luther King, Jr., and his fight for civil rights for blacks in the 1960s:

> Like most people, I had heard of Gandhi, but I had never studied him seriously. As I read I became deeply fascinated by his campaigns of non-violent resistance. I was particularly moved by his Salt March to the Sea and his numerous fasts. The whole concept of Satyagraha (Satya is truth which equals love, and agraha is force; Satyagraha, therefore, means truth force or love force) was profoundly significant to me. As I delved deeper into the philosophy of Gandhi, my

skepticism concerning the power of love gradually diminished, and I came to see for the first time its potency in the area of social reform.

Re-enactment of Dandi March

To commemorate the Great Salt March, the Mahatma Gandhi Foundation proposed a re-enactment on the 75th anniversary. The event was known as the "International Walk for Justice and Freedom". Mahatma Gandhi's great-grandson Tushar Gandhi and several hundred fellow marchers followed the same route to Dandi. The start of the march on March 12, 2005 in Ahmedabad was attended by Sonia Gandhi, Chairperson of the National Advisory Council, as well as several Indian Cabinet Ministers, many of whom walked for the first few kilometres. The participants halted at Dandi on the night of April 5, with the commemoration ending on April 7.

A series of commemorative stamps were issued on the centenary of the Dandi March — denomination INR 5, Date of Issue: April 5, 2005.

Elections and Lahore Resolution

The Government of India Act 1935, the voluminous and final constitutional effort at governing British India, articulated three major goals: establishing a loose federal structure, achieving provincial autonomy, and safeguarding minority interests through separate electorates. The federal provisions, intended to unite princely states and British India at the centre, were not implemented because of ambiguities in safeguarding the existing privileges of Princes. In February 1937, however, provincial autonomy became a reality when elections were held; the Congress emerged as the dominant party with a clear majority in five provinces and held an upper hand in two, while the Muslim League performed poorly.

In 1939, the Viceroy Linlithgow declared India's entrance into World War II without consulting provincial governments. In protest, the Congress asked all of its elected representatives to resign from the government. Jinnah, the president of the Muslim League, persuaded participants at the annual Muslim League session at Lahore in 1940 to adopt what later came to be known as the Lahore Resolution, demanding the division of India into two separate sovereign states, one Muslim, the other Hindu; sometimes referred to as Two Nation Theory. Although the idea of Pakistan had been introduced as early as 1930, very few had responded to it. However, the volatile political climate and hostilities between the Hindus and Muslims transformed the idea of Pakistan into a stronger demand.

Arrest and Imprisonment

The Government seized the opportunity for which it was waiting. On the evening of March 10, 1922, Gandhi was arrested in his ashram. The trial was held before Broomfield, District and Sessions Judge of Ahmedabad. The British judge behaved with great consideration, nodding respectfully to the accused in the dock before taking his seat. He acknowledged that Gandhi was in a different category from any person that he had ever tried or was likely to try. Gandhi made his task easy by pleading guilty. He was sentenced to six years' imprisonment.

An observer noted that Gandhi was not only serene but 'festively joyful' during the 100-minute trial. "So far as the sentence is concerned," he told the judge "I certainly consider that it is as light as any judge would inflict on me; and so far as the whole proceedings are concerned, I must say that I could not have expected greater courtesy." He was lodged in the Yeravda prison in Poona. He was not allowed to sleep in the open. He was denied a pillow but he devised one with books and spare clothes. Among the 150 and odd books he read during this term were Henry James' The Varieties of Religious Experience, Bernard Shaw's Man and Superman, Buckle's History of Civilization, Wells' Outline of History, Goethe's Faust and Kipling's Barrack Room Ballads. He kept up his daily routine of morning and evening prayers, and spinning. His literary and religious studies which had been neglected in the midst of other activities were resumed. There is no doubt that in spite of occasional pinpricks, prison life proved for Gandhi, as Tagore once put it, "arrest cure".

Reaction and Recovery

Soon after Gandhi's imprisonment, signs of a serious rift appeared among his followers. Some prominent Congressmen including Motilal Nehru and C.R. Das declared themselves in favour of lifting the boycott of the councils. They formed the Swaraj Party to contest elections to the provincial and central legislative councils and to "carry the fight into the enemy's camp". Vallabhbhai Patel, Rajagopalachari and others who were opposed to any change in the original non-cooperation programme came to be known as 'No-Changers'. During the whole of 1923, Congress politics were extremely fluid. There were a number of resignations from the Working Committee and the All India Congress Committee, bona fides were questioned; 'points of order' were raised, and the Constitution of Congress discussed threadbare. In September 1923, at a special session of the Congress, it was decided that the Swarajists should be allowed to put up candidates at the election, which were scheduled in November. The Swarajists had barely two months to fight the elections, but they succeeded in capturing a solid bloc of seats in the Central Legislative Assembly, a substantial representation in provincial legislatures and even a majority in the Central Provinces Council. Motilal Nehru led the party in the Central Assembly, while C. R. Das took up the leadership of the party in Bengal Council.

In February, after he had served only two years in jail, Gandhi, after an operation for appendicitis, was released. He did not, as his faithful No-Changers hoped, throw his weight in their favour. On the contrary, he did everything to avoid a split in the party. He made a series of gestures to the "rebels" — the Swarajists — and let them dominate the political stage. The Viceroy wrote home: "Gandhi is now attached to the tail of Das and Nehru, although they try their utmost to make him and his supporters think that he is one of the heads, if not the head."

If the rift in the Congress ranks on Council entry was one disappointment to Gandhi, after his release from jail, the division between Hindus and Muslims was another and greater. The Hindu-Muslim unity of the heyday of Non-cooperation Movement was now a mere memory. Trust had given way to distrust. Apart from the riots which periodically disfigured several towns, there was a new bitterness in politics and in the press. There were not a few who put down the new tension to the Non-cooperation Movement and its alliance with the 'Khilafat" cause, and blamed Gandhi for having played with the masses and roused them prematurely. "The awakening of the masses," wrote Gandhi, "was a necessary part of the training. I would do nothing to put the people to sleep again." However, he wanted this awakening to be diverted into constructive channels. The two communities had to be educated out of the mental morass into which they had slipped. His doctrine of non-violence held the key not only to the political freedom of the country but also to peace between the communities. Hearts could never be united by breaking heads. A civilized society which had given up violence as a means of settling individual disputes could also eschew violence for reconciling differences between groups. Disagreements could be resolved by mutual tolerance and compromise.

In September 1924, Gandhi went on a twenty-one day fast to "purify" himself and "to recover the power to react on the people." The fast had a soothing effect, but only for a while; India had not yet seen the last of communal wrangles. The problem had really been reduced to the struggle for fruits of political power between the professional classes of the two communities. It was a scramble for crumbs which the British offered to political India. Gandhi had declared that "majorities must set the example of self-sacrifice." The blank cheque which he later offered to the Muslims was ridiculed by them and resented by the Hindus, but it epitomised his approach to this squabble for seats in legislatures and jobs under the Government. Unfortunately in the course of the negotiations, the Hindus tended to deal with Muslims as the British Government dealt with nationalist India: they made concessions but it was often a case of too little and too late.

During the next three years, while national politics were dominated by communal issues and controversies in legislatures, Gandhi retired from the political scene; to be precise, he retired only from the political controversies of the day to devote his time to the less spectacular but more important task of nation-building "from the bottom up". He toured the country extensively from one end to the other, using every mode of transport from railway trains to bullock-carts. He exhorted the people to shake off the age-old social evils such as child-marriage and untouchability, and to ply the spinning wheel. Primarily advocated as a solution of the chronic under-employment in the villages, the spinning-wheel in Gandhi's hands became something more than a simple tool of a cottage industry. In his efforts to "sell" the spinning wheel to the people, he romanticised it. He put in forward not only as a panacea for economic ills but also for national unity and freedom. It became a symbol of defiance of foreign rule; Khadi, the cloth made from yarn spun on the spinning wheel, became the nationalist garment, the 'livery of freedom', as Jawaharlal Nehru once picturesquely described it.

By 1929 Indian politics began to recover from the malaise which had affected them after the collapse of the Non-cooperation Movement seven years before. This recovery was assisted by discontent among industrial workers, peasants and middle class youth. The trade unions became militant bodies. The peasantry was in distress because of an unprecedented economic depression; there was a dramatic no-tax campaign in Bardoli in Gujarat, Gandhi's home province, under his able lieutenant, Vallabhbhai Patel. The Swaraj Party which had professed an alternative to the Gandhian programme was deeply disillusioned by 1928; dissensions and defections had emasculated it.

In November 1927, the British Government announced the appointment of a royal Commission headed by Sir John Simon, to report on the working of the Constitutional reforms of 1919, and on the possibilities of further advance towards self-government. The commission included representatives of the British political parties, but no Indian. The "all-white" commission came to be looked upon in India as an inquisition by foreigners into India's fitness for self-government. The Indian National Congress decided to boycott the commission "at every stage and in every form". Even moderate and Muslim politicians, whose cooperation the Government had taken for granted, were unanimous in denouncing the commission.

A challenge from Birkenhead, the Conservative Secretary of State, stung Indian leaders to seek an agreed solution of the constitutional problem. An All-Party committee headed by Motilal Nehru drafted a Constitution for a self-governing India. The "Nehru Report" adopted Dominion Status as he basis of its recommendations: it represented the lowest measure of agreement among the Congress, the "Liberals" and the other political groups. The younger wing of the Congress led by Subhash Chandra Bose, the brilliant young leader from Bengal, and Motilal Nehru's own son, Jawaharlal, repudiated Dominion Status. A rift was avoided at the Calcutta Congress in December 1928 by a compromise formula framed by Gandhi. A resolution was passed endorsing the Nehru Report on the condition that, if by December 31, 1929, it was not accepted by the Government, the Congress would fight for complete independence, if necessary, by resorting to non-violent non-cooperation.

The Calcutta Congress opened the way for Gandhi's return to politics. If the British Government did not concede that demand of the Congress — and there was little prospect of their doing so — the Congress was committed to a Non-cooperation Movement and it was obvious to all that Gandhi alone could conduct it.

In May 1929, as the result of the British General Election, a Labour Government headed by Ramsay McDonald came into office. The Viceroy, Lord Irwin, visited England and, on return to India towards the end of October 1929, issued a statement that it "is implied in the declaration of 1917 that the natural issue of India's constitutional progress, as there contemplated, is the attainment of Dominion Status". The statement had a favourable reception in India, but a storm broke over Irwin and the Labour Government in England. The British press and Parliament subjected the announcement to a protracted post-mortem. The official spokesmen were on the defensive, explained away the statement, and asserted that there had been no radical departure from past policy. The breach between the Government and the Congress thus remained unhealed. No more success attended an eleventh-hour effort at an understanding between Gandhi and the Viceroy through an interview arranged at Delhi on December 23, just before the Congress session at Lahore.

Declaration of Complete Independence

The Lahore session proved a momentous one. At Gandhi's instance, the All India Congress Committee had elected Jawaharlal Nehru as its president. The Congress, instinct with new hope and energy, needed a young man at the helm. The forty-year-old Jawaharlal whom Gandhi described, *"pure as crystal.... truthful beyond suspicion... a knight sans peur et sans reproche"* was to be in fullness of time the Mahatma's political heir. There was a bond of deep affection between the two men in spite of the twenty years and widely differing intellectual backgrounds which separated them.

The year of grace which the Calcutta Congress had granted had drawn to a close. Dominion Status had not been conceded;

the offer of the minimum national demand embodied in the Nehru Report lapsed. At midnight on December 31, 1929, as the new year dawned, the Indian National Congress unfurled the flag of independence on the bank of the river Ravi. The Congress called upon its members in central and provincial legislatures to resign their seats and authorised the launching of a civil disobedience campaign.

In January 1930, Gandhi wrote that he was "furiously thinking night and day" The first step he took was to call for the celebration of an "Independence Day" on January 26. On that day, in the towns and villages of India, hundreds of thousands of people took a pledge that "it was a crime against man and God to submit to British rule." Gandhi was encouraged by the latent enthusiasm in the country revealed by the observance of the Independence Day; he felt the country was ripe for a mass movement. He suggested the inauguration of the movement with the breach of Salt Laws. The salt tax, though relatively light in incidence, hit the poorest in the land. But salt did not quite seem to fit into the plan of a national struggle for liberation. And when Gandhi announced that he would walk the 241 miles from his ashram in Ahmedabad to Dandi on the Arabian Sea, the first impulse of the Government, as of the Congress intellectual, was to ridicule the "kindergarten stage of political revolution", and to laugh away the idea that the King-Emperor could be unseated by boiling sea-water in a kettle.

Events were to show that those who had scoffed at Salt Satyagraha and failed to see any connection between salt and swaraj (independence) had underrated Gandhi's knack for organising the Indian masses for corporate action. Gandhi was arrested on May 5. Just before his arrest he had planned a more "aggressive" phase of his non-violent rebellion by raiding and taking possession of the salt depots at Dharasana. The raid took place a fortnight after Gandhi's arrest. There were 2,500 volunteers. Before they advanced, Sarojini Naidu, the poetess, led them in prayer and appealed to them to be true to Gandhi's teaching and to abstain from violence. Round the depot, a barrier of barbed wire had been erected and a ditch dug. As the first column of volunteers advanced, police officers ordered them to disperse. The volunteers advanced in silence even though scores of policemen fell on them and rained blows upon them. Not one man so much as raised his arm to fend off the blows. Webb Miller, an American correspondent, who witnessed the scene, wrote: "In eighteen years of reporting in twenty two countries, I have never witnessed such harrowing scenes as at Dharasana. Sometimes the scenes were so painful that I had to turn away momentarily. One surprising feature was the discipline of volunteers. It seemed they were thoroughly imbued with Gandhi's non-violent creed."

The Satyagraha campaign was extended by the Congress to include breach of salt as well as forest laws, the non-payment of taxes and the boycott of foreign cloth, banks and shipping. The Government replied by issuing "ordinances" which conferred extraordinary powers on the executive authority for arrest and prosecution of Congress workers.

Gandhi-Irwin Pact

The Viceroy, Lord Irwin, was at this time directing the sternest repression which Indian nationalism had known, but he did not really relish the role. The British civil service and the commercial community were in favour of even harsher measures. But Premier Ramsay McDonald and Secretary of State Benn were eager for peace, if they could secure it without weakening the position of the Labour Government; they wanted to make a success of the Round Table Conference and they knew that this body without the presence of Gandhi and the Congress could not carry much weight. In January 1931, at the closing session of the Round Table Conference, Ramsay McDonald went so far as to express the hope that the Congress would be represented at the next session.

The Viceroy took the hint and promptly ordered the unconditional release of Gandhi and all members of the Congress Working Committee. To this gesture Gandhi responded by agreeing to meet the Viceroy.

"The Two Mahatmas" — as Sarojini Naidu described Gandhi and Irwin — had eight meetings which lasted for a total of 24 hours. Gandhi was impressed by Irwin's sincerity. The terms of the "Gandhi-Irwin Pact" fell manifestly short of those which Gandhi had prescribed as the minimum for a truce. Some of his colleagues considered the Gandhi-Irwin Pact a clever manoeuvre, and Suspected that Irwin had led the Mahatma upon the garden path of the Viceroy's House.

On the other hand, it is fair to record that British officials in India, and Tory politicians in England, were outraged by the idea of a pact with a party whose avowed purpose was the destruction of the British Raj. Winston Churchill publicly expressed his disgust "at the nauseating and humiliating spectacle of this one-time Inner Temple lawyer, now seditious fakir, striding half-naked up the steps of the Viceroy's palace, there to negotiate and parley on equal terms with the representative of the King Emperor".

Gandhi's motives in concluding a pact with the Viceroy can be best understood in terms of his technique. The Satyagraha movements were commonly described as "struggles", "rebellions" and "wars without violence". Owing, however, to the common connotation of these words, they seemed to lay a disproportionate emphasis on the negative aspect of the movements, namely, opposition and conflict. The object of Satyagraha was, however, not to achieve the physical elimination or moral breakdown of an adversary, but, through suffering at his hands, to initiate those psychological processes which could make it possible for minds and hearts to meet. In such a struggle a compromise with an opponent was neither heresy nor treason, but a natural and necessary step. And if it turned out that the compromise was premature and the adversary was unrepentant, there was nothing to prevent the Satyagrahi from returning to non-violent battle.

Round Table Conference

On August 29, 1931, Gandhi sailed for England in the S. S. Rajputana to attend the Second Round Table Conference, He went as the sole representative of the Indian National Congress. All the delegates were nominees of the British Government; they had a sprinkling of able individuals, but most of them were drawn from the princely order, the landlords, the titled gentry and the leaders of communal groups and vested interests.

What with its composition and what with its procedure, which the British Government controlled, the conference side-tracked its energies into secondary issues and particularly the communal problem. Gandhi was prepared to give a "blank cheque" to Muslims and other minorities to remove their legitimate fears, provided they were willing to press the national demand for freedom. Most of the Hindu delegates were not ready for this gesture, and the Muslim nationalists were not represented at the conference.

Gandhi pleaded for an honourable and equal partnership between Britain and India, held not by force but "by the silken cord of love" He found the odds against him. There was a financial crisis and a change of government in Britain; in the new Ministry, the Conservatives were heavily represented. The British public was preoccupied with domestic issues; for it, the financial crisis was a more urgent issue than the niceties of an Indian Constitution. Inevitably, even if imperceptibly, there was a change in emphasis. Sir Samuel Hoare, the new Secretary of State, told Gandhi that he sincerely believed that Indians were unfit for complete self-government.

In London

Meanwhile Gandhi was, as he put it, "doing the real round table work, getting to know the people of England". He had accepted Muriel Lester's invitation to stay in Kingsley Hall in the East end, in order to be "among the same sort of people to whom I have given my life" Every morning the light appeared in his room at four for the morning prayer. He had his morning walk in the main streets of the East End; he visited his neighbours in Bow; he made friends with the children. "Uncle Gandhi" became a popular figure. He explained to the children why he had chosen to stay in the East End and why he wore his meagre dress. He advised them to return good for evil.

There was an interesting sequel to this advice, when the father of a four-year-old girl told the Mahatma that he had a bone to pick with him. "And what is it?" asked Gandhi. "Well my little Jane comes every morning to me, hits me and wakes me up and says: Now, don't you hit back, for Gandhi told us not to hit back". On October 2, Gandhi's birth day, the children presented him with 'two woolly dogs, three pink birthday candles, a tin plate, a blue pencil and some jelly sweets' — gifts which he especially treasured and took to India.

One of the most pleasant surprises of the tour was the courtesy and even affection Gandhi received from the cotton operatives of Lancashire, which had been hit the hardest by the boycott of

British goods in India. He listened with obvious attention and sympathy to the tale of woe of those who were jobless. Many of them saw the background of the boycott which he had sponsored, when he told them: "You have three million unemployed, but we have 200 million unemployed for half the year. Your average unemployment dole is seventy shillings. Our average income is 7s. 6d. a month."

Gandhi's homely logic and transparent sincerity left an indelible impression on some of those whom he met. They formed clearer impressions of him than the loin cloth and goat's milk version with which the popular press regaled them. While his opinions might appear utopian or revolutionary, he could no longer be dismissed as "humbug", the appellation with which Truth had heralded his arrival in England.

Meanwhile, the news from India had been far from reassuring. The compromise which had been patched up between the Congress and the Government before Gandhi's departure for England had virtually broken down. Gandhi was anxious to return home; he declined invitations to prolong his itinerary in Europe and to visit America, but he decided to spend a few days in Switzerland with his biographer, Romain Rolland. In Rome, where he spent a day, he walked through the Vatican galleries; in the Sistine Chapel he was spell-bound: "I saw a figure of Christ there. It was wonderful. I could not tear myself away. The tears sprang to my eyes as I gazed."

5

Resumption of Struggle

On December 28, 1931, Gandhi landed at Bombay. Within a week he was in jail and civil disobedience was resumed; the Indian National Congress was outlawed and the Gandhi-Irwin Pact had gone to pieces.

While Gandhi was on the high seas, the arrests of Jawaharlal Nehru and Abdul Ghaffar Khan, two of his ablest lieutenants, had created a crisis. Most of the British officers in India had really been unhappy at the rapprochement which Irwin had attempted with Gandhi; they won over his successor Lord Willingdon to a tougher policy towards the Mahatma. Gandhi sought an interview with the Viceroy to smooth away difficulties but was rebuffed. The Government of India was not in a conciliatory mood. Indeed it struck with lightning speed to deprive the Indian National Congress of its leaders, organisation and resources. Despite the suddenness and severity of the repression, 61,551 persons came forward and were convicted for civil disobedience in the first nine months of the movement in 1932; this figure was a little higher than that of the earlier campaign in 1930-31.

Campaign against Untouchability

A new twist to the Civil Disobedience Movement came in September 1932 when Gandhi, who was in Yeravda Jail, went on a fast as a protest against the segregation of the so-called "untouchables" in the electoral arrangement planned for the new Indian Constitution. Uncharitable critics described the fast as a form of coercion, a political blackmail. Gandhi was aware that his fast did exercise a moral pressure, but the pressure was directed not against those who disagreed with him, but against those who loved him and believed in him. He did not expect his critics to react in the same way as his friends and co-workers, but if his self-crucifixion could demonstrate his sincerity to them, the battle would be more than half-won. He sought to prick the conscience of the people and to convey to them something of his own inner anguish at a monstrous social tyranny. The fast dramatised the issues at stake; ostensibly it suppressed reason, but in fact it was designed to free reason from that mixture of inertia and prejudice which had permitted the evil of untouchability, which condemned millions of Hindus to humiliation, discrimination and hardship.

The news that Gandhi was about to fast shook India from one end to the other. September 20, 1932, when the fast began, was observed as a day of fasting and prayer. At Shantiniketan, poet Tagore, dressed in black, spoke to a large gathering on the significance of the fast and the urgency of fighting an age-old evil. There was a spontaneous upsurge of feeling; temples, wells and public places were thrown open to the "untouchables". A number of Hindu leaders met the representatives of the untouchables; an alternative electoral arrangement was agreed upon, and received the approval of the British Government before Gandhi broke his fast.

More important than the new electoral arrangement was the emotional catharsis through which the Hindu community had passed. The fast was intended by Gandhi "to sting the conscience of the Hindu community into right religious action". The scrapping of separate electorates was only the beginning of the end of untouchability. Under Gandhi's inspiration, while he was still in prison, a new organisation, Harijan Sevak Sangh was founded to combat untouchability and a new weekly paper, the Harijan, was started. Harijan means "children of God"; it was Gandhi's name for the "untouchables"

After his release Gandhi devoted himself almost wholly to the campaign against untouchability. On November 7, 1933, he embarked on a country-wide tour which covered 12,500 miles and lasted for nine months. The tour evoked great enthusiasm for the breaking down of the barriers which divided the untouchables from the rest of the Hindu community, but it also provoked the militancy of the orthodox Hindus. On June 25, while Gandhi was on his way to the municipal hall in Poona, a bomb was thrown at his party. Seven persons were injured, but Gandhi was unhurt. He expressed his "deep pity" for the unknown thrower of the bomb. "I am not aching for martyrdom," he said, "but if it comes in my way in the prosecution of what I consider to be the supreme duty in defence of the faith I hold in common with millions of Hindus, I shall have well earned it."

Gandhi's fast had aroused public enthusiasm, but diverted it from political to social issues. In May 1933, he suspended civil disobedience for six weeks. He revived it later, but confined it to himself. A year later he discontinued it: this was a recognition of the fact that the country was fatigued and in no mood to continue a campaign of defiance. These decisions disconcerted many of his adherents, who did not relish his moral and religious approach to political issues, and chafed at his self-imposed restraints. Gandhi sensed the critical mood in the Congress party and in October 1934, announced his retirement from it. For the next three years, not politics but village economics was his dominant interest.

A New Deal for the Villages

Ever since Gandhi had entered Indian public life in 1915, he had been pleading for a new deal for the village. The acute pressure on land and the absence of supplementary industries had caused chronic unemployment and under-employment among the peasants whose appalling poverty never ceased to weigh upon Gandhi's mind. His advocacy of the spinning wheel really derived from its immediate value as a palliative. Since eighty-five per cent of the population of India lived in villages, their economic and social resuscitation seemed to Gandhi to be a *sine qua non* for freedom from foreign rule. The growing gap in economic standards and social amenities between the village and the town had to be bridged. This could best be done by volunteers from the towns who spread themselves in the countryside to help revive dead or dying village industries, and to improve standards of nutrition, education and sanitation.

It was not Gandhi's habit to preach what he did not practise; he decided to settle in a village. His choice fell upon Segaon which was situated near Wardha. It had a population of six hundred, and lacked such bare amenities as a pucca road, a shop and a post office. Here, on land owned by his friend and disciple Jamnalal Bajaj, Gandhi occupied a one-room hut. Those who came to see him during the rains had to wade through ankle-deep mud. The climate was inhospitable; there was not an inhabitant of this village who had not suffered from dysentery or malaria. Gandhi himself fell sick but was resolved not to leave Segaon. He hoped he would draw his team for village uplift from Segaon itself, but could not prevent his disciples, old and new, from collecting around him. When Dr. John Mott interviewed him in 1937, Gandhi's was the solitary hut; before long a colony of mud and bamboo grew up. Among its residents were Prof. Bhansali, who had roamed in forests naked and with sealed lips, subsisting on *neem* leaves; Maurice Frydman, a Pole, who became a convert to the Gandhian of a handicraft civilization based on non-violence; a Sanskrit scholar who was a leper and was housed next to Gandhi's hut so that he could tend him; a Japanese monk who (in the words of Mahadev Desai, Gandhi's Secretary) worked like a horse and lived like a hermit.

Sevagram (as Segaon came to be known) was not planned as an ashram. Gandhi never conceived it as such and did not impose any formal discipline upon it. It became a centre of the Gandhian scheme of village welfare. A number of institutions grew up in and around it to take up he various strands of economic and social uplift. The All India Village Industries Association supported and developed such industries as could easily be fostered, required little capital and did not need help from outside the village. The Association set up a school for training village workers and published its own periodical, the Gram Udyog Patrika. There were other organisations such as the Goseva Sangh, which sought to improve the condition and breed of the Hindustani Talimi Sangh, which experimented in Gandhi's ideas on education.

The educational system in India had always struck Gandhi as inadequate and wasteful. The vast majority of the population could not get the rudiments of education, but even those who went to village primary schools soon unlearnt what was taught to them because it had little to do with their daily lives and environment. Gandhi suggested that elementary education suited to the Indian village could best be imparted through handicrafts so as to substitute a coordinated training in the use of the hand and the eye for a notoriously bookish and volatile learning. His ideas found an expression in the scheme of "Basic Education" which stirred the stagnant pools of the Indian educational system and stimulated administrators and educationists along new lines.

Work in the village was an arduous and slow affair; it was plodder's work, as Gandhi once put it. It did not earn banner headlines in the press and did not seem to embarrass the Government. Many of Gandhi's colleagues did not see how this innocuous activity could help India in advancing to the real goal — that of political freedom. On the other hand, the first official reaction to Gandhi's village uplift work was to consider it a well-laid plan to spread sedition among the rural masses; the government of India warned the provincial governments to be on their guard and to start counter-propaganda in the villages.

Preparation of a New Constitution

Indian politics were in the doldrums during the years 1934-35, but as the time came for elections to the provincial legislatures in accordance with the Act of 1935, political excitement rose to a high pitch. From the point of view of the Indian National Congress, the new Constitution was the inadequate and unsatisfactory. The scheme of the Indian Federation gave a sizeable representation to the princely states, and since their representatives, because of the absence of elective bodies, were likely to be the nominees of the Princes, (who in turn were dependant for their very existence on the British Government) Indian nationalists viewed the new Constitution with a feeling bordering on dismay. In the provinces a wider field was permitted to Ministers responsible to elected legislatures, but even here the Governors had been invested with over-riding and preventive authority.

Because of these limitations, there was a large and vocal section in the Congress led by Jawaharlal Nehru which did not want to have anything to do with the new Constitution. Nevertheless, the Congress decided to contest the elections, which were held early in 1937. It acquitted itself very well indeed, and was in a position to form ministries in six out of eleven provinces. A section of the Congress even favoured acceptance of office and its hands were strengthened by the moral support it received from Gandhi. The Mahatma felt that with all its deficiencies, the new Constitution could promote the programme of village uplift. He saw no reason why Congress ministries in the provinces could not encourage village industries, introduce prohibition, reduce the burden on the peasantry, promote the use of hand-spun cloth, extend education and combat untouchability.

The acceptance of office by the Congress party was facilitated by a statement issued by the Viceroy, Lord Linlithgow, which did not change the legal position or the powers of the Governors, but breathed a spirit of conciliation to which the Congress responded by deciding to form ministries.

For a political party which had remained so long in opposition, to get into the seat of power was a novel, and even a hazardous experience. The left wing in the Congress, which opposed formation of ministries, had in fact stressed the possibilities of internal dissensions and scramble for loaves and fishes among Congressmen. Gandhi found himself inundated with requests for jobs and minister ships; he expressed his surprise and distress at this trend, because to him the legislatures and ministerships were only one and a limited medium of serving the country. He felt that for the majority of Congressmen the work lay in the villages in the constructive fields of social and economic reform. The caucus system, the struggle for power and pressure politics, which are accepted as part of political democracy, were repellent to Gandhi. As an 'experienced servant and general', he deprecated the struggle for "the spoils of office", and the dissipation of energy in factional rivalries.

Hindu-Muslim Antagonism

During these years Gandhi was also much distressed by the rise in communal tension. To some extent this increased tension was attributable to the elections to the legislatures. The religious minorities were allowed to elect their representatives only from a purely communal electorate, from which adherents of all other religions were excluded. It was only natural that Muslim candidates should raise religious issues which could make the widest and easiest appeal to a largely illiterate electorate. It so happened that from 1937 onwards it suited the All India Muslim League, under the leadership of M. A. Jinnah, to whip up religious feeling. The League had done badly in the elections, but it sought to retrieve its position by launching a tirade against the Congress and Gandhi. Gandhi was alleged to be 'Enemy Number One' of the Muslim community and the British Governors were accused of conniving at a systematic oppression of the Muslim minority by the Hindus. Vague and exaggerated accusations were made about "atrocities" on the Muslims.

The Muslim League's antagonism to the Congress acquired a progressively sharper edge. Jinnah began even to question the suitability of a democratic system of government for India, in 1940 came out with the theory that Hindus and Muslims were two separate nations and the Muslim nation needed a 'homeland' of its own in the northwest and northeast of the subcontinent.

Gandhi's reaction to the two-nation theory and the demand for Pakistan was one of bewilderment, almost of incredulity. Was it the function of religion to separate men or to unite them? He described the two-nation theory as an "untruth"; in his dictionary there was no stronger word. He discussed the attributes of nationality. A change of religion did not change nationality; the religious divisions did not coincide with cultural differences. A Bengali Muslim, He wrote, "speaks the same tongue that a Bengali Hindu does, cats the same food, has the same amusements as his Hindu neighbour. They dress alike. His (Jinnah's) name could be that of any Hindu. When I first met him, I did not know he was a Muslim."

To divide India was to undo the centuries of work done by Hindus and Muslims. Gandhi's soul rebelled against the idea that Hinduism and Islam represented antagonistic cultures and doctrines, and that eighty million of Muslims had really nothing in common with their Hindu neighbours. And even if there were religious and cultural differences, what clash of interests could there be on such matters as revenue, industry, sanitation or justice? The differences could only be in religious usage and observances with which a secular state should have no concern.

Non-violence in a Violent World

The separatist ideology was to receive a fillip from the outbreak of the Second by Nehru in international affairs, Gandhi sympathised with the victims of Fascist and Nazi aggression. Gandhi's own life had been one long struggle against the forces of violence. For more then thirty years he had been experimenting with technique — Satyagraha — which, while eschewing violence, was designed to resolve conflicts.

Gandhi's ideas on non-violence had matured over many years. In the Boer War and the Fist World War he had raised ambulance units and enlisted soldiers for the British Empire. The fact that he not handled a gun himself did not, in his opinion, make a material difference. As he confessed later: "There is no defence for my conduct only in the scales of non-violence (ahimsa). I draw no distinction between those who wield weapons of destruction and those who do Red Cross work. Both participate in war and advance its cause. Both are guilty of the crime of war. But even after introspection during all these years, I feel that in the circumstances in which I found myself I was bound to adopt the course I did."

The Indians whom Gandhi led in the battle fronts of the Boer War or exhorted to join the British Indian army in 1914-18 did not believe in non-violence; it was not repugnance to violence, but indifference or cowardice which had kept them from bearing arms. Believing as he did in those days in the British Empire, as a benign institution, Gandhi also thought that as citizens of the Empire, Indians had duties as well as rights; one of these duties was to participate in the defence of the Empire.

In the twenty years which spanned the First and Second World Wars, Gandhi's faith in the British Empire had been irrevocably shaken. At the same time his own belief in the power of non-violence had grown. As the threat of war grew and the forces of violence gathered momentum in the late-30, he felt more strongly than ever that at that moment of crisis in world history, he had a message for India and India had a message for the bewildered humanity. Through the pages of Harijan, his weekly paper, he expounded the non-violent approach to military aggression and political tyranny He advised the weaker nations to defend themselves not by seeking protection from better armed states, but by non-violent resistance to the aggressor. A non-violent Abyssinia, he explained, needed no arms and succour from the League of Nations; if every Abyssinian man, woman and child refused cooperation, willing or forced, with the Italians, the aggressor would have to walk over the dead bodies of their victims and to occupy the country without the people.

It may be argued that Gandhi was making a heavy overdraft upon human endurance. It required supreme courage for a whole people to die to the last man, woman and child, rather than surrender to the enemy. Gandhi's non-violent resistance was thus not a soft doctrine — a convenient refuge from a dangerous situation. Nor was it an offer on a silver platter to the dictators of what they plotted to wrest by force. Those who offered non-violent resistance had to be prepared for the extreme sacrifice.

Cripps Mission

Gandhi was thus firmly anchored to pacifism when the war broke out in 1939, but many of his closest colleagues and the rank and file in the Indian National Congress could not bring themselves to accept the feasibility of defending the country against aggression without resort to arms. Twice during the war — after the fall of France in 1940, and the collapse of the British position in South East Asia in 1941 — when there was a possibility of a rapprochement between the Congress and the Government for a united war effort, Gandhi stepped aside rather than be a party to organised violence. The rapprochement did not come. The only serious British effort for a compromise was made in the Spring of 1942 with the dispatch of the Cripps Mission to India; it proved abortive.

For nearly two and a half years, Gandhi had resisted pressure from a section of his following for the launching of a mass movement. It became clear that the British Government first under Chamberlain, and then under Churchill, was reluctant to assure Indian freedom in the future, or to offer a practical token of it in the present Gandhi had endeavoured to restrain the radical wing of the Congress party, and diverted its discontent into "individual Satyagraha", a subdued form of civil resistance confined to "selected individuals"

After the failure of the Cripps Mission, Gandhi noted with concern that in the face of grave peril posed by the Japanese advance in South East Asia, the mood of the people of India was not one of resolute defiance, but of panic, frustration and helplessness. If India was not to go the way of Malaya and Burma, something had to be done, and done quickly. He came to the conclusion that only an immediate declaration of Indian independence by the British Government could give the people of India a stake in the defence of their country.

World War II

World War II broke out in 1939 when Nazi Germany invaded Poland. Initially, Gandhi had favoured offering "non-violent moral support" to the British effort, but other Congressional leaders were offended by the unilateral inclusion of India into the war, without consultation of the people's representatives. All Congressmen elected to resign from office *en masse*. After lengthy deliberations, Gandhi declared that India could not be party to a war ostensibly being fought for democratic freedom, while that freedom was denied to India itself. As the war progressed, Gandhi intensified his demand for independence, drafting a resolution calling for the British to Quit India. This was Gandhi's and the Congress Party's most definitive revolt aimed at securing the British exit from Indian shores.

Gandhi was criticised by some Congress party members and other Indian political groups, both pro-British and anti-British. Some felt that opposing Britain in its life or death struggle was immoral, and others felt that Gandhi wasn't doing enough. Quit India became the most forceful movement in the history of the struggle, with mass arrests and violence on an unprecedented scale. Thousands of freedom fighters were killed or injured by police gunfire, and hundreds of thousands were arrested. Gandhi and his supporters made it clear they would not support the war effort unless India were granted immediate independence. He even clarified that this time the movement would not be stopped if individual acts of violence were committed, saying that the "ordered anarchy" around him was "worse than real anarchy." He called on all Congressmen and Indians to maintain discipline via ahimsa, and *Karo Ya Maro* (Do or Die) in the cause of ultimate freedom.

Gandhi and the entire Congress Working Committee were arrested in Bombay by the British on August 9, 1942. Gandhi was held for two years in the Agha Khan Palace in Pune. It was here that Gandhi suffered two terrible blows in his personal life. His

50-year old secretary Mahadev Desai died of a heart attack 6 days later and his wife Kasturba died after 18 months imprisonment in February 22, 1944; six weeks later Gandhi suffered a severe malaria attack. He was released before the end of the war on 6 May 1944 because of his failing health and necessary surgery; the Raj did not want him to die in prison and enrage the nation. Although the Quit India Movement had moderate success in its objective, the ruthless suppression of the movement brought order to India by the end of 1943. At the end of the war, the British gave clear indications that power would be transferred to Indian hands. At this point Gandhi called off the struggle, and around 100,000 political prisoners were released, including the Congress's leadership.

Quit India Movement

The "Quit India" resolution passed by the All-India Congress Committee brought it into a head-on collision with the Government in August 1942. The Viceroy, with the strong backing of the British Cabinet, struck hard. Gandhi, Nehru and almost all the Congress leaders were imprisoned; the severest repression was launched against the Congress — its funds were frozen offices sealed and publicity media plugged. This "blitzkrieg" had violent repercussions. In the last speech before the All India Congress Committee before his arrest, Gandhi had made non-violence the basic premise of the struggle which he proposed to launch; this advice remained unheeded between the frenzy of the people and the hammer blows of the Government. In several parts of the country, in Bihar, in UP, in Bengal and in Bombay, the fury of the people burst the dykes and turned on the instruments and symbols of British rule. "The Congress Party", Churchill told the House of Commons, "has now abandoned the policy which Mr. Gandhi had so long inculcated in theory and has come into the open as a revolutionary movement." In India and abroad official propaganda attributed violence to a plot carefully laid by Congress leaders. Gandhi was even accused of being pro-Axis, and assisting a Japanese conquest of India. Official propaganda held the field for a time, but not for long. "It is sheer nonsense," Smuts, Gandhi's old antagonist in South Africa, told a press conference in London in November 1942, "to talk of Mahatma Gandhi as a fifth columnist. He is a great man. He is one of the great men of the world."

Mahadev Desai, who had served as Gandhi's secretary for 25 years, died of a heart attack within a week of his imprisonment and Kasturba, the Mahatma's wife, passed away in 1944 after a long illness. Early in 1944, his health began to cause concern to the Government. He had contracted malaria and had been running a high temperature. The tide of the war had already turned in favour off the Allies, and the risks of his release seemed to the Government immeasurably less than those of his possible death in jail.

After his release in May 1944, Gandhi tried to break the political deadlock. Neither Churchill, who still headed the British Cabinet, nor Jinnah, who had the commanding voice in the counsels of the Muslim League, seemed eager for a political detente. The British seemed reluctant to part with power, and the Muslim League evidently was waiting for an opportunity for driving a harder bargain. A formula suggested by C. Rajagopalachari, which Gandhi discussed with Jinnah, conceded the substance of the Muslim League's demand for Pakistan, but the offer was turned down by the League leader.

Shimla Conference

In the summer of 1945, a conference was convened at Shimla by the Viceroy, Lord Wavell, who had recently returned from England with the approval of the Newspaper report of the outcome of the Shimla Conference British Cabinet to a proposal for reconstituting the Executive Council in consultation with Indian leaders. Gandhi was not a delegate to the conference, though he was consulted by the Viceroy and the Congress working committee.

The conference broke down on the insistence of Jinnah that his party should have an exclusive right to nominate Muslim members of the Viceroy's Executive Council. This was something which the Congress could not concede without repudiating its national composition.

The Shimla Conference failed to break the deadlock, but two important events took place in the wake of the conference which made a new initiative possible. With the surrender of Japan on August 15, 1945, the Second World War came to an end, and the Labour Party came to power in Britain. Lord Wavell visited London, and on return to India, announced on September 19, 1942, that the British Government was still working "in the spirit of he Cripps Offer of 1942" and intended to convene a Constitution-making body. Elections to the central and provincial legislatures, which were in any case overdue, were announced. Indian politics were again deeply stirred and entered a period of intense excitement, interminable negotiations and bitter controversy.

Cabinet Mission

Early in 1946, the Labour Government dispatched an all-party parliamentary delegation to India to meet Indian leaders and convince them of the British desire for an early settlement of the Indian constitutional issue. However, it was only in March 1946 that with the arrival of three Cabinet Ministers, Lord Pethick-Lawrence, Sir Stafford Cripps and Mr. A. V. Alexander, a crucial stage was reached in the negotiations between the British Government and the Indian political parties. The negotiations were conducted on behalf of the Congress by Abul Kalam Azad who was assisted by Nehru and Patel. Gandhi was, however, frequently consulted. The negotiations were bogged down on the basic question whether India was to remain united or to be split up to satisfy the Muslim League's demand for Pakistan.

The Congress opposed to the partition of the country, but was prepared to go to the farthest limit in conceding cultural, economic and regional autonomy to various regions. A conference at Shimla failed to resolve the Congress-League differences. The Cabinet Mission then offered a compromise plan in their statement of May 16,1946. They sketched a three-tier constitutional structure for India. On the top was to be a Union of India embracing British India as well as the Indian States, but dealing only with foreign affairs, defence and communications.

The bottom tier was to consist of Provinces and States in which were to vest all residuary powers. The intermediate tier was to comprise "groups" to be formed by Provinces (if they chose) to deal with certain common subjects. The Muslim League avowed its acceptance of the Cabinet Mission Plan, but this acceptance was more apparent than real, The League and its leaders made no secret of their hope and design that the new Constitution would be used to effect a partition of the country. "Let me tell you," Jinnah told the Muslim League Council on June

5, 1946 "that Muslim India will not rest content until we have established full, complete and sovereign Pakistan." It was this apparent contradiction in the League's stand, which made Gandhi and his colleagues in the Congress uneasy about the "grouping of provinces", which the League wanted to make compulsory and a stepping-stone to Pakistan. The controversy on this issue wrecked the Cabinet Mission Plan.

The three-tier Constitution was a delicate mechanism with numerous checks and balances. Without the fullest cooperation between the major parties it was impossible to draft a new Constitution, much less to work it. This cooperation was, however, lacking. The Cabinet Mission Plan was a compromise but it did not really bring the two parties together. The result was that questions presumed to have been settled by the Cabinet Mission were reopened soon after the return of its three members to England. Controversy rose to a fever pitch on two crucial issues, that of the "grouping" of provinces and the composition of the "interim government".

Communal Conflagration

At a time when tension was mounting, it was imperative that the country should have a strong and stable government at the centre. The Cabinet Mission had failed in the formation of a national interim government. In July 1946, the Viceroy, Lord Wavell, once again took the initiative and called upon Jawaharlal Nehru to form the Government. Jinnah, who was approached by Nehru, refused to cooperate, was bitterly critical and announced that August 16 would be observed by the Muslim League as "the Direct Action Day". On that day Calcutta witnessed a communal riot, the scale and intensity of which had never been known in living memory. "The Great Calcutta Killing" touched off a chain reaction of violent communal explosions in East Bengal, Bihar and the Punjab.

As the news of disturbances in Bengal came through, Gandhi cancelled all his plans and decided to leave for the riot-affected areas. In East Bengal he noticed how fear, hatred and violence had come to pervade the countryside. He toured the villages, saw things at first hand, and tried to lift the issue of peace from the plane of politics to that of humanity. Whatever the political map of the future, he pleaded, it should be common ground among all parties that standards of civilized life would not be thrown overboard.

Gandhi's presence acted as a soothing balm on the villages of East Bengal; he eased tensions, assuaged anger and softened. In March 1947, he left for Bihar where the Hindu peasants had wreaked a terrible vengeance on the Muslim minority for the misdeeds of the Muslim majority in East Bengal. In Bihar, Gandhi's refrain was the same as in East Bengal: the majority community must repent and make amends; the minority must forgive and make a fresh start. He would not accept any apology for what had happened, and chided those who sought in the misdeeds. Of the rioters in East Bengal, a justification for what had happened in Bihar. Civilized conduct, he argued, was the duty of every individual and every community irrespective of what others did.

Alarmed by the increasing lawlessness, Lord Wavell brought the Muslim League into the Interim Government. The formation of the coalition between the Congress and the League fanned political controversy instead of putting it out. The Constituent Assembly had been summoned to meet on December 9, 1946, but the Muslim League refused to participate in its deliberations. The constitutional impasse looked complete when in the last week of November in an eleventh hour bid to bring the parties together, the British Government invited Wavell, Nehru, Jinnah, Liaquat Ali and Baldev Singh to London. The discussion proved abortive, but the British Government issued a statement to clarify the points at dispute. Though this clarification largely met its objections, the Muslim League did not lift its boycott of the Constituent Assembly.

The year 1947 dawned with the darkest possible prospects on the political horizon. To check the drift to chaos, Clement Attlee, the British Premier, came to the conclusion that what was needed was a new policy and a new Viceroy to carry it out. He announced in the House of Commons on February 20, 1947 that the British Government definitely intended to quit India by June 1948, and if by that date the Indian parties did not agree on an all-India Constitution, power would be transferred to "some form of Central Government in British India or in some areas to the existing Provincial Governments." Simultaneously it was announced that Lord Mountbatten would succeed Lord Wavell as Viceroy.

The British withdrawal had been decided and dated by the February 20th statement. Lord Mountbatten arrived in India in March and one of his first acts as Viceroy was to invite Gandhi for a discussion. The Mahatma interrupted his peace mission in Bihar and travelled to New Delhi. During the next few weeks it became evident that a solution of the political deadlock would be sought through the division of India. The Muslim League led by Jinnah was adamant, but there was also a re-orientation of the Congress attitude towards partition. Hitherto the Congress had insisted that partition should, if at all, follow and not precede political liberation, that there could be "no divorce before marriage". But the few months of stormy courtship in the Interim Government had cured Nehru, Patel and other Congress leaders of the desire for a closer union with the Muslim League. In the spring of 1947, the choice seemed to them to be between anarchy and partition; they resigned themselves to the latter in order to salvage three-fourths of India from the chaos which threatened the whole.

6

Freedom of India

Gandhi advised the Congress to reject the proposals the British Cabinet Mission offered in 1946, as he was deeply suspicious of the grouping proposed for Muslim-majority states — Gandhi viewed this as a precursor to partition. However, this became one of the few times the Congress broke from Gandhi's advice (though not his leadership), as Nehru and Patel knew that if the Congress did not approve the plan, the control of government would pass to the Muslim League. Between 1946 and 1948, over 5,000 people were killed in violence.

Gandhi was vehemently opposed to any plan that partitioned India into two separate countries. An overwhelming majority of Muslims living in India, side by side with Hindus and Sikhs, were in favour of Partition. Additionally Muhammad Ali Jinnah, the leader of the Muslim League, commanded widespread support in West Punjab, Sindh, North-West Frontier Province and East Bengal. The partition plan was approved by the Congress leadership as the only way to prevent a wide-scale Hindu-Muslim civil war. Congress leaders knew that Gandhi would viscerally oppose partition, and it was impossible for the Congress to go ahead without his agreement, for Gandhi's support in the party and throughout India was strong. Gandhi's closest colleagues had accepted partition as the best way out, and Sardar Patel endeavoured to convince Gandhi that it was the only way to avoid civil war. A devastated Gandhi gave his assent.

He conducted extensive dialogue with Muslim and Hindu community leaders, working to cool passions in northern India, as well as in Bengal. Despite the Indo-Pakistani War of 1947, he was troubled when the Government decided to deny Pakistan the Rs. 55 crores due as per agreements made by the Partition Council. Leaders like Sardar Patel feared that Pakistan would use the money to bankroll the war against India. Gandhi was also devastated when demands resurged for all Muslims to be deported to Pakistan, and when Muslim and Hindu leaders expressed frustration and an inability to come to terms with one another. He launched his last fast-unto-death in Delhi, asking that all communal violence be ended once and for all, and that the payment of Rs. 55 crores be made to Pakistan. Gandhi feared that instability and insecurity in Pakistan would increase their anger against India, and violence would spread across the borders. He further feared that Hindus and Muslims would renew their enmity and precipitate into an open civil war. After emotional debates with his life-long colleagues, Gandhi refused to budge, and the Government rescinded its policy and made the payment to Pakistan. Hindu, Muslim and Sikh community leaders, including the Rashtriya Swayamsevak Sangh and Hindu Mahasabha assured him that they would renounce violence and call for peace. Gandhi thus broke his fast by sipping orange juice.

Partition of India

The stage was thus set for the June 3 Plan under which power was to be transferred by the British to two successor states on August 15, 1947. What Gandhi has feared had come to pass. India was to be divided, but partition was not being imposed; it had been accepted by Nehru, Patel and a majority of the Congress leaders. Gandhi had serious doubts on the wisdom of this decision. The very violence, which in the opinion of his Congress colleagues and that of the British Government provided a compelling motive for partition was, for him an irresistible argument against it; to accept partition because of the fear of civil war was to acknowledge that "everything was to be got if mad violence was perpetrated in sufficient measure"

Partitions having become a fait accompli, Gandhi's efforts from now on were directed to mitigating its risks. He paid brief visits to Kashmir, the Punjab and Bengal. In Calcutta, just before the transfer of power, his presence had a magical effect; the communal tensions and hatreds of the preceding twelve months vanished almost overnight. When there was a recrudescence of trouble a fortnight later, he went on a fast which electrified the town, moved the Muslims and shamed the Hindus. The leaders of all communities pledged themselves to peace and begged Gandhi to break the fast. The Calcutta fast was rightly acclaimed as a miracle; in the of-quoted words of the London Times, it did what several divisions of troops could not have done.

Gandhi now felt free to turn to Punjab which was witnessing one of the major migrations of population in history. Seized with fantastic hopes and fears, the villages and town of the Punjab had been dreading, and at the same time, preparing for a battle of the barricades. The administrative paralysis caused by the reshuffling of administrative cadres on a communal basis, and the infection of the police and military with communal virus had, by the end of August, led to a situation in which it was impossible for the Hindu minority to stay in West Punjab and the Muslim minority to stay in the East Punjab.

As the interminable caravans of refugees with their tales of woes crawled to their destinations, violence spread. When Gandhi arrived in Delhi early in September, he found it paralysed by communal tension. The Government, led by Nehru, had acted energetically and impartially. Gandhi was not content with a peace imposed by the police and the military; he wanted violence to be purged form the hearts of Hindus and Muslims. It was an uphill task. Delhi had a number of refugee camps, some of which housed Hindus and Sikhs from West Pakistan, while others sheltered Muslims fleeing from Delhi for a passage across the border.

Mission of Peace

The tales of woe that Gandhi heard burned themselves into his soul, but he did not falter in his conviction that only non-violence and love could end this spiral of hate and violence. In his prayer speech every evening, he touched on this problem. He stressed the futility of retaliation. He wore himself out in an effort to re-educate the people; he heard grievances, suggested solutions, encouraged or admonished his numerous interviewers, visited refugee camps, remained in touch with local officials.

On January 13, 1948, he began a fast; "my greatest fast," he wrote to Miraben, his English disciple. It was also to be his last. The fast was not to be broken until Delhi became peaceful. The fast had a refreshing impact upon Pakistan. In India there was an emotional shake-up. The fast compelled people to think afresh on the problem on the solution of which he had staked his life. On January 18, representatives of various communities and parties in Delhi signed a pledge in Gandhi's presence that they would guarantee peace in Delhi.

After this fast the tide of violence showed definite signs of ebbing. Gandhi felt free to make his plans for the future. He thought he should visit Pakistan to promote the process of reconciliation between the two countries and the two communities.

Even as he had grappled with communal violence, the real problems of India, the social and economic uplift of her people, had never been absent from his mind. Political freedom having become a fact, Gandhi's mind was switching more and more to constructive work, and to the refurbishing of his non-violent technique.

The End

However, he was not destined to pick up the threads of his constructive Programme. He had a narrow escape on January 20, 1948, when a bomb exploded in Birla House in New Delhi where he was addressing his prayer meeting. He took no notice of the explosion. Next day he referred to the congratulations which he had received for remaining unruffled after the explosion. He would deserve them, he said, if he fell as a result of such an explosion and yet retained a smile on his face and no malice against the assailant. He described the bomb-thrower as a misguided youth and advised the police not to "molest" him but to convert him with persuasion and affection. "The misguided youth" was Madan Lal, a refugee from West Punjab, who was a member of a gang which had plotted Gandhi's death. These highly-strung Youngman saw Hinduism menaced by Islam from without and by Gandhi from within. Madan Lal having missed his aim, a fellow conspirator from Poona, Nathu Ram Godse, came to Gandhi's prayer meeting on the evening of January 30, whipped out his pistol and fired three shots. Gandhi fell instantly with the words 'He Rama' (Oh! God).

Assassination of the Mahatma

Mahatma Gandhi was assassinated on January 30, 1948, shot at point-blank range by Nathuram Godse, an activist of the Hindu Nationalist Hindu Mahasabha. Since 1934, there had been five unsuccessful attempts to kill Gandhi.

The Assassination

After the failed attempt at Birla House, Nathuram Godse and Narayan Apte returned to Pune via Bombay. With the help of Dr. Dattatraya Parchure and Gangadhar Dandavate they purchased a Beretta automatic and eleven rounds of ammunition at Gwalior and reached Delhi on January 29, 1948. On January 30, 1948, at around 5:10 p.m., Nathuram Godse got close enough to Mahatma Gandhi and shot him three times in his chest at point-blank range. Many have also said that sweets were distributed in Pune and other places of India, when the news of Gandhi's assassination reached them through the supporters of Hindu Mahasabha.

Shri Dharam Jit Jigyasu gave an account of that tragic day in world history to Muni Jaitly, his grandson, in 2000. He was standing next to the assassin, Nathuram Godse, when all who were present kneeled before Gandhi to greet him.

Godse shot Gandhi three times. Dharam Jit Jigyasu heard Gandhi utter the words, "Hai Ram [Oh God] ... Hai Ram ... Hai Ram" as he hit the ground.

Failed Attempts

First Attempt: On June 25, 1934, Mahatma Gandhi was in Pune along with Kasturba to deliver a speech at "Corporation Auditorium". They were travelling in a motorcade of two cars. *En route,* they came across a railway level crossing. The car in which the couple was travelling was left behind and the first car reached the auditorium. Just when the first car arrived at the auditorium, a huge bomb was thrown, which exploded near the car. This caused grievous injury to the Chief Officer of the Pune Municipal Corporation, two policemen and seven others.

Nevertheless, no account or records of the investigation nor arrests made can be found. Gandhi's secretary, Pyarelal Nayyar believes that the attempt failed due to lack of planning and coordination. Many have alleged that Nathuram Godse and Narayan Apte were involved in the attack.

Second Attempt: The second attempt on the life of Mahatma Gandhi may not have been an attempt to assassinate as much as a demonstration of anger by an angry young man. In May 1944, Gandhi was released from Agha Khan Palace prison and soon after he contracted malaria. On the advice of doctors, he took a vacation to Panchgani, a hill station near Pune. During his stay at Panchgani, Gandhi was staying at Dilkush Bungalow. A group of 15-20 young men came to Panchgani after realising that Gandhi was staying there. This young crowd, led by Nathuram Godse, came through a chartered bus. These youth held a day long protest demonstration, but declined to talk with Gandhi when invited. However, by evening, during the prayer meeting, Nathuram Godse rushed towards Gandhi with a dagger shouting anti-Gandhi slogans. He was unable to reach Gandhi as he was overpowered by Mani Shankar Purohit (proprietor of Surti Lodge, Pune) and D. Billare Guruji of Satara (who later became a Congress legislator from Mahabaleshwar).

The documentary evidence of this attack can be found in the depositions made by Mani Shankar Purohit and D. Billare Guruji before the Kapoor Commission set up to investigate the assassination of Gandhi. However, the Kapoor Commission rejected this theory as many of the close associates of Gandhi were not present during that time.

Third Attempt: The third attempt was also a demonstration. However, people who testified before the Kapoor Commission referred it as an attempt to murder. Mahatma Gandhi began his talks with Muhammad Ali Jinnah on 9 September 1944 which lasted for 14 days. While leaving for Bombay from Sevagram Ashram, a group of Hindu activists stopped him. They did not want him to go to Bombay to hold talks with Jinnah. However, these protesters were stopped by volunteers of the ashram.

The leader of this group, Nathuram Godse, was again found in possession of a dagger. The policeman who found the dagger then looked up to him and joked, "Why do you want to kill Gandhi? Let's leave it to the leaders themselves... perhaps (Veer) Savarkar will finish off the job!" At which Godse retorted, "Gandhi does not require such an honour. Even the jamadar (sweeper) is enough for that!"

Dr. Sushila Nayyar testified to this effect before the Kapoor Commission and she considered this an attempt at assassination. This incident has also been portrayed in the film Gandhi by Sir Richard Attenborough. However, it is not portrayed as an attempt to murder but as a peaceful demonstration in which the demonstrators were waving black flags.

Fourth Attempt: June 29, 1946, the train carrying Mahatma Gandhi called Gandhi Special derailed between Neral and Karjat stations of Bombay Section. The report submitted by the motorman or driver of the train claimed that boulders were placed on the tracks of the train, with the intention to derail it. The train had crashed into the boulders. The Pune police claimed that the boulders were placed by looters to stop trains carrying goods. The police have not disclaimed sabotage. Since the Gandhi Special was the only train on that route at that time, and there were no goods trains on the section, either before or after, it is highly plausible that Gandhi must have been the target.

> By the grace of God I have escaped from the jaws of death seven times. I have not hurt anybody nor do I consider anybody to be my enemy. I can't understand why there are so many attempts on my life. Yesterday's attempt on my life has failed. I will not die just yet. I aim to live till the age of 125.
>
> *Mohandas K. Gandhi, at a prayer meeting in Pune.*

Fifth Attempt: On January 14, 1948, Madanlal Pahwa, Shankar Kistaiyya, Digambar Badge, Vishnu Karkare, Gopal Godse, Nathuram Godse, and Narayan Apte came to Birla Bhavan (aka Birla House) in Delhi to carry out an attack on Mahatma Gandhi. Except for Madanlal Pahwa and Vishnu Karkare, everyone else reached the venue through the rear entrance in a cab. Surjeet Singh was the cab driver. Madanlal Pahwa tried to bribe the driver at Birla Bhavan, named Choturam, to let him go behind the podium to take pictures of Gandhi. However, Choturam became suspicious and asked Madanlal Pahwa, why he needed photographs from behind, and enquired about the absence of a camera. Madanlal Pahwa just left, having Choturam think he was going back to the taxi; however, he placed a cotton ball enclosing a bomb on the wall behind the podium and ignited it. The bomb went off without creating any panic. The team had left after abandoning Madanlal Pahwa.

On interrogation, Madanlal Pahwa admitted that he was part of a seven member gang who wanted to kill him. The plan was that Madanlal Pahwa would explode the bomb as close to the podium as possible while Digambar Bagde or Shankar Kishtaiyya would shoot Gandhi in the head, ensuing panic and stampede, using the chaotic situation to effect their escape. Vishnu Karkare was to compound the chaos by hurling hand grenades. However, faced with Choturam's suspicious attitude, Digambar Bagde decided not to act at the last minute, and also instructed Shankar Kishtaiyya (who was his servant) to do the same.

Later, Madanlal Phawa led the police to the Marina Hotel where Nathuram Godse and Narayan Apte were staying and also to Sharief Hotel where all other gang members were staying. Everyone had left by that time and the police were only able to recover some letters and clothes which had the initials "NVG" on it. By this time they were able to ascertain that the members of that team were from Maharashtra; however they were not able to establish the identity and the involvement of Nathuram Godse.

During the Mahatma Gandhi murder trial, Madanlal Pahwa was identified by Mrs. Sulochana Devi, who had come to Birla Bhavan in search of her three year old son (who used to play in the servant quarters). She was the fifteenth witness in the trial, and Surjeet Singh, the driver was the fourteenth witness.

> Is it true that on the day of the bomb blast during the search of the room at Marina Hotel clothes were found bearing the initials N.V.G. – Nathuram Vinayak Godse? On the basis of which the police went to Bombay and requested the Bombay police to look for this person, the Bombay police assured the Delhi police

to do the needful and asked them to return, but did nothing. Is it true that the Bombay Police failed in tracing Nathuram Vinayak Godse?

— *Balkrishna Sharma, during the debate on murder of Mahatma Gandhi in the Constituent Assembly of India.*

To comment on matters under investigation is both difficult and unwarranted. I can only say that after the arrest and interrogation of the bomber, an officer of Delhi police went to Bombay and briefed the CID in Bombay. After the briefing, it was decided that some people should be arrested but to arrest them immediately would lead to the other conspirators going underground. So the Delhi police and Bombay CID decided to defer the arrests for some time to enable them to uncover the conspiracy and all who were involved in it. It is true that the police were on a look out for them but all of them were not in Bombay

— *Sardar Patel, during the debate on murder of Mahatma Gandhi in the Constituent Assembly of India.*

If I am to die by the bullet of a mad man, I must do so smiling. There must be no anger within me. God must be in my heart and on my lips..

— *Mohandas K. Gandhi, on January 28, 1948, two days prior to his assassination.*

Controversy over 'Hey Ram'

The last word(s) uttered by Mahatma Gandhi are still a matter of debate. Venkita Kalyanam, former personal assistant to Mr. Gandhi, said that he was present at the spot and Gandhi did not utter a single word.

New Delhi's Tughlaq Road police station's assistant subinspector Dhalu Ram recorded Nand Lal Mehta's statement

> ...suddenly a man, who was later identified as Nathu Ram Godse took steps out of the crowd and fired three shots at Mahatmaji. Bullets hit him on the

> stomach and chest. The Mahatma fell down saying Ram-Ram...
>
> — *Nand Lal Mehta, in the First Information Report recorded on January 30, 1948, at 9.45 p.m.*

In the First Information Report we find no statement that any doctor was called. We have no explanation of why he was not rushed to hospital and was instead taken to Birla House, where he died later.

7

Gandhi's Principles

Gandhi and Non-violence

Gandhi did not claim to be a prophet or even a philosopher. "There is no such thing as Gandhism," he warned, "and I do not want to leave any sect after me." There was only one Gandhian, he said, an imperfect one at that: himself.

The real significance of the Indian Freedom Movement in Gandhi's eyes was that it was waged non-violently. He would have had no interest in it if the Indian National Congress had not adopted Satyagraha and subscribed to non-violence. He objected to violence not only because an unarmed people had little chance of success in an armed rebellion, but because he considered violence a clumsy weapon which created more problems than it solved, and left a trail of hatred and bitterness in which genuine reconciliation was almost impossible.

This emphasis on non-violence jarred alike on Gandhi's British and Indian critics, though for different reasons. To the former, non-violence was a camouflage; to the latter, it was sheer sentimentalism. To the British who tended to see the Indian struggle through the prism of European history, the professions of non-violence rather than on the remarkably peaceful nature of Gandhi's campaigns. To the radical Indian politicians, who had browsed on the history of the French and Russian revolutions or the Italian and Irish nationalist struggles, it was patent that force would only yield to force, and that it was foolish to miss opportunities and sacrifice tactical gains for reasons more relevant to ethics than to politics.

Gandhi's total allegiance to non-violence created a gulf between him and the educated elite in India which was temporarily bridged only during periods of intense political excitement. Even among his closest colleagues there were few who were prepared to follow his doctrine of non-violence to its logical conclusion: the adoption of unilateral disarmament in a world armed to the teeth, the scrapping of the police and the armed forces, and the decentralisation of administration to the point where the state would "wither away".

Nehru, Patel and others on whom fell the task of organising the administration of independent India did not question the superiority of the principle of non-violence as enunciated by their leader, but they did not cope rider it practical politics. The Indian Constituent Assembly include a majority of members owing allegiance to Gandhi or at least holding him in high esteem, but the Constitution which emerged from their labours in 1949 was based more on the Western parliamentary than on he Gandhian model. The development of the Indian economy during the last four decades cannot be said to have conformed to Gandhi's conception of "self-reliant village republics". On the other hand, it bears the marks of a conscious effort to launch an Indian industrial revolution.

Jawaharlal Nehru — Gandhi's "political heir" — was thoroughly imbued with the humane values inculcated by the Mahatma. But the man who spoke Gandhi's language, after his death, was Vinoba Bhave, the "Walking Saint", who kept out of politics and government, Bhave's Bhoodan (land gift) Movement was designed as much as a measure of land reform as that of a spiritual renewal. Though more than five million acres of land were distributed to the landless, the movement, despite its early promise, never really spiralled into a social revolution by consent. This was partly because Vinoba Bhave did not command Gandhi's extraordinary genius for organising the masses for a national crusade, and partly because in independent India the tendency grew for the people to look up to the government rather than to rely on voluntary and cooperative effort for effecting reforms in society.

Soon after Gandhi's death in 1948, a delegate speaking at the United Nations predicted that "the greatest achievements of the Indian sage were yet to come" "Gandhi's times," said Vinoba Bhave, "were the first pale dawn of the sun of Satyagraha." Forty years after Gandhi's death, this optimism would seem to have been too high-pitched. The manner in which Gandhi's techniques have sometimes been invoked even in the land of his birth in recent years would appear to be a travesty of his principles. And the world has been in the grip of a series of crises in Korea, the Congo, the Vietnam, the Middle East, and South Africa with a never-ending trail of blood and bitterness.

The shadow of a thermo-nuclear war with its incalculable hazards continues to hang over mankind. From this predicament, Gandhi's ideas and techniques may suggest a way out. Unfortunately, his motives and methods are often misunderstood, and not only by mobs in the street, Not long ago, Arthur Koestler described Gandhi's attitude as one "of passive submission to bayonetting and raping, to villages without sewage, septic childhood's and trachoma." Such a judgement is of course completely with the same tenacity with which he battled with the British Raj. He advocated non-violence not because it offered an easy way out, but because he considered violence a crude and in the long run, an ineffective weapon. His rejection of violence stemmed from choice, not from necessity.

Horace Alexander, who knew Gandhi and saw him in action, graphically describes the attitude of the non-violent resister to his opponent: "On your side you have all the mighty forces of the modern State, arms, money, a controlled press, and all the rest. On my side, I have nothing but my conviction of right and truth, the unquenchable spirit of man, who is prepared to die for his convictions than submit to your brute force. I have my comrades in armlessness. Here we stand; and here if need be, we fall." Far from being a craven retreat from difficulty and danger, non-violent resistance demands courage of a high order, the courage to resist injustice without rancour, to unite the utmost firmness with the utmost gentleness, to invite suffering but not to inflict it, to die but not to kill.

Gandhi did not make the facile division of mankind into "good" and "bad". He was convinced that every human being — even the "enemy" — had a kernel of decency: there were only evil acts, no wholly evil men. His technique of Satyagraha was designed not to coerce the opponent, but to set into motion forces which could lead to his conversion. Relying as it did on persuasion and compromise, Gandhi's method was not always quick in producing results, but the results were likely to be the more durable for having been brought about peacefully. "It is my firm conviction," Gandhi affirmed, "that nothing enduring can be built upon violence." The rate of social change through the non-violent technique was not in fact likely to be much slower than that achieved by violent methods; it was definitely faster than that expected from the normal functioning of institutions which tended to fossilise and preserve the *status quo*.

Gandhi did not think it possible to bring about radical changes in the structure of society overnight. Nor did he succumb to the illusion that the road to a new order could be paved merely with pious wishes and fine words. It was not enough to blame the opponent or bewail the times in which one's lot was cast. However, heavy the odds, it was the Satyagrahi's duty never to feel helpless. The least he could do was to make a beginning with himself. If he was crusading for a new deal for peasantry, he could go to a village and live there, If he wanted to bring peace to a disturbed district, he could walk through it, entering into the minds and hearts of those who were going through the ordeal, If an age-old evil like untouchability was to be fought, what could be a more effective symbol of defiance for a reformer than to adopt an untouchable child? If the object was to challenge foreign rule, why not act on the assumption that the country was already free, ignore the alien government and build alternative institutions to harness the spontaneous, constructive and cooperative effort of the people? If the goal was world peace, why not begin today by acting peacefully towards the immediate neighbour, going more than half way to understand and win him over?

Though he may have appeared a starry-eyed idealist to so me, Gandhi's attitude to social and political problems was severely practical. There was a deep mystical streak in him, but even his mysticism seemed to have little of the ethereal about it. He did not dream heavenly dreams nor see things unutterable in trance;

when "the still small voice" spoke to him, it was often to tell how he could fight a social evil or heal a rift between two warring communities. Far from distracting him from his role in public affairs, Gandhi's religious quest gave him the stamina to play it more effectively. To him true religion was not merely the reading of scriptures, the dissection of ancient texts, or even the practice of cloistered virtue: it had to be lived in the challenging context of political and social life.

Gandhi used his non-violent technique on behalf of his fellow-countrymen in South Africa and India, but he did not conceive it only as a weapon in the armoury of Indian nationalism. On the other hand, he fashioned it as an instrument for righting wrongs and resolving conflicts between opposing groups, races and nations. It is a strange paradox that though the stoutest and perhaps the most successful champion of the revolt against colonialism in our time, Gandhi was frees from the taint of narrow nationalism. As early as 1924, he had declared that "the better mind of the world desires today, not absolutely independent states, warring one against another, but a federation of independent, of friendly interdependent states".

Even before the First World War had revealed the disastrous results of the combination of industrialism and nationalism, he had become a convert to the idea that violence between nation-states must be completely abjured.

In 1931, during his visit to England, a cartoon in the Star depicted him in a loin cloth besides Mussolini, Hitler, de Valera and Stalin, who were clad in black, brown, green and red shirts respectively. The caption, "And he was not wearing any blooming' shirt at all" was not only literally but figuratively true. For a man of non-violence, who believed in the brotherhood of man, there was no superficial division of nations into good and bad, allies and adversaries. This did not, however, mean that Gandhi did not distinguish between the countries which inflicted and the countries which suffered violence. His own life had been one struggle against the forces of violence, and Satyagraha was designed at once to eschew violence and to fight injustice.

In the years immediately preceding the Second Word war, when the tide of Nazi and Fascist aggression was relentlessly rolling forward, Gandhi had reasserted his faith in non-violence and commended it to the smaller nation which were living in daily dread of being overwhelmed by superior force. Through the pages of his weekly paper the Harijan, he expounded the non-violent approach to military aggression and political tyranny. He advised the weaker nations to defend themselves not by increasing their fighting potential, but by non-violent resistance to the aggressor. When Czechoslovakia was blackmailed into submission in September 1938, Gandhi suggested to the unfortunate Czechs: "There is no bravery greater than a resolute refusal

To bend the knee to an earthly power, no matter how great, and that without bitterness of spirit, and in the fullness of faith that the spirit alone lives, nothing else does."

Seven years later when the first atomic bombs exploded over Hiroshima and Nagasaki, Gandhi's reaction was characteristic: "I did not move a muscle. On the contrary, I said to myself that unless now the adopts non-violence, it will spell certain suicide for mankind." The irony of the very perfection of the weapons of war rendering them useless as arbiters between nations has become increasingly clear during the last forty years. The atomic stockpiles which the major nuclear powers have already built up are capable of destroying civilization, as we know it several time over and peace has been precariously preserved by, what has been grimly termed, "the balance of atomic terror." The fact is that with the weapons of mass destruction, which are at hand now, to attack another nation is tantamount to attacking oneself. This is a bitter truth which old habits of thought have prevented from going home. "This splitting of the atoms has changed everything" bewailed Einstein, "save our modes of thinking and thus we drift towards unparalleled catastrophe."

Non-violence, as Gandhi expounded it, has ceased to be a pious exhortation, and become a necessity. The advice he gave to the unfortunate Abyssinians and Czechs during the twilight years before the Second Word War, may have seemed utopian thirty years ago. Today, it sounds commonsense. Even some hardheaded military strategists such as Sir Stephen King-Hall have begun to see in Gandhi's method a possible alternative to suicidal violence.

Gandhi would have been the first to deny that his method offered an instant or universal panacea for world peace. His method is capable of almost infinite evolution to suit new situations in a changing world. It is possible that "applied non-violence" is at present at the same stage of development "as the invention of electricity was in the days of Edison and Marconi." The lives-and deaths-of Chief Lithuli and Dr. Martin Luther King have proved that there is nothing esoteric about non-violence, limiting it to a particular country or a particular period. Indeed Tagore, the great contemporary and friend of Gandhi, prophesies that the West would accept Gandhi before the East "for the West has gone through the cycle of dependence on force and material things of life and has become disillusioned. They want a return to the spirit. The East has not yet gone through materialism and hence has not become so disillusioned."

Truth

Gandhi dedicated his life to the wider purpose of discovering truth, or Satya. He tried to achieve this by learning from his own mistakes and conducting experiments on himself. He called his autobiography The Story of My Experiments with Truth.

Gandhi stated that the most important battle to fight was overcoming his own demons, fears, and insecurities. Gandhi summarised his beliefs first when he said "God is Truth". He would later change this statement to "Truth is God". Thus, Satya (Truth) in Gandhi's philosophy is "God".

Non-violence

Mahatma Gandhi was in no way the originator of the principle of non-violence. But he was the first to apply it in the political field on a huge scale. The concept of non-violence (ahimsa) and non-resistance has a long history in Indian religious thought and has had many revivals in Hindu, Buddhist, Jain, Jewish and Christian contexts. Gandhi explains his philosophy and way of life in his autobiography The Story of My Experiments with Truth. He was quoted as saying:

> "When I despair, I remember that all through history the way of truth and love has always won. There have been tyrants and murderers and for a time they seem invincible, but in the end, they always fall — think of it, always."

"What difference does it make to the dead, the orphans, and the homeless, whether the mad destruction is wrought under the name of totalitarianism or the holy name of liberty and democracy?"

"An eye for an eye makes the whole world blind."

"There are many causes that I am prepared to die for but no causes that I am prepared to kill for."

In applying these principles, Gandhi did not balk from taking them to their most logical extremes in envisioning a world where even government, police and armies were non-violent. The quotations below are from the book "For Pacifists."

The science of war leads one to dictatorship, pure and simple. The science of non-violence alone can lead one to pure democracy...Power based on love is thousand times more effective and permanent than power derived from fear of punishment....It is a blasphemy to say non-violence can be practiced only by individuals and never by nations which are composed of individuals...The nearest approach to purest anarchy would be a democracy based on non-violence...A society organised and run on the basis of complete non-violence would be the purest anarchy

I have conceded that even in a non-violent state a police force may be necessary...Police ranks will be composed of believers in non-violence. The people will instinctively render them every help and through mutual cooperation they will easily deal with the ever decreasing disturbances...Violent quarrels between labour and capital and strikes will be few and far between in a non-violent state because the influence of the non-violent majority will be great as to respect the principle elements in society. Similarly, there will be no room for communal disturbances....

A non-violent army acts unlike armed men, as well in times of peace as in times of disturbances. Theirs will be the duty of bringing warring communities together, carrying peace propaganda, engaging in

> activities that would bring and keep them in touch with every single person in their parish or division. Such an army should be ready to cope with any emergency, and in order to still the frenzy of mobs should risk their lives in numbers sufficient for that purpose. ...Satyagraha (truth-force) brigades can be organised in every village and every block of buildings in the cities. [If the non-violent society is attacked from without] there are two ways open to non-violence. To yield possession, but non-cooperate with the aggressor...prefer death to submission. The second way would be non-violent resistance by the people who have been trained in the non-violent way...The unexpected spectacle of endless rows upon rows of men and women simply dying rather than surrender to the will of an aggressor must ultimately melt him and his soldiery...A nation or group which has made non-violence its final policy cannot be subjected to slavery even by the atom bomb.... The level of non-violence in that nation, if that even happily comes to pass, will naturally have risen so high as to command universal respect.

In accordance with these views, in 1940, when invasion of the British Isles by Nazi Germany looked imminent, Gandhi offered the following advice to the British people (Non-Violence in Peace and War):

> "I would like you to lay down the arms you have as being useless for saving you or humanity. You will invite Herr Hitler and Signor Mussolini to take what they want of the countries you call your possessions...If these gentlemen choose to occupy your homes, you will vacate them. If they do not give you free passage out, you will allow yourselves, man, woman, and child, to be slaughtered, but you will refuse to owe allegiance to them."

In a post-war interview in 1946, he offered a view at an even further extreme:

> "The Jews should have offered themselves to the butcher's knife. They should have thrown themselves into the sea from cliffs."

However, Gandhi was aware that this level of non-violence required incredible faith and courage, which he realised not everyone possessed. He therefore advised that everyone need not keep to non-violence, especially if it were used as a cover for cowardice:

> "Gandhi guarded against attracting to his Satyagraha Movement those who feared to take up arms or felt themselves incapable of resistance. 'I do believe,' he wrote, 'that where there is only a choice between cowardice and violence, I would advise violence."
>
> "At every meeting I repeated the warning that unless they felt that in non-violence they had come into possession of a force infinitely superior to the one they had and in the use of which they were adept, they should have nothing to do with non-violence and resume the arms they possessed before. It must never be said of the Khudai Khidmatgars that once so brave, they had become or been made cowards under Badshah Khan's influence. Their bravery consisted not in being good marksmen but in defying death and being ever ready to bare their breasts to the bullets."

Vegetarianism

As a young child, Gandhi experimented with meat-eating. This was due partially to his inherent curiosity as well as his rather persuasive peer and friend Sheikh Mehtab. The idea of vegetarianism is deeply ingrained in Hindu and Jain traditions in India, and, in his native land of Gujarat, most Hindus were vegetarian and so are all Jains. The Gandhi family was no exception. Before leaving for his studies in London, Gandhi made a promise to his mother, Putlibai and his uncle, Becharji Swami that he would abstain from eating meat, taking alcohol, and engaging in promiscuity. He held fast to his promise and gained more than a diet: he gained a basis for his life-long philosophies. As Gandhi grew into adulthood, he became a strict vegetarian. He wrote the book The Moral Basis of Vegetarianism and several articles on the subject, some of which were published in the London Vegetarian Society's publication, The Vegetarian. Gandhi, himself, became inspired by many great minds during this period and befriended the chairman of the London Vegetarian Society, Dr. Josiah Oldfield.

Having also read and admired the work of Henry Stephens Salt, the young Mohandas met and often corresponded with the vegetarian campaigner. Gandhi spent much time advocating vegetarianism during and after his time in London. To Gandhi, a vegetarian diet would not only satisfy the requirements of the body, it would also serve an economic purpose as meat was, and still is, generally more expensive than grains, vegetables, and fruits. Also, many Indians of the time struggled with low income, thus vegetarianism was seen not only as a spiritual practice but also a practical one. He abstained from eating for long periods, using fasting as a form of political protest. He refused to eat until his death or his demands were met. It was noted in his autobiography that vegetarianism was the beginning of his deep commitment to Brahmacharya; without total control of the palate, his success in Bramacharya would likely falter.

Gandhi had been a frutarian, but started taking goat's milk on the advice of his doctor. He never took dairy products obtained from cows because of his view initially that milk is not the natural diet of man, disgust for cow blowing, and, specifically, because of a vow to his late mother.

Brahmacharya

When Gandhi was 16 his father became very ill. Being very devoted to his parents, he attended to his father at all times during his illness. However, one night, Gandhi's uncle came to relieve Gandhi for a while. He retired to his bedroom where carnal desires overcame him and he made love to his wife. Shortly afterwards a servant came to report that Gandhi's father had just died. Gandhi felt tremendous guilt and never could forgive himself. He came to refer to this event as "double shame." The incident had significant influence in Gandhi becoming celibate at the age of 36, while still married.

This decision was deeply influenced by the philosophy of Brahmacharya — spiritual and practical purity — largely associated with celibacy and asceticism. Gandhi saw brahmacharya as a means of becoming close with God and as a primary foundation for self realisation. In his autobiography he tells of his battle against lustful urges and fits of jealousy with his childhood bride, Kasturba. He felt it his personal obligation to remain celibate so that he could learn to love, rather than lust. For

Gandhi, brahmacharya meant "control of the senses in thought, word and deed."

Simplicity

Gandhi earnestly believed that a person involved in social service should lead a simple life which he thought could lead to Brahmacharya. His simplicity began by renouncing the western lifestyle he was leading in South Africa. He called it "reducing himself to zero," which entailed giving up unnecessary expenditure, embracing a simple lifestyle and washing his own clothes. On one occasion he returned the gifts bestowed to him from the natals for his diligent service to the community

Gandhi spent one day of each week in silence. He believed that abstaining from speaking brought him inner peace. This influence was drawn from the Hindu principles of *mauna* (silence) and *shanti* (peace). On such days he communicated with others by writing on paper. For three and a half years, from the age of 37, Gandhi refused to read newspapers, claiming that the tumultuous state of world affairs caused him more confusion than his own inner unrest.

After reading John Ruskin's Unto This Last, he decided to change his lifestyle and create a commune called Phoenix Settlement.

Upon returning to India from South Africa, where he had enjoyed a successful legal practice, he gave up wearing Western-style clothing, which he associated with wealth and success. He dressed to be accepted by the poorest person in India, advocating the use of homespun cloth (khadi). Gandhi and his followers adopted the practice of weaving their own clothes from thread they themselves spun, and encouraged others to do so.

While Indian workers were often idle due to unemployment, they had often bought their clothing from industrial manufacturers owned by British interests. It was Gandhi's view that if Indians made their own clothes, it would deal an economic blow to the British establishment in India. Consequently, the spinning wheel was later incorporated into the flag of the Indian National Congress. He subsequently wore a dhoti for the rest of his life to express the simplicity of his life.

Faith

Gandhi was born a Hindu and practised Hinduism all his life, deriving most of his principles from Hinduism. As a common Hindu, he believed all religions to be equal, and rejected all efforts to convert him to a different faith. He was an avid theologian and read extensively about all major religions. He had the following to say about Hinduism:

> "Hinduism as I know it entirely satisfies my soul, fills my whole being...When doubts haunt me, when disappointments stare me in the face, and when I see not one ray of light on the horizon, I turn to the Bhagavad Gita, and find a verse to comfort me; and I immediately begin to smile in the midst of overwhelming sorrow. My life has been full of tragedies and if they have not left any visible and indelible effect on me, I owe it to the teachings of the Bhagavad Gita."

Gandhi wrote a commentary on the Bhagavad Gita in Gujarati. The Gujarati manuscript was translated into English by Mahadev Desai, who provided an additional introduction and commentary. It was published with a Foreword by Gandhi in 1946.

Gandhi believed that at the core of every religion was truth and love (compassion, non-violence and the Golden Rule). He also questioned hypocrisy, malpractices and dogma in all religions and was a tireless social reformer. Some of his comments on various religions are:

> "Thus, if I could not accept Christianity either as a perfect, or the greatest religion, neither was I then convinced of Hinduism being such. Hindu defects were pressingly visible to me. If untouchability could be a part of Hinduism, it could but be a rotten part or an excrescence. I could not understand the *raison d'etre* of a multitude of sects and castes. What was the meaning of saying that the Vedas were the inspired Word of God? If they were inspired, why not also the Bible and the Koran? As Christian friends were endeavouring to convert me, so were Muslim friends. Abdullah Sheth had kept on inducing me to study

> Islam, and of course he had always something to say regarding its beauty."
>
> "The sayings of Muhammad are a treasure of wisdom, not only for Muslims but for all of mankind:"

Later in his life when he was asked whether he was a Hindu, he replied:

> "Yes I am. I am also a Christian, a Muslim, a Buddhist and a Jew."

In spite of their deep reverence to each other, Gandhi and Rabindranath Tagore engaged in protracted debates more than once. These debates exemplify the philosophical differences between the two most famous Indians at the time. On 15 January 1934, an earthquake hit Bihar and caused extensive damage and loss of life. Gandhi maintained this was because of the sin committed by upper caste Hindus by not letting untouchables in their temples (Gandhi was committed to the cause of improving the fate of untouchables, referring to them as Harijans, people of Krishna). Tagore vehemently opposed Gandhi's stance, maintaining that an earthquake can only be caused by natural forces, not moral reasons, however repugnant the practice of untouchability may be.

Books on Gandhi

Several biographers have undertaken the task of describing Gandhi's life. Among them, two works stand out: D. G. Tendulkar with his "Mahatma: Life of Mohandas Karamchand Gandhi" in eight volumes, and Pyarelal and Sushila Nayar with their "Mahatma Gandhi" in 10 volumes. Colonel G. B. Singh from US Army is said of have spent 20 years collecting Gandhi's original speeches and writings for his factual research book "Gandhi: Behind the Mask of Divinity".

Followers and Influence

Gandhi influenced important leaders and political movements. Leaders of the civil rights movement in the United States, including Martin Luther King and James Lawson, drew from the writings of Gandhi in the development of their own theories about non-violence. Anti-apartheid activist and former President of South

Africa, Nelson Mandela, was inspired by Gandhi. Others include Khan Abdul Ghaffar Khan, Steve Biko, and Aung San Suu Kyi.

Gandhi's life and teachings inspired many who specifically referred to Gandhi as their mentor or who dedicated their lives to spreading Gandhi's ideas. In Europe, Romain Rolland was the first to discuss Gandhi in his 1924 book Mahatma Gandhi, and Brazilian anarchist and feminist Maria Lacerda de Moura wrote about Gandhi in her work on pacifism. In 1931, notable European physicist Albert Einstein exchanged written letters with Gandhi, and called him "a role model for the generations to come" in a later writing about him. Lanza del Vasto went to India in 1936 intending to live with Gandhi; he later returned to Europe to spread Gandhi's philosophy and founded the Community of the Ark in 1948 (modelled after Gandhi's ashrams). Madeleine Slade (known as "Mirabehn") was the daughter of a British admiral who spent much of her adult life in India as a devotee of Gandhi.

In addition, the British musician John Lennon referred to Gandhi when discussing his views on non-violence. At the Cannes Lions International Advertising Festival in 2007, former US Vice-President and environmentalist Al Gore spoke of Gandhi's influence on him.

His Legacy

Gandhi's birthday, 2 October, is a national holiday in India, Gandhi Jayanti. On 15 June 2007, it was announced that the "United Nations General Assembly" has "unanimously adopted" a resolution declaring 2 October as "the International Day of Non-Violence."

The word Mahatma, while often mistaken for Gandhi's given name in the West, is taken from the Sanskrit words *maha* meaning Great and *atma* meaning Soul. Most sources, such as Dutta and Robinson's Rabindranath Tagore: An Anthology, state that Rabindranath Tagore first accorded the title of Mahatma to Gandhi. Other sources state that Nautamlal Bhagavanji Mehta accorded him this title on 21 January 1915. In his autobiography, Gandhi nevertheless explains that he never felt worthy of the honour. According to the manpatra, the name Mahatma was given in response to Gandhi's admirable sacrifice in manifesting justice and truth.

Time magazine named Gandhi the Man of the Year in 1930. Gandhi was also the runner-up to "Person of the Century" at the end of 1999. Time Magazine named The Dalai Lama, Lech Walesa, Dr. Martin Luther King, Jr., Cesar Chavez, Aung San Suu Kyi, Benigno Aquino, Jr., Desmond Tutu, and Nelson Mandela as Children of Gandhi and his spiritual heirs to non-violence. The Government of India awards the annual Mahatma Gandhi Peace Prize to distinguished social workers, world leaders and citizens. Nelson Mandela, the leader of South Africa's struggle to eradicate racial discrimination and segregation, is a prominent non-Indian recipient.

In 1996, the Government of India introduced the Mahatma Gandhi series of currency notes in rupees 5, 10, 20, 50, 100, 500 and 1000 denomination. Today, all the currency notes in circulation in India contain a portrait of Mahatma Gandhi. In 1969, the United Kingdom issued a series of stamps commemorating the centenary of Mahatma Gandhi.

The Martyr's Column at the Gandhi Smriti in New Delhi, marks the spot where he was assassinated.

In the United Kingdom, there are several prominent statues of Gandhi, most notably in Tavistock Square, London near University College London where he studied law. January 30 is commemorated in the United Kingdom as the "National Gandhi Remembrance Day." In the United States, there are statues of Gandhi outside the Union Square Park in New York City, and the Martin Luther King, Jr. National Historic Site in Atlanta, and on Massachusetts Avenue in Washington, D. C., near the Indian Embassy. The city of Pietermaritzburg, South Africa — where Gandhi was ejected from a first-class train in 1893 — now hosts a commemorative statue. There are wax statues of Gandhi at the Madame Tussaud's wax museums in London, New York, and other cities around the world.

Gandhi never received the Nobel Peace Prize, although he was nominated five times between 1937 and 1948, including the first-ever nomination by the American Friends Service Committee. Decades later, the Nobel Committee publicly declared its regret for the omission, and admitted to deeply divided nationalistic opinion denying the award. Mahatma Gandhi was to receive the Prize in 1948, but his assassination prevented the award. The war breaking out between the newly created states of India and Pakistan could have been an additional complicating factor that year. The Prize was not awarded in 1948, the year of Gandhi's death, on the grounds that "there was no suitable living candidate" that year, and when the Dalai Lama was awarded the Prize in 1989, the chairman of the committee said that this was "in part a tribute to the memory of Mahatma Gandhi."

In New Delhi, the Birla Bhavan (or Birla House), where Gandhi was assassinated on January 30, 1948, was acquired by the Government of India in 1971 and opened to the public in 1973 as the Gandhi Smriti or "Gandhi Remembrance". It preserves the room where Mahatma Gandhi lived the last four months of his life and the grounds where he was shot while holding his nightly public walk. A Martyr's Column now marks the place where Mohandas Gandhi was assassinated.

On January 30 every year, on the anniversary of the death of Mahatma Gandhi, in schools of many countries is observed the School Day of Non-violence and Peace (DENIP), founded in Spain in 1964. In countries with a Southern Hemisphere school calendar, it can be observed on March 30 or thereabouts.

Gandhi Jayanti

Gandhi Jayanti is national holiday celebrated in India to mark the occasion of the birthday of Mahatma Gandhi, the "Father of the Nation". It is celebrated on October 2, every year. It is one of the three official declared National Holidays of India and is observed in all its states and union territories. The United Nations General Assembly announced on 15 June 2007 that it adopted a resolution which declared that October 2 will be celebrated as the International Day of Non Violence.

Cultural Impact

The day is marked by prayer services and tributes all over India, especially at Raj Ghat, Gandhi's memorial in New Delhi where he was cremated. Popular celebration includes prayer meetings, commemorative ceremonies in different cities by colleges, local government institutions and socio-political institutions. Painting and essay competitions are conducted and best awards are awarded for projects in schools and the community, on themes of glorifying peace, non-violence and Gandhi's effort in Indian Freedom Struggle. Usually, Gandhi's favourite devotional song, Raghupati Raghava Raja Ram is sung in memory of him.

Ideals and Criticisms

Gandhi's rigid *ahimsa* implies pacifism, and is thus a source of criticism from across the political spectrum.

Gandhi's Writings

Gandhi was a prolific writer. For decades he edited several newspapers including Harijan in Gujarati, Hindi and English; Indian Opinion while in South Africa and, Young India, in English, and Navajivan, a Gujarati monthly, on his return to India. Later Navajivan was also published in Hindi. In addition, he wrote letters almost every day to individuals and newspapers.

Gandhi also wrote a few books including his autobiography, An Autobiography or My Experiments with·Truth, Satyagraha in South Africa about his struggle there, Hind Swaraj or Indian Home Rule, a political pamphlet, and a paraphrase in Gujarati of John Ruskin's Unto This Last. This last essay can be considered his programme on economics. He also wrote extensively on vegetarianism, diet and health, religion, social reforms, etc. Gandhi usually wrote in Gujarati, though he also revised the Hindi and English translations of his books.

Gandhi's complete works were published by the Indian government under the name The Collected Works of Mahatma Gandhi in the 1960s. The writings comprise about 50,000 pages published in about a hundred volumes. In 2000, a revised edition of the complete works sparked a controversy, as Gandhian followers accused the government of incorporating changes for political purpose.

Concept of Partition

As a rule, Gandhi was opposed to the concept of partition as it contradicted his vision of religious unity. Of the partition of India to create Pakistan, he wrote in Harijan on 6 October 1946:

> The demand for Pakistan, as put forth by the Muslim League is un-Islamic and I have not hesitated to call it sinful. Islam stands for unity and the brotherhood

> of mankind, not for disrupting the oneness of the human family. Therefore, those who want to divide India into possibly warring groups are enemies alike of India and Islam. They may cut me into pieces but they cannot make me subscribe to something which I consider to be wrong [...] we must not cease to aspire, in spite of [the] wild talk, to befriend all Muslims and hold them fast as prisoners of our love.
>
> However, as Homer Jack notes of Gandhi's long correspondence with Jinnah on the topic of Pakistan: "Although Gandhi was personally opposed to the partition of India, he proposed an agreement...which provided that the Congress and the Muslim League would cooperate to attain independence under a provisional government, after which the question of partition would be decided by a plebiscite in the districts having a Muslim majority."

These two positions on the topic of the partition of India opened Gandhi up to criticism from both Hindus and Muslims. Muhammad Ali Jinnah and contemporary Pakistanis condemned Gandhi for undermining Muslim political rights. Vinayak Damodar Savarkar and his allies condemned Gandhi, accusing him of politically appeasing Muslims while turning a blind eye to their atrocities against Hindus, and for allowing the creation of Pakistan (despite Gandhiji having publicly declared that "before partitioning India, my body will have to be cut into two pieces").

This continues to be politically contentious: some, like Pakistani-American historian Ayesha Jalal argue that Gandhi and the Congress' unwillingness to share power with the Muslim League hastened partition; others, like Hindu nationalist politician Pravin Togadia have also criticised Gandhi's leadership and actions on this topic, but indicating that excessive weakeness on his part led to the division of India.

Views on Palestine

Gandhi also expressed his dislike for partition during the late-1930s in response to the topic of the partition of Palestine to create Israel. He stated in Harijan on 26 October 1938:

> Several letters have been received by me asking me to declare my views about the Arab-Jew question in Palestine and persecution of the Jews in Germany. It is not without hesitation that I venture to offer my views on this very difficult question. My sympathies are all with the Jews. I have known them intimately in South Africa. Some of them became life-long companions. Through these friends I came to learn much of their age-long persecution. They have been the untouchables of Christianity [...] But my sympathy does not blind me to the requirements of justice. The cry for the national home for the Jews does not make much appeal to me. The sanction for it is sought in the Bible and the tenacity with which the Jews have hankered after return to Palestine. Why should they not, like other peoples of the earth, make that country their home where they are born and where they earn their livelihood? Palestine belongs to the Arabs in the same sense that England belongs to the English or France to the French. It is wrong and inhuman to impose the Jews on the Arabs. What is going on in Palestine today cannot be justified by any moral code of conduct.

Rejection of Violent Resistance

Gandhi also came under some political fire for his criticism of those who attempted to achieve independence through more violent means. His refusal to protest against the hanging of Bhagat Singh, Sukhdev, Udham Singh and Rajguru were sources of condemnation among some parties.

Of this criticism, Gandhi stated, "There was a time when people listened to me because I showed them how to give fight to the British without arms when they had no arms...but today I am told that my non-violence can be of no avail against the [Hindu–Muslim riots] and, therefore, people should arm themselves for self-defence."

He continued this argument in a number of articles reprinted in Homer Jack's "The Gandhi Reader: A Sourcebook of His Life and Writings". In the first, "Zionism and anti-Semitism," written in 1938, Gandhi commented upon the 1930s persecution of the

Jews in Germany within the context of Satyagraha. He offered non-violence as a method of combating the difficulties Jews faced in Germany, stating:

> If I were a Jew and were born in Germany and earned my livelihood there, I would claim Germany as my home even as the tallest Gentile German might, and challenge him to shoot me or cast me in the dungeon; I would refuse to be expelled or to submit to discriminating treatment. And for doing this I should not wait for the fellow Jews to join me in civil resistance, but would have confidence that in the end the rest were bound to follow my example. If one Jew or all the Jews were to accept the prescription here offered, he or they cannot be worse off than now. And suffering voluntarily undergone will bring them an inner strength and joy...the calculated violence of Hitler may even result in a general massacre of the Jews by way of his first answer to the declaration of such hostilities. But if the Jewish mind could be prepared for voluntary suffering, even the massacre I have imagined could be turned into a day of thanksgiving and joy that Jehovah had wrought deliverance of the race even at the hands of the tyrant. For to the God-fearing, death has no terror.

Gandhi was highly criticised for these statements and responded in the article "Questions on the Jews" with : "Friends have sent me two newspaper cuttings criticising my appeal to the Jews. The two critics suggest that in presenting non-violence to the Jews as a remedy against the wrong done to them, I have suggested nothing new...what I have pleaded for is renunciation of violence of the heart and consequent active exercise of the force generated by the great renunciation. He responded to the criticisms in "Reply to Jewish Friends" and "Jews and Palestine." By arguing that "What I have pleaded for is renunciation of violence of the heart and consequent active exercise of the force generated by the great renunciation."

Gandhi's statements regarding Jews facing the impending Holocaust have attracted criticism from a number of commentators. Martin Buber, himself an opponent of a Jewish state, wrote a sharply critical open letter to Gandhi on February 24, 1939. Buber asserted that the comparison between British treatment of Indian subjects and Nazi treatment of Jews was inapposite; moreover, he noted that when Indians were the victims of persecution, Gandhi had, on occasion, supported the use of force.

Gandhi commented upon the 1930s persecution of the Jews in Germany within the context of Satyagraha. In the November 1938 article on the Nazi persecution of the Jews quoted above, he offered non-violence as a solution:

> The German persecution of the Jews seems to have no parallel in history. The tyrants of old never went so mad as Hitler seems to have gone. And he is doing it with religious zeal. For he is propounding a new religion of exclusive and militant nationalism in the name of which any inhumanity becomes an act of humanity to be rewarded here and hereafter. The crime of an obviously mad but intrepid youth is being visited upon his whole race with unbelievable ferocity. If there ever could be a justifiable war in the name of and for humanity, a war against Germany, to prevent the wanton persecution of a whole race, would be completely justified. But I do not believe in any war. A discussion of the pros and cons of such a war is therefore outside my horizon or province. But if there can be no war against Germany, even for such a crime as is being committed against the Jews, surely there can be no alliance with Germany. How can there be alliance between a nation which claims to stand for justice and democracy and one which is the declared enemy of both?"

Early South African Articles

Some of Gandhi's early South African articles are controversial. As reprinted in "The Collected Works of Mahatma Gandhi", Gandhi wrote in the "Indian Opinion" in 1908 of his time in a South African prison: "Many of the native prisoners are only one degree removed from the animal and often created rows and fought among themselves." Also as reprinted in The Collected Works of Mahatma Gandhi, Gandhi gave a speech on 26 September 1896 in which he referred to the "raw kaffir, whose occupation is hunting and whose sole ambition is to collect a certain number of cattle to buy a wife with, and then pass his life in indolence and nakedness". The term Kaffir is considered a derogatory term today (it is worth noting, however, that during Gandhi's time, the term Kaffir had a different connotation than its present-day usage). Remarks such as these have led some to accuse Gandhi of racism.

Two professors of history who specialise in South Africa, Surendra Bhana and Goolam Vahed, examined this controversy in their text, The Making of a Political Reformer: Gandhi in South Africa, 1893-14. "Gandhi, Africans and Indians in Colonial Natal" on the relationship between the African and Indian communities under "White rule" and policies which enforced segregation (and, they argue, inevitable conflict between these communities). Of this relationship they state that, "the young Gandhi was influenced by segregationist notions prevalent in the 1890s."

At the same time, they state, "Gandhi's experiences in jail seemed to make him more sensitive to their plight...the later Gandhi mellowed; he seemed much less categorical in his expression of prejudice against Africans, and much more open to seeing points of common cause. His negative views in the Johannesburg jail were reserved for hardened African prisoners rather than Africans generally."

Former President of South Africa Nelson Mandela is a follower of Gandhi, despite efforts in 2003 on the part of Gandhi's critics to prevent the unveiling of a statue of Gandhi in Johannesburg. Bhana and Vahed commented on the events surrounding the unveiling in the conclusion to The Making of a Political Reformer: Gandhi in South Africa, 1893-14.

In the section "Gandhi's Legacy to South Africa," they note that "Gandhi inspired succeeding generations of South African activists seeking to end White rule. This legacy connects him to Nelson Mandela...in a sense Mandela completed what Gandhi started." They continue by referring to the controversies which arose during the unveiling of the statue of Gandhi. In response to these two perspectives of Gandhi, Bhana and Vahed argue: "Those who seek to appropriate Gandhi for political ends in post-apartheid South Africa do not help their cause much by ignoring certain facts about him; and those who simply call him a racist are equally guilty of distortion."

Anti-Statism

Gandhi was an anti-Statist in the sense that his vision of India meant India without an underlying government. His idea was that true self rule in a country means that every person rules himself and that there is no state which enforces laws upon the people. On occasions he described himself as a philosophical anarchist. A free India for him meant existence of thousands of self sufficient small communities (an idea possibly from Tolstoy) who rule themselves without hindering others. It did not mean merely transferring a British established administrative structure into Indian hands which he said was just making Hindustan into Englistan. He wanted to dissolve the Congress Party after independence and establish a system of direct democracy in India, having no faith in the British styled parliamentary system.

Swaraj

Swaraj can mean generally self-governance or "home-rule" (*swa-* "self", *raj-* "rule") but the word usually refers to Mahatma Gandhi's concept for Indian independence from foreign domination. Swaraj lays stress on governance not by a hierarchical government, but self governance through individuals and community building. The focus is on political decentralisation. Since this is against the political and social systems followed by Britain, Gandhi's concept of Swaraj laid stress on India discarding British political, economic, bureaucratic, legal, military, and educational institutions.

Key Concepts: Swaraj is a kind of Individualist Anarchism. It warrants a stateless society as according to Gandhi the overall impact of the state on the people is harmful. He called the state a "soulless machine" which, ultimately, does the greatest harm to mankind. Adopting Swaraj means implementing a system whereby state machinery is virtually nil, and the real power directly resides in the hands of people. Gandhi said, "Power resides in the people, they can use it at any time." This philosophy rests inside an individual who has to learn to be master of his own self and spreads upwards to the level of his community which must be dependent only on itself. Gandhi said, "In such a state (where swaraj is achieved) everyone is his own ruler. He rules himself in such a manner that he is never a hindrance to his neighbour"; and also "It is Swaraj when we learn to rule ourselves."

Gandhi explained his vision in 1946:

> "Independence begins at the bottom... A society must be build in which every village has to be self sustained and capable of managing its own affairs... It will be trained and prepared to perish in the attempt to defend itself against any onslaught from without... This does not exclude dependence on and willing help from neighbours or from the world. It will be a free and voluntary play of mutual forces... In this structure composed of innumerable villages, there will be ever widening, never ascending circles. Life will not be a pyramid with the apex sustained by the bottom. But it will be an oceanic circle whose centre will be the individual. Therefore, the outermost circumference will not wield power to crush the inner circle but will give strength to all within and derive its own strength from it."

Thus, basically a nation is said to have achieved its Swaraj, when its people govern themselves directly, are entirely self sufficient not only as a whole but as individuals as well, and have an innate sense of nationhood that is identified by themselves and not their government.

Gandhi was undaunted by the task of implementing such a utopian vision in India. He believed that by transforming enough individuals and communities society at large would change. He said, "It may be taunted with the retort that this is all Utopian and, therefore not worth a single thought... Let India live for the true picture, though never realisable in its completeness. We must have a proper picture of what we want before we can have something approaching it."

Efforts for Implementation

In 1917, Gandhi asked Indians nationwide to sign a petition demanding Swaraj. This petition was supported by, among others, Sardar Vallabhbhai Patel, Vinayak Damodar Savarkar, Maulana Abul Kalam Azad and Ram Manohar Lohia. Critics include Muhammad Ali Jinnah (who said that only a constitutional struggle could lead to independence) and Rabindranath Tagore.

In 1919, the Navajivan Trust, a publishing house, was founded by Gandhi to educate through publications common Indians about the principles of Swaraj, in their native tongue. The trust is still in existence today and according to its initial promises is totally self reliant having accepted absolutely no donation or grant throughout its existence.

Gandhi also decided to popularise the spinning wheel in India around the same time to make hand-spun cloth out of Khadi. This was part of an economically inclined plan to make Indians work towards self sufficiency, a key component of Swaraj. Gandhi believed that anything that would help India get out of its grinding poverty would in the end help in attaining Swaraj. This movement called The Khadi Movement later gained fame by the term Swadeshi. The spinning wheel or the Charkha became a symbol of the Indian freedom struggle, and was incorporated into many flags.

At the Indian National Congress annual session in September 1920, delegates supported Swaraj, and in the same year they agreed with Khilafat leaders to work and fight together for both causes. This can be regarded as the official launching of the Swaraj Movement by the Congress. However, over the years, political ideas gained momentum in the Congress and in 1927, Jawaharlal Nehru introduced a resolution demanding "complete national independence" called Purna Swaraj which was a more politically inclined goal. The Payyannur Conference in May 1928 passed a resolution requesting the Indian National Congress to adopt "Complete Independence" instead of Swaraj as its goal. Another political group the Swaraj Party which also was against the British merged with the Congress soon after.

After Gandhi: It is generally believed that Gandhi's model of Swaraj has not been followed by the Indian government. He had wanted a system of a classless, stateless direct democracy. For achieving this he wanted to disband the Congress Party after independence. He said, "Its task is done. The next task is to move into villages and revitalise life there to build a new socio-economic structure from the bottom upwards." However, none of these objectives were achieved when India became independent. India, although a federation, got a strong central government. Representative democracy, rather than direct democracy was adopted. The Congress Party was not disbanded. Rather it went on to become one of the frontrunners in running the government of India.

'Sarvodaya'

Gandhiji formed an Ashram near Ahmedabad. It was called 'Satyagraha Ashram'. The way of life that he practised there was known as 'Sarvodaya' — the well being of all. It was the way of life that he practiced in South Africa. In South Africa, he had started two institutions — the Phoenix Settlement and the Tolstoy Farm. The aim of these Ashrams was plain living and high thinking. He believed that by such a way of life the well being of all men could be secured. 'A tooth for a tooth and an eye for an eye' was not true religion, that is, revenge was not religion. His desire was that the individual should lead a truthful, religious and loving life. Man should strive to establish truth, piety and love in human society. It was Gandhiji's belief that the power of goodness that comes from such a life could transform the worst power on earth.

8

Greatest Leader of His Times

In early twentieth century, the people of India were carrying on a struggle for freedom from the British rule. The Indian National Congress was striving for it. In 1919, British soldiers had acted in a brutal manner against an innocent and unarmed assembly of people, who had gathered for a meeting at Jalianwala Bagh in Punjab. There were walls around with only a small passage to go out of the Bagh. The soldiers fired on the assembly, and killed and wounded many people mercilessly.

Lokamanya Tilak, the great Indian national leader, passed away at that time. The nation was looking for an able leader. The Mahatma, the hero of the Satyagraha struggle in South Africa, had attracted the attention of many Indians. Thus, leadership courted him naturally. There was great charm in his words. His conduct was flaw- less and crystal clear. He filled the nation with a new spirit. Under his leadership the weakest man, woman and child, as well as innocent ryots, were ready for a non-violent fight. They were ready to sacrifice their all. Self-sacrifice and service became the religion of the nation.

The Indian National Congress carried on five major struggles for freedom, during three decades, under the leadership of Gandhiji. In 1920-22, it was called 'The Non-cooperation Movement'. Government schools and colleges, courts and

Legislatures were all boycotted. Gandhiji himself was arrested, and was sentenced to six years imprisonment. His trial in the court at that time drew the attention of the entire civilized world.

In 1922, there was Hindu-Muslim disturbances in Bombay. Many were injured and killed on account of religiousmadness. Gandhiji was shocked to the core, He called his son Devadas and advised him: "Go and tell Hindus and Muslims, wherever they may be fighting, that this hatred is bad. It does not matter even if they kill you. I would be happy to sacrifice my son for the cause of Hindu-Muslim amity."

The Salt Satyagraha of 1930-31 became world-famous. It was known as the 'Dandi March'. Manufacturing salt from sea water was the monopoly of the Government. By breaking the Salt Law Gandhiji desired to show that the Indians were a free nation. On March 12, he went on foot with seventy-nine trusted disciples, from his Ashram at Sabarmati to Dandi, a sea-side place 241 miles away. Staff in hand he walked about 10 to 15 miles each day. The determination of the 62-year-old 'young man' was wonderful. He was like one in quest of Truth. His action shook the foundations of the British Empire. The courage and the spirit of self-sacrifice with which he filled the hearts of millions of Indians were amazing. There was Civil Disobedience or non-violent breaking of the law throughout the country. Cities, towns and villages were all scenes of Satyagraha. Heroism was the order of the day. The British Government put Gandhiji in prison again.

In 1932, when Gandhi was behind the bars, an extraordinary event took place. In the name of political reforms, the British Government planned to cut away millions of Indians called 'untouchables' from the Hindu Society. Their principle was to 'Divide and Rule'. In 1924, Gandhiji had fasted for 21 days to bring about Hindu- Muslim unity. He had been saying that un touchability was a shame to Hindu Society. Hinduism should be purged of that guilt. When he saw what the Government was doing, he became unhappy, and decided to fast unto death. There was great commotion in the entire country. The Government realised its folly and gave up the plan. There was an awakening among the people. Government temples, wells and public places were declared open to the untouchables. Gandhiji called the untouchables — 'Harijans' (men dear to God). He started three periodicals 'Harijan Sevak', 'Harijan-Bandhu' and 'Harijan' — all devoted to the service of the Harijans. He took a vow not to re-enter his Ashrarn at Sabarmati until untouchability became a thing of the past in India. He settled down at Sevagram, (near Wardha) a new Ashram, which he started there.

In 1941, the Satyagraha struggle took a different shape. It was called the 'Symbolic Satyagraha', and was different from the previous mass Satyagrahas. Only the individuals, whom Gandhiji selected or permitted, had to offer Satyagraha. This change was made because Gandhiji, the Truth-seeker, knew that the past mass Satyagrahas had not been entirely free from violence. Thus, he conducted this experiment to make Satyagraha free and from violence as far as humanly possible.

In 1942, there came the final struggle for freedom. The call was 'Britishers, Quit India'. For this struggle, Gandhiji gave the inspiring message, 'Do or Die'. Gandhiji expected that the struggle would be purely non-violent. It did not happen that way. Out there was great national upsurge for freedom. Thousands were put into prison. They faced the lath and the bullet, and gave up their lives. A whole nation rose up against an alien empire. It took all the suffering on itself cheerfully, without a word of demur or hatred or ill will. The way India got her freedom is unique in the history of the world. And all the glory of this unique struggle goes to the great leader Gandhiji.

Ordeal by Fire

On August 15, 1947, India became a free country. But it was divided into two independent States — India that is Bharat and Pakistan. Gandhiji was totally opposed to this division of the country. Though the country was divided, the Hindu-Muslim riots did not cease. They increased. Lakhs of people were rendered homeless. Many lost their near and dear ones, and became orphans, In Noakhali and Thippera of East Bengal, the killings of Hindus and the shameful acts committed on women were a blot on humanity. It looked as if man had become a demon. For half a century Gandhi had tried to put into action the principles of love and non-violence in his personal life and in public life; now it seemed to him that those principles had totally failed. Naked violence ruled every where. In that fearful situation, Gandhiji tried to test his great principles. He decided to go to those areas, as a messenger of peace. Political madness and religious unreason had reached the height of cruelty. He decided to bring about peace between the Hindus and the Muslims. Though he was seventy-seven years old, he walked from village to village. He brought hope and courage to the suffering, unhappy people. He addressed prayer meetings. He advised both the Hindus and the Muslims. It was a noble mission of compassion. It shines as a noble proof of the heights of divinity to which frail man can soar.

Peace returned to the unfortunate area. The people of both the communities had realised the shame of their senseless acts. Gandhiji returned to Delhi. He was staying at the Birla House.

It was Friday, January 30. 1948. Gandhiji used to hold prayer meetings every evening at 5:30. Prayer was his sole strength. That evening too he was on his way to the prayer meeting A man called Nathuram Vinayak Godse had come to think that Gandhiji was partial to the Muslims and that he would be saving Hinduism by killing him. As Gandhiji was walking to the prayer meeting Godse bowed to him in respect, and then fired three bullets at point blank range.

Gandhiji, the embodiment of the eternal message of the Gita, was no more.

The tragedy sent tremors the world over. A great and noble spirit that showed the path of piety to man, disappear from the world- stage; all who had a heart to feel shed tears of sorrow.

Gandhiji's Heritage

The Swaraj or Freedom that Gandhiji dreamed was not merely of a political character. It was to be a means to create a new man, who would strive to create a new society, a new civilization and a new culture. He called the new social order 'Ramraj' — 'the Kingdom of God on Earth'. Love would be the sole law there. All would be dutiful. There would be no distinction of caste, religion and community. No one would be treated as untouchables. All would be equal in the eyes of religion, All would live by the sweat of their brow. The intellectual worker and the manual worker would be equals; neither could claim superiority. There would be no intoxicating drinks. Women would be honoured. Every one would be ready to give up his life for the good of his country. Gandhiji called such a state of society 'Sarvodaya (The Prosperity of All).

To realise Sarvodaya, man has to live with fellow men, with other living beings and nature in understanding and harmony.

Service to the lowly and the lost in society was Gandhiji's first step towards Sarvodaya.

Gandhiji taught that knowledge and wealth devoid of religion and morals led to the fall of men. He died as a martyr in the cause of true religion.

A leader's responsibilities are high. He has to examine himself severely time and again, to convince himself that he is fit to lead others. He has to bear all the moral responsibility for all that his followers do. If he feels unable to do so, he has to retire from the field of action. Through self- criticism and self-confidence, he has to work to lead this imperfect world in the way of perfection. This is the deathless message that Gandhiji has left us.

Single-minded devotion to the God of Truth and prayer are lights that Gandhiji has bequeathed to us. He could not remain without prayer even for a single day. 'Silent prayer is my greatest strength' — he used to say.

> 'Raghupathi Raghava Rajaram, Pathitha Pavana Seetharam.'

Whenever we hear this prayer Gandhiji's memory becomes alive. His soul will be present there unseen, and blesses all. It is the task of religion to purify the fallen; it is the power of goodness in man. What does it matter what name we give it? Let us all is blessed with goodness. This is the perennial message that Gandhiji has left to mankind.

As a boy Gandhiji was afraid of ghosts and devils. A good nurse, Rambha by name, taught him to repeat the name of Shri Rama to get over this fear. It brought him hope and courage. He chanted it day in and day out. It is significant that, when the assassin shot at him and his body slumped to find eternal rest in the lap of Mother Earth, the last words he uttered were 'Rama', 'Rama'.

Mahatma Gandhiji, called 'Bapu' by his loving countrymen, will ever be remembered as a saint and a great leader of men.

Gandhism

Gandhism (or Gandhianism) is a collection of inspirations, principles, beliefs and philosophy of Mohandas Karamchand Gandhi (known as Mahatma Gandhi), who was a major political and spiritual leader of the country and the Indian Independence Movement.

It is a body of ideas and principles that describes the inspiration, vision and the life work of Gandhi. The term also encompasses what Gandhi's ideas, words and actions mean to people around the world, and how they used them for guidance in building their own future. Gandhism also permeates into the realm of the individual human being, non-political and non-social. A Gandhian can mean either an individual who follows, or a specific philosophy which is attributed to, Gandhism.

Satyagraha

Satya is the Sanskrit word for "truth," and aagraha (from the Sanskrit root aagrah cognate with English word "grab") can be rendered as "effort/endeavour/insist." The term was popularised during the Indian Independence Movement, and is used in many Indian languages including Hindi.

Gandhi stated that "I have nothing new to teach the world. Truth and non-violence are as old as the hills."

The pivotal and defining element of Gandhism is satya, a Sanskrit word usually translated into English as truth, whose literal meaning is 'what actually is' (deriving from the root verb as meaning 'to be'). Truth must pervade all considerations of politics, ego, society and convention. Gandhi did not consider himself to be a pacifist, socialist or on any definable spectrum of politics. He professed to adhere to the pure, existing facts of life to make his decisions.

Gandhi's commitments to non-violence, human freedom, equality and justice arose from his personal examination.

Truth is interpreted subjectively. Gandhism does not demand that its adherents agree to Gandhi's own principles to the letter, but in spirit. If one honestly believes that violence is sometimes necessary, it is truthful to believe in it. When Gandhi returned to India in the middle of World War I, he said he would have supported the British in the war. It would have been wrong, according to Gandhi, to demand equal rights for Indians in the Empire, and not contribute to its defence. On the other hand, by the time of the advance of the Japanese in World War II, Gandhi had given up notions of fighting alongside the British and argued for non-violence instead.

Gandhi developed his vision, thought and way of life by his constant "experimenting with truth" — a phrase that formed the subtitle to his autobiography. He was prepared to learn through trial and error, often admitting to mistakes and changing his behaviour accordingly. This was particularly notable when Gandhi stopped all nationwide civil resistance in 1922 after the Chauri Chaura incident. He would forsake political independence for truth — believing that Indians should not become murderers and commit the very evils they were accusing the British of perpetrating in India.

Gandhism is more about the spirit of Gandhi's journey to discover the truth, than what he finally considered to be the truth. It is the foundation of Gandhi's teachings, and the spirit of his whole life to examine and understand for oneself, and not take anybody or any ideology for granted.

Gandhi said: "The Truth is far more powerful than any weapon of mass destruction."

Gandhi's philosophy encompassed ontology and its association with truth. For Gandhi, "to be" did not mean to exist within the realm of time, as it has in the past with the Greek philosophers. But rather, "to exist" meant to exist within the realm of truth, or to use the term Gandhi did, satya. Gandhi summarised his beliefs first when he said "God is Truth", which his experimenting later prompted him to change to "Truth is God". The first statement seemed insufficient to Gandhi, as the mistake could be made that Gandhi was using truth as a description of God, as opposed to God as an aspect of satya. Satya (truth) in Gandhi's philosophy is God. It shares all the characteristics of the Hindu concept of God, or Brahman, and is believed by Gandhians to live within each person as their conscience while at the same time guiding the universe.

Birla House

Birla House or Birla Bhavan, in New Delhi, is the location where Mahatma Gandhi spent the last 144 days of his life and was assassinated on January 30, 1948. It was originally the house of the Indian business tycoons, the Birlas.

It was acquired by the Government of India in 1971 and opened for the public on August 15, 1973, renamed the Gandhi Smriti (or Gandhi Remembrance). The museum in the building houses a number of articles associated with Gandhi's life and death. Visitors can tour the building and grounds, viewing the preserved room where Gandhi lived and the place on the grounds where he was shot while holding his nightly public walk.

The Martyr's Column now marks the place where Gandhi, the "Father of the Nation" was assassinated.

The Gandhi Smriti or Birla House is located at 5 Tees January Marg, a couple of kilometres from the Connaught Place, one of the CBDs of New Delhi. Nathuram Godse killed Gandhi.

Gandhian Economics

Gandhian economics is a school of economic thought based on the socio-economic principles expounded by Indian leader Mohandas Gandhi. It is largely characterised by its affinity to the principles and objectives of socialism, but with a rejection of class war and promotion of socio-economic harmony. Gandhi's economic ideas also aim to promote spiritual development and harmony with a rejection of materialism. The term "Gandhian economics" was coined by J. C. Kumarappa, a close supporter of Gandhi.

Gandhi's Economic Ideas: Gandhi's thinking on socio-economics issues was greatly influenced by the American writer Henry David Thoreau. Throughout his life, Gandhi sought to develop ways to fight India's extreme poverty, backwardness and socio-economic challenges as a part of his wider involvement in the Indian Independence Movement. Gandhi's championing of Swadeshi and non-cooperation were centred on the principles of economic self-sufficiency. Gandhi sought to target European-made clothing and other products as not only a symbol of British colonialism but also the source of mass unemployment and poverty, as European industrial goods had left many millions of India's workers, craftsmen and women without a means of living. By championing homespun khadi clothing and Indian-made goods, Gandhi sought to incorporate peaceful civil resistance as a means of promoting national self-sufficiency. Gandhi led farmers of Champaran and Kheda in a satyagraha (civil disobedience and tax resistance) against the mill owners and landlords supported by the British government in an effort to end oppressive taxation and other policies that forced the farmers and workers and defend their economic rights. A major part of this rebellion was a commitment from the farmers to end caste discrimination and oppressive social practices against women while launching a cooperative effort to promote education, health care and self-sufficiency by producing their own clothes and food.

Gandhi and his followers also founded numerous ashrams in India (Gandhi had pioneered the ashram settlement in South Africa). The concept of an ashram has been compared with the commune, where its inhabitants would seek to produce their own food, clothing and means of living, while promoting a lifestyle of self-sufficiency, personal and spiritual development and working for wider social development. The ashrams included small farms and houses constructed by the inhabitants themselves. All inhabitants were expected to help in any task necessary, promoting the values of equality. Gandhi also espoused the notion of "trusteeship," which centred on denying material pursuits and coveting of wealth, with practitioners acting as "trustees" of other individuals and the community in their management of economic resources and property. Contrary to many Indian socialists and communists, Gandhi was averse to all notions of class warfare and concepts of class-based revolution, which he saw as causes of social violence and disharmony. Gandhi's concept of egalitarianism was centred on the preservation of human dignity rather than material development. Some of Gandhi's closest supporters and admirers included industrialists such as Ghanshyamdas Birla, Ambalal Sarabhai, Jamnalal Bajaj and J. R. D. Tata, who adopted several of Gandhi's progressive ideas in managing labour relations while also personally participating in Gandhi's ashrams and socio-political work.

Implementation in India: During India's freedom struggle as well as after India's independence in 1947, Gandhi's advocacy of homespun khadi clothing, the khadi attire (which included the Gandhi cap) developed into popular symbols of nationalism and patriotism. India's first Prime Minister, Jawaharlal Nehru was a socialist as well as a close supporter of Gandhi. While Nehru was influenced by Gandhi's aversion to the brand of socialism practised in the Soviet Union, he was also an exponent of industralisation and critical of Gandhi's focus on rural economics.

Gandhian activists such as Vinoba Bhave and Jayaprakash Narayan were involved in the Sarvodaya Movement, which sought to promote self-sufficiency amidst India's rural population by encouraging land redistribution, socio-economic reforms and promoting cottage industries. The movement sought to combat the problems of class conflict, unemployment and poverty while attempting to preserve the lifestyle and values of rural Indians, which were eroding with industrialisation and modernisation. Sarvodaya also included Bhoodan, or the gifting of land and agricultural resources by the landlords (called *zamindars*) to their tenant farmers in a bid to end the medieval system of zamindari. Bhave and others promoted Bhoodan as a just and peaceful method of land redistribution in order to create economic equality, land ownership and opportunity without creating class-based conflicts. Bhoodan and Sarvodaya enjoyed notable successes in many parts of India, including Maharashtra, Gujarat, Karnataka and Uttar Pradesh. Bhave would become a major exponent of discipline and productivity amongst India's farmers, labourers and working classes, which was a major reason for his support of the controversial Indian Emergency (1975-77). Jayaprakash Narayan also sought to use Gandhian methods to combat organised crime, alcoholism and other social problems.

Modern Interpretations: Gandhi's ideas have inspired socio-economic policies in post-colonial Africa and Asia, but have also been criticised as impractical and idealistic, especially on the macroeconomic scale. The main attempts at implementation have centred on microeconomic initiatives. The proximity of Gandhian economic thought to socialism has also evoked criticism from the advocates of free-market economics. To many, Gandhian economics represent an alternative to mainstream economic ideologies as a way to promote economic productivity without an emphasis on material pursuits or compromising human development. Gandhi's emphasis on peace, "trusteeship" and cooperation has been touted as an alternative to competition as well as conflict between different economic and income classes in societies. Gandhian focus on human development is also seen as an effective emphasis on the eradication of poverty, social conflict and backwardness in developing nations. Gandhian socio-economic ideas have gained the interest and attention of an increasing number of people across the world.

Khadi: Gandhi also adopted the clothing style of most Indians in the early-20th century. His adoption of khadi, or homespun cloth, was intended to help eradicate the evils of poverty, social and economic discrimination. It was also aimed as a challenge to the contrast that he saw between most Indians, who were poor and traditional, and the richer classes of educated, liberal-minded Indians who had adopted Western mannerisms, clothing and practices.

The clothing policy was designed to protest against the violence of British economic policies in India. Millions of poor Indian workers had been left unemployed and entrenched in poverty, owing to the industrialisation of cotton processing in Britain. Gandhi promoted khadi as a direct boycott of the Lancashire cotton industry, linking British imperialism to Indian poverty. He focused on persuading all members of the Indian National Congress to spend some time each day hand-spinning on the charkha (spinning wheel). In addition to its point as an economic campaign, the drive for hand-spinning was an attempt to connect the privileged Indian Brahmins and lawyers of Congress to connect with the mass of Indian peasantry.

Many prominent figures of the Indian Independence Movement, including Motilal Nehru, were persuaded by Gandhi to renounce their smart London-made clothes in favour of khadi.

Weapon of Fasting

To Gandhi, fasting was an important method of exerting mental control over base desires. In his autobiography, Gandhi analyses the need to fast to eradicate his desire for delicious, spicy food. He believed that abstention would diminish his sensual faculties, bringing the body increasingly under the mind's absolute control. Gandhi was opposed to the partaking of meat, alcohol, stimulants, salt and most spices, and also eliminated different types of cooking from the food he ate.

Fasting would also put the body through unusual hardship, which Gandhi believed would cleanse the spirit by stimulating the courage to withstand all impulses and pain. Gandhi undertook a "Fast Unto Death" on three notable occasions:

- When he wanted to stop all revolutionary activities after the Chauri Chaura incident of 1922;
- When he feared that the 1934 communal award giving separate electorates to Untouchable Hindus would politically divide the Hindu people;
- And in 1947, when he wanted to stop the bloodshed between Hindus and Muslims in Bengal and Delhi.

In all three cases, Gandhi was able to abandon his fast before death. There was some controversy over the 1934 fast, which brought him into conflict with the Untouchable leader B. R. Ambedkar. In the end, Gandhi and Ambedkar both made some concessions to negotiate the Poona Pact, which abandoned the call for separate electorates in turn for voluntary representation and a commitment to abolish untouchability.

Gandhi also used the fasts as a penance, blaming himself for inciting Chauri Chaura and the divisive communal politics of both 1934 and 1947, especially the Partition of India. Gandhi sought to purify his soul and expiate his sins, in what he saw as his role in allowing terrible tragedies to happen. It took a heavy toll on his physical health and often brought him close to death.

Religious Philosophy

Hindu Universalism denotes the ideology that all religions are true and therefore worthy of toleration and respect. It was articulated by Gandhi:

> "After long study and experience, I have come to the conclusion that all religions are true; all religions have some error in them; all religions are almost as dear to me as my own Hinduism, in as much as all human beings should be as dear to one as one's own close relatives. My own veneration for other faiths is the same as that for my own faith; therefore no thought of conversion is possible." (M. K. Gandhi, All Men

> Are Brothers: Life and Thoughts of Mahatma Gandhi, as told in his own words, Paris, UNESCO 1958, p 60).

Gandhi believed that at the core of every religion was truth (satya), non-violence (ahimsa) and the Golden Rule. He was deeply influenced by the Christian teaching of "turning the other cheek", once stating that if Christianity practised the Sermon on the Mount, he would indeed be a Christian. Gandhi felt that one should be aware of worshipping the symbols and idols of the religion and not its teachings, such as worshipping the crucifix whilst ignoring its significance as a symbol for self-sacrifice.

Although Gandhi was raised as a Hindu he was critical of most religions, including Hinduism. He wrote in his autobiography:

> "Thus, if I could not accept Christianity either as a perfect, or the greatest religion, neither was I then convinced of Hinduism being such. Hindu defects were pressingly visible to me. If untouchability could be a part of Hinduism, it could but be a rotten part or an excrescence. I could not understand the *raison d'etre* of a multitude of sects and castes. What was the meaning of saying that the Vedas were the inspired Word of God? If they were inspired, why not also the Bible and the Koran? As Christian friends were endeavouring to convert me, so were Muslim friends. Abdullah Sheth had kept on inducing me to study Islam, and of course he had always something to say regarding its beauty".

He then went on to say:

> "As soon as we lose the moral basis, we cease to be religious. There is no such thing as religion over-riding morality. Man, for instance, cannot be untruthful, cruel or incontinent and claim to have God on his side".

Gandhi was critical of the hypocrisy in organised religion, rather than the principles on which they were based. He also said the following about Hinduism:

> "Hinduism as I know it entirely satisfies my soul, fills my whole being... When doubts haunt me, when

> disappointments stare me in the face, and when I see not one ray of light on the horizon, I turn to the Bhagavad Gita, and find a verse to comfort me; and I immediately begin to smile in the midst of overwhelming sorrow. My life has been full of tragedies and if they have not left any visible and indelible effect on me, I owe it to the teachings of the Bhagavad Gita".

The concept of Islamic *jihad* can also be taken to mean a non-violent struggle or satyagraha, in the way Gandhi practiced it. On Islam he said:

> "The sayings of Muhammad are a treasure of wisdom, not only for Muslims but for all of mankind".

Later in his life when he was asked whether he was a Hindu, he replied:

> "Yes I am. I am also a Christian, a Muslim, a Buddhist and a Jew".

Gandhi's religious views are reflected in the hymns his group often sang:

- Vaishnav jan to Call them Vishnava, those who understand the sufferings of others...
- Raghupati Raghava Raja Ram Call him Rama or God or Allah...

Nehru's India

Gandhi was assassinated in 1948, but his teachings and philosophy would play a major role in India's economic and social development and foreign relations for decades to come.

Sarvodaya is a term meaning 'universal uplift' or 'progress of all'. It was coined by the Gandhian leader Vinoba Bhave to refer to the struggle of post-independence Gandhians to ensure that self-determination and equality reached the masses and the downtrodden. Sarvodaya workers associated with Vinoba, including Jaya Prakash Narayan and Dada Dharmadhikari, undertook various projects aimed at encouraging popular self-organisation during the 1950s and 1960s. Many groups descended from these networks continue to function locally in India today.

While the problem of the desperate poverty of tens of millions of landless farmers across the country had to be addressed, Gandhi did not believe that class warfare was inevitable, as Lenin, Mao Zedong and Stalin did. Bhave and other Gandhi disciples organised the Bhoodan campaign encouraging landlords across the country to award land to their farmers. They were encouraged to acknowledge the desperate poverty and mistreatment of these farmers, to accept them as fellow Indians and their brethren. This peaceful land distribution programme was frowned upon by supporters of free-market economics, the Communists and socialists alike, but did enjoy notable successes.

The Prime Minister of India, Jawaharlal Nehru, was often considered Gandhi's successor, although he was not religious and often disagreed with Gandhi. He was, however, deeply influenced by Gandhi personally as well as politically, and used his premiership to pursue ideological policies based on Gandhi's principles.

Nehru's foreign policy was staunch anti-colonialism and neutrality in the Cold War. Nehru backed the Independence Movement in Tanzania and other African nations, as well as the American Civil Rights Movement led by Martin Luther King Jr. and the anti-apartheid struggle of Nelson Mandela and the African National Congress in South Africa. Nehru refused to align with either the United States or the Soviet Union, and helped found the Non-aligned Movement.

Nehru also pushed through major legislation that granted legal rights and freedoms to Indian women, and outlawed untouchability and many different kinds of social discrimination, in the face of strong opposition from orthodox Hindus.

Not all of Nehru's policies were Gandhian. Nehru refused to condemn the USSR's 1956-57 invasion of Hungary to put down an anti-communist, popular revolt. Some of his economic policies were criticised for removing the right of property and freedoms from the landowing peasants of Gujarat for whom Gandhi had fought for in the early-1920s. Nehru's socialism sometimes conflicted with Gandhism.

Nehru's biggest failure is often considered to be the 1962 Sino-Indian War, though his policy is said to have been inspired by Gandhian pacifism. In this instance, it led to the defeat of the Indian Army against a surprise Chinese invasion. Nehru had neglected the defence budget and disallowed the Army to prepare, which caught the soldiers in India's north eastern frontier off-guard with lack of supplies and reinforcements.

Freedom: Gandhi's deep commitment and disciplined belief in non-violent civil disobedience as a way to oppose tyranny, oppression and injustice has inspired many subsequent political figures, including Martin Luther King Jr. of the United States, Julius Nyerere of Tanzania, Nelson Mandela and Steve Biko of South Africa, Lech Wa³êsa of Poland and Aung San Suu Kyi of Myanmar.

Gandhi's early life work in South Africa between the years 1910 and 1915, for the rights of Indian residents oppressed by the racist, white minority South African regime inspired the later work of the African National Congress. From the 1950s, the ANC organised non-violent civil disobedience akin to the campaign advanced by the Indian National Congress under the inspiration of Gandhi between the 1920s and 1940s. ANC activists braved the sticks and bullets of the police, water-hoses, tear gas and dogs to protest against tyranny, racism and oppression in South Africa. Many, especially Mandela, languished for decades in jail, while the world outside was divided in its effort to remove apartheid. Steve Biko, perhaps the most vocal adherent to non-violent civil resistance, was allegedly murdered in 1977 by agents of the regime.

When the first universal, free elections were held in South Africa in 1994, the ANC was elected and Mandela became President. Mandela made a special visit to India and publicly honoured Gandhi as the man who inspired the freedom struggle of black South Africans. Statues of Gandhi have been erected in Natal, Pretoria and Johannesburg.

Martin Luther King Jr., a young Christian minister and leader of the American Civil Rights Movement seeking the liberation of African Americans from racial segregation in the American South, and also from economic and social injustice and political disenfranchisement, travelled to India in 1962 to meet Jawaharlal Nehru. The two discussed Gandhi's teachings, and the methodology of organising peaceful resistance. The graphic imagery of black protestors being hounded by police, beaten and brutalised, evoked admiration for King and the protestors across America and the world, and precipitated the 1964 Civil Rights Act.

The non-violent Solidarity Movement of Lech Walesa of Poland overthrew a Soviet-backed communist government after two decades of peaceful resistance and strikes in 1989, beginning the downfall of the Soviet Communist empire.

Myanmar's Aung San Suu Kyi remains under house arrest, and her National League for Democracy suppressed in their non-violent quest for democracy and freedom in military-controlled Myanmar. This struggle was inaugurated when the military dismissed the results of the 1991 democratic elections and imposed military rule.

"Without Truth, nothing": Mohandas Gandhi's early life was a series of personal struggles to decipher the truth about life's important issues and discover the true way of living. He admitted in his autobiography to beating his young wife, and indulging in carnal pleasures out of lust, jealousy and possessiveness, not genuine love. He had eaten meat, smoked a cigarette, and almost visited a prostitute. It was only after much personal turmoil and repeated failures that Gandhi developed his philosophy.

Gandhi disliked having a cult following, and was averse to being addressed to as Mahatma, claiming that he was not a perfect human being.

In 1942, while he had already condemned Adolf Hitler, Benito Mussolini and the Japanese militarists, Gandhi took on an offensive in civil resistance, called the Quit India Movement, which was even more dangerous and definitive owing to its direct call for Indian independence. Gandhi did not see the British as defenders of freedom giving their continuance of imperialist domination in India. He did not feel a need to take sides with world powers.

Gandhism is brutal adherence to truth. If it means condemning the practice of untouchability in Hindu society, it means condemning the victimisation of Muslim women and coerced conversions to Islam and Christianity in the same breath. Gandhism has no respect for power. No institution or individual is infallible, save God.

Gandhi believed that all humans are susceptible to sinful actions and behaviour, and the worst of dictators were essentially the same despite the difference in their lives, beliefs and actions. Despite this, he held firmly that humans had no right to punish each other. He believed punishment to be the responsibility of God.

Gandhians Today: Despite Gandhi's adherence to Hindu cultural and religious values, Gandhism is broad over everything save the truth, which is definite and inviolable. There have been Muslim Gandhians, such as Khan Abdul Ghaffar Khan, known as the "Frontier Gandhi"; Christian Gandhians, such as Horace Alexander; Jewish Gandhians, such as Herman Kallenbach; and atheist Gandhians, such as Jawaharlal Nehru.

To become a Gandhian, one must set upon the same personal journey to seek truth and build one's life around it. It is not necessary to arrive at the same conclusions as Gandhi. But undergoing personal challenges, travails and the testing of one's spirit, resolve and fundamental values is a definitive element.

9

Mahatma Gandhi's Speeches

Speech at the Johannesburg Banquet

[A Banquet was given at Johannesburg to Mr. and Mrs. Gandhi on the eve of their departure for India, by a large number of Europeans and Indians]

Mr. Gandhi said that they or circumstances had placed him that evening in a most embarrassing position. Hitherto those who had known him in Johannesburg had known him in the capacity of one of many hosts at a gathering of that kind, but that evening they had placed him in the unfortunate position of being a guest, and he did not know how he would be able to discharge that duty. For the other he thought long experience had fitted him, if he might say so with due humility, most admirably; but the present position was entirely new to him and Mrs. Gandhi, and he was exceedingly diffident as to how he was going to discharge the new duty that had been imposed upon him. So much had been said about Mrs. Gandhi and himself, their so-called devotion, their so-called self-sacrifice, and many other things. There was one injunction of his religion, and he thought it was true of all religions, and that was that when one's praises were sung one should fly from those praises, and, if one could not do that, one should stop one's ears, and if one could not do either of these things one should dedicate, everything that was said in connection with one to the Almighty, the Divine Essence, which pervaded everyone and everything in the Universe, and he hoped that Mrs. Gandhi and he would have the strength to dedicate all that had been said that evening to that Divine Essence.

Of all the precious gifts that had been given to them those four boys were the most precious, and probably Mr. Chamney could tell them something, of the law of adoption in India and what Mr. and Mrs. Naidoo, both of them old gaolbirds, had done. They had gone through the ceremony of adoption, and they had surrendered their right to their four children and given them (Mr. and Mrs. Gandhi) the charge. He did not know that they were worthy to take charge of those children. He could only assure them that they would try to do their best. The four boys had been his pupils when he had been conducting a school for Passive Resisters at Tolstoy Farm and Jater on at Phoenix. Then when Mrs. Naidoo had sought imprisonment, the boys had been taken over to Johannesburg, and he thought that he had lost those four pearls, but the pearls had returned to him. He only hoped that Mrs. Gandhi and he would be able to take charge of the precious gift.

Johannesburg was not a new place to him. He saw many friendly faces there, many who had worked with him in many struggles in Johannesburg. He had gone through much in life. A great deal of depression and sorrow had been his lot, but he had also learnt during all those years to love Johannesburg even though it was a Mining Camp. It was in Johannesburg that he had found his most precious friends. It was in Johannesburg that the foundation for the great struggle of Passive Resistance was laid in the September of 1906. It was in Johannesburg that he had found a friend, a guide, and a biographer in the late Mr. Doke. It was in Johannesburg that he had found in Mrs. Doke a loving sister, who had nursed him back to life, when he had been assaulted by a countryman who had misunderstood his mission and who misunderstood what he had done. It was in Johannesburg that he had found a Kallenbach, a Polak, a Miss Schlesin, and many another who had always helped him, and always cheered him and his countrymen. Johannesburg, therefore had the holiest associations of all the holy associations that Mrs. Gandhi and he would carry back to India, and, as he had already said on many another platform, South Africa, next to India, would be the holiest land to him and to Mrs. Gandhi and to his children, for, in spite of all the bitternesses, it had given them those life-long companions. It was in Johannesburg again that the European Committee had been formed, when Indians were going through the darkest stage m their history, presided over then, as it still was, by Mr. Hosken. It was last, but not least, Johannesburg that had given Valiamma, that young girl, whose picture rose before him even as he spoke, who had died in the cause of truth. Simple-minded in faith — she had not the knowledge that he had, she did not know what Passive Resistance was, she did not know what it was the community would gain but she was simply taken up with unbounded enthusiasm for her people — went to gaol, came out of it a wreck, and within a few days died. It was Johannesburg again that produced a Nagappan and Narayanswamy, two lovely youths hardly out of their teens, who also died. But both Mrs. Gandhi and he stood living before them. He and Mrs. Gandhi had worked in the lime light; those others had worked behind the scenes, not knowing where they were going, except this, that what they were doing was right and proper, and, if any praise was due anywhere at all, it was due to those three who died. They had the name of Harbatsingh given to them. He (the speaker) had the privilege of serving imprisonment with him. Harbatsingh was 75 years old. He was an ex-indentured Indian, and when he (the speaker) asked him why he had come there, that he had gone there to seek his grave the brave man replied, "What does it matter ? I know what you are fighting for. You have not to pay the £3 tax, but my fellow ex-indentured Indians have to pay that tax, and what more glorious death could I meet ?" He had met that death in the gaol at Durban.

No wonder if Passive Resistance had fired and quickened, the conscience of South Africa ! And therefore, whenever he had spoken, he had said that, if the Indian community had gained anything through this settlement it was certainly due to Passive Resistance; but it was certainly not due to Passive Resistance alone. He thought that the cablegram that had been read that evening showed that they had to thank that noble Viceroy, Lord Hardinge, for his great effort. He thought, too, that they had to thank the Imperial Government, who, during the past few years, in season and out of season, had been sending despatches after despatches to General Botha, and asking him to consider their standpoint — the Imperial standpoint. They had to thank also the Union Government for the spirit of justice they had adopted that time. They had, too, to thank the noble members of both Houses of the Legislature who had made those historic speeches and brought about the settlement; and, lastly, they had to thank the Opposition also for their cooperation with the Government in bringing about the passage of the Bill, in spite of the jarring note produced by the Natal Members. When one considered all those things, the service that he and Mrs. Gandhi might have rendered could be only very little. They were but two out of many instruments that had gone to make this settlement. And what was that settlement?

In his humble opinion, the value of the settlement, if they were to examine it, would consist not in the intrinsic things they had received, but in the sufferings and the sorrows long drawn out that were necessary in order to achieve those things. If an outsider were to come there and find that there was a banquet given to two humble individuals for the humble part they played in a settlement which freed indentured Indians from a tax which they should never have been called upon to pay, and if he were told also that some redress were given in connection with their marriages, and that their wives who were lawfully married to them according to their own religions had not hitherto been recognised as their wives, but by this settlement those wives were recognised as valid wives according to the law of South Africa, that outsider would laugh, and consider that those Indians, or those Europeans who had joined them in having a banquet, and giving all those praises and so on, must be a parcel of fools. What was there to gloat over in having an intolerable burden removed which might have been removed years ago? What was there in a lawful wife's being recognised in a place like South Africa ? But, proceeded Mr. Gandhi, he concurred with Mr. Duncan in an article he wrote some years ago, when he truly analysed the struggle, and said that behind that struggle for concrete rights lay the great spirit which asked for an abstract principle, and the fight which was undertaken in 1906, although it was a fight against a particular law, was a fight undertaken in order to combat the spirit that was seen about to overshadow the whole of South Africa and to undermine the glorious British Constitution, of which the Chairman had spoken so loftily that evening, and about which he (the speaker) shared his views.

It was his knowledge, right or wrong, the British Constitution bound him to the Empire. Tear that Constitution to shreds and his loyalty also would be torn to shreds. Keep that Constitution intact, and they held him bound a slave to that Constitution. He had felt that the choice lay for himself and his fellow-countrymen between two courses, when this spirit was brooding over South Africa, either to sunder themselves from the British Constitution, or to fight in order that the ideals of that Constitution might be preserved — but only the ideals. Lord Ampthill had said, in a preface to Mr. Doke's book, that the theory of the British Constitution must be preserved at any cost if the British Empire was to be saved from the mistakes that all the previous Empires had made. Practise might bend to the temporary aberration through which local circumstances might compel them to pass, it might bend before unreasoning or unreasonable prejudice, but theory once recognised could never be departed from, and this principle must be maintained at any cost. And it was that spirit which had been acknowledged now by the Union Government, and acknowledged how nobly and loftily. The words that General Smuts so often emphasised still rang in his ears. He had said, "Gandhi, this time we want no misunderstanding, we want no mental or other reservations, let all the cards be on the table, and I want you to tell me wherever you think that a particular passage or word does not read in accordance with your own reading," and it was so. That was the spirit in which he approached the negotiations. When he remembered General Smuts of a few years ago, when he told Lord Crewe that South Africa would not depart from its policy of racial distinction, that it was bound to retain that distinction, and that, therefore the sting that lay in this Immigration Law would not be removed, many a friend, including Lord Ampthill, asked whether they could not for the time being suspend their activity. He had said "No". If they did that it would undermine his loyalty, and even though he might be the only person he would still fight on.

Lord Ampthill had congratulated him, and that great nobleman had never deserted the cause even when it was at its lowest ebb, and they saw the result that day. They had not by any means to congratulate themselves on a victory gained. There was no question of a victory gained, but the question of the establishment of the principle that, so far as the Union of South Africa at least was concerned, its legislation would never contain the racial taint, would never contain the colour disability. The practice would certainly be different. There was the Immigration Law — it recognised no racial distinctions, but in practice they had arranged, they had given a promise, that there should be no undue influx from India as to immigration. That was a concession to present prejudice. Whether it was right or wrong was not for him to discuss then. But it was the establishment of that principle which had made the struggle so important in the British Empire, and the establishment of that principle which had made those sufferings perfectly justifiable and perfectly honourable, and he thought that, when they considered the struggle from that standpoint, it was a perfectly dignified thing for any gathering to congratulate itself upon such a vindication of the principles of the British Constitution.

One word of caution he wished to utter regarding the settlement. The settlement was honourable to both parties. He did not think there was any room left for misunderstanding, but whilst it was final in the sense that it closed the great struggle, it was not final in the sense that it gave to Indians all that they were entitled to. There was still the Gold Law which had many a sting in it. There was still the Licensing Laws throughout the Union, which also contained many a sting. There was still a matter which the Colonial-born Indians especially could not understand or appreciate, namely, the water-tight compartments in which they had to live; whilst there was absolutely free inter-communication and inter-migration between the Provinces for Europeans, Indians had to be cooped up in their respective Provinces. Then there was undue restraint on their trading activity. There was the prohibition as to holding landed property in the Transvaal, which was degrading, and all these things took Indians into all kinds of undesirable channels. These restrictions would have to be removed. But for that, he thought, sufficient patience would have to be exercised. Time was now at their disposal, and how wonderfully the tone had been changed ! And here he had been told in Capetown, and he believed it implicitly, the spirit of Mr. Andrews had pervaded all those statesmen and leading men whom he saw. He came and went away after a brief period, but he certainly fired those whom he saw with a sense of their duty to the Empire of which they were members. But, in any case, to whatever circumstances that healthy tone was due, it had not escaped him. He had seen it amongst European friends whom he met at Capetown; he had seen it more fully in Durban, and this time it had been his privilege to meet many Europeans who were perfect strangers even on board the train, who had come smilingly forward to congratulate him on what they had called a great victory. Everywhere he had noticed that healthy tone. He asked European friends to continue that activity, either through the European Committee or through other channels, and to give his fellow-countrymen their help and extend that fellow-feeling to them also, so that they might be able to work out their own salvation.

To his countrymen he would say that they should wait and nurse the settlement, which he considered was all that they could possibly and reasonably have expected, and that they would now live to see, with the cooperation of their European friends, that what was promised was fulfilled, that the administration of the existing laws was just, and that vested rights were respected in the administration; that after they had nursed these things, if they cultivated European public opinion, making it possible for the Government of the day to grant a restoration of the other rights of which they had been deprived, he did not think that there need be any fear about the future. He thought that, with mutual cooperation, with mutual goodwill, with due response on the part of either party, the Indian community need never be a source of weakness to that Government or to any Government. On the contrary, he had full faith in his countrymen that, if they were well treated, they would always rise to the occasion and help the Government of the day. If they had insisted on their rights on many an occasion, he hoped that the European friends who where there would remember that they had also discharged the responsibilities which had faced them.

And now it was time for him to close his remarks and say a few words of farewell only. He did not know how he could express those words. The best years of his life had been passed in South Africa. India, as his distinguished countryman, Mr. Gokhale had reminded him, had become a strange land to him. South Africa he knew, but not India. He did not know what impelled him to go to India, but he did know that the parting from them all the parting from the European friends who had helped him through thick and thin, was a heavy blow, and one he was least able to bear; yet he knew he had to part from them. He could only say farewell and ask them to give him their blessing, to pray for them that their heads might not be turned by the praise they had received, that they might still know how to do their duty to the best of their ability, that they might still learn that first, second, and last should be the approbation of their own conscience, and that then whatever might be due to them would follow in its own time.

Speech At Verulam

[One of the most important gatherings held just before Mr. Gandhi left South Africa was the great meeting of indentured Indians and employers at Verulani, In his address, Mr. Gandhi took pains to make the position under the Relief Act absolutely clear to the Indian labourers, and addressed a few earnest words at the close to the European Employers of the neighbourhood]

He asked his countrymen to understand that it was wrong for them to consider that the relief that had been obtained had been obtained because he had gone to gaol, or his wife, or those who were immediately near and dear to him. It was because they had the good sense and courage to give up their own lives and to sacrifice themselves, and in these circumstances he had also to tell them that many causes led to that relief, and one of these was certainly also the most valuable and unstinted assistance rendered by Mr. Marshall Campbell of Mount Edgecombe. He thought that their thanks and his thanks were due to him for the magnificent work that he did in the Senate whilst the Bill was passing through it. They would now not have to pay the £3 Tax, and the arrears would also be remitted. That did not mean that they were free from their present indentures. They were bound to go through their present indentures faithfully and honestly, but when those indentures terminated, they were just as free as any other free Indian, and they were entitled, if they would go to the Protector's office, to the same discharge certificate as was granted to those who came before 1895, under Law 25 of 1891. They were not bound to re-indenture nor to return to India. The discharge certificates would be issued to them free of charge. If they wanted, after having gone to India, to return, they could only do so after they had lived for full three years in the Province as free men after serving their indentures. If any of them wished to have assistance for going to India, they could obtain it from the Government if they did not wish to return from India. If, therefore, they wanted to return from India, they would fight shy of that assistance which was given to them by the Government, but would find their own money or borrow it from friends. If they re-indentured, they could come under the same law, namely, Law 25 of 1891. His own advice to them was not to re-indenture, but by all means to serve their present masters under the common law of the country. If ever occasion arose, which he hoped would never happen, they now knew what it was possible for them to do. But he wanted to remind them of this one thing, that Victoria Country, as also the other Districts of Natal, had not been so free from violence on their own part as the Newcastle District had been. He did not care that provocation had been offered to them or how much they had retaliated with their sticks or with stones, or had burned the sugarcane — that was not Passive Resistance, and, if he had been in their midst, he would have repudiated them entirely and allowed his own head to be broken rather than permit them to use a single stick against their opponents. And he wanted them to believe him when he told them that Passive Resistance pure and simple was an infinitely finer weapon than all the sticks and gunpowder put together.

They might strike work, but they might compel nobody else to strike work, and, if, as a result of their strike, they were sentenced to be imprisoned, whipped, or to both, they must suffer even unto death — that was Passive Resistance, nothing else. Nothing else, and nothing less than that, would satisfy the requirements of Passive Resistance. If, therefore, he was indentured to Mr. Marshall Campbell, or Mr. Sanders, or any friends about there, and if he found that he was being persecuted or not receiving justice, in their case he would not even go to the Protector, he would sit tight and say, "My master, I want justice or I won't work. Give me food if you want to, water if you want to; otherwise, I sit here hungry and thirsty," and he assured them that the hardest, stoniest heart would be melted. Therefore, let that sink deeply into themselves, that whenever they were afraid of any injury being done to them all, that was the sovereign remedy and that alone was the most effective remedy. If they wanted advice and guidance, and many of them had complained that he was going away, and that his advice would not be at their disposal, all he could suggest to them was that, although he was going away Phoenix was not leaving, and, therefore if they had any difficulty for which they did not wish to pay Mr. Langston or other lawyers, they should go to Phoenix and ask Mr. West or Mr. Chhaganlal Gandhi what was to be done in a particular case. If Mr. West or Mr. Chhaganlal could help them, they would do so free of charge, and if they could not they would send them to Mr. Langston or his other brothers in the law, and he had no doubt that, if they went to Mr. Langston with a certificate from Mr. West that they were too poor, he would render them assistance free of charge. But, if they were called upon to sign any document whatsoever, his advice to them was not to sign it unless they went to Phoenix and got advice. If Phoenix ever failed them and wanted a farthing from them, then they should shun Phoenix.

The scene before him that morning would not easily fade from his memory, even though the distance between him and them might be great. He prayed that God might help them in all the troubles that might be in store for them, and that their conduct might be such that God might find it possible to help them. And to the European friends living in this country be wished to tender his thanks, and he wished also to ask them to forgive him if they had ever considered that during that awful time he was instrumental in bringing about any retaliation at all on the part of his countrymen. He wished to give them this assurance that he had no part or parcel in it, and that, so far as he knew, not a single leading Indian had asked the men to retaliate. There were times in a man's life when he lost his senses, his self-control, and under a sense of irritation, fancied or real, began to retaliate when the brute nature in him rose, and he only went by the law of "might is right," or the law of retaliation — a tooth for a tooth. If his countrymen had done so, whether under a real sense of wrong or fancied, let them forgive him and let them keep a kind corner in their hearts; and, if there were any employers of indentured labour there present who would take that humble request to them, he did ask them not to think always selfishly, though he knew it was most difficult to eradicate self, and let them consider these indentured Indians not merely as cattle which they had to deal with, but as human beings with the same fine feelings, the same fine sentiments as themselves. Let them credit them to the fullest extent with their weaknesses, as also at least with the possibility of all the virtues. Would they not then treat their Indian employees even as brothers? It was not enough that they were well treated as they well treated their cattle. It was not enough that they looked upon them with a kindly eyes merely; but it was necessary that employers should have a much broader view of their own position, that they should think of their employees as fellow human beings and not as Asiatics who had nothing in common with them who were Europeans, and they would also respond to every attention that might be given to them. Then they would have an intelligent interest not merely in the material or physical well-being of their men, but in their moral well-being. They would look after their morality, after their children, after their education, after their sensation, and, if they were herding together in such a manner that they could not but indulge in hideous immorality, that they would themselves recoil with horror from the very imagination that the men who were for the time being under their control should indulge in these things because they had been placed in these surroundings. Let them not consider that because these men were drawn from the lowest strata of society that they were beyond reclamation. No, they would respond to every moral pressure that might be brought to bear upon them, and they will certainly realise the mortal height that it is possible for every human being, no matter who he is, no matter what tinge of colour his skin possesses.

Speech at Madras Public Reception

[The following is the speech delivered by Mr. M. K. Gandhi on the occasion of his visit to Madras in 1915. Sir S. Subramania Aiyar presided on the occasion]

Mr. Chairman and Friends! On behalf of my wife and myself I am deeply grateful for the honour that you here, and Madras, and, may I say, this Presidency, have done to us and the affection that has been lavished upon us in this great and enlightened, not benighted. Presidency. If there is anything that we have deserved, as has been stated in this beautiful address, I can only say I lay it at the feet of my Master under whose inspiration I have been working all this time under exile in South Africa. In so far as the sentiments expressed in this address are merely prophetic, Sir, I accept them as a blessing and as a prayer from you and from this great meeting, that both my wife and I myself may possess the power, the inclination, and the life to dedicate whatever may be developed in us by this sacred land of ours to the service of the Motherland. It is no wonder that we have come to Madras. As my friend, Mr. Natesan, will perhaps tell you, we have been long overdue and we seem to have neglected Madras. But we have done nothing of the kind. We knew that we had a corner in your hearts and we knew that you will not misjudge us if we did not hasten to Madras before going to other Presidencies and other towns. It was in 1896 that I found in Mr. Gokhale my Rajya Guru, and it was here that I found that deep abiding sense of religion which has carried me through all trials. I appeared in 1896 before you as a stranger pleading a forlorn cause, and then discovered that Madras, this Presidency, had that instinctive power to distinguish between a right cause and a wrong cause which marks the religious, and it was here that you appreciated in its fullest measure the gravity of the situation that I was then endeavouring to place before my countrymen throughout India. And the impressions that I took with me to South Africa in 1896 have been more than amply verified throughout my experience in South Africa. The drafters of this beautiful address have, I venture to say, exaggerated out of all proportion the importance of the little work that I was able to do in South Africa. As I have said on so many platforms, India is still suffering under the hypnotic influence produced upon it by that great saintly politician, Mr. Gokhale. He assured in my favour a certificate which you have taken at its surface value and it is that certificate which has placed me in a most embarrassing position, embarrassing because I do not know that I shall be able to answer the expectations that have been raised about myself and about my wife in the work that lies before us in the future on behalf of this country.

But, Sir, if one-tenth of the language that has been used in this address is deserved by us, what language do you propose to use for those who have lost their lives, and therefore finished their work, on behalf of your suffering countrymen in South Africa? What language do you propose to use for Nagappan and

Narayanaswamy, lads of seventeen or eighteen years, who braved in simple faith all the trials, all the sufferings, and all the indignities for the sake of the honour of the

Motherland? (Applause) What language do you propose to use with reference to Valliamma, that sweet girl of seventeen years, who was discharged from Maritzburg prison, skin and bone, suffering from fever to which she succumbed after about a month's time ? (Cries of Shame) It was the Madrasis, who, of all Indians, were singled out by the great Divinity that rules over us for this great work. Do you know that in the great city of Johannesburg, the Madrasis look on a Madrasi dishonoured if he has not passed through the gaols once or twice during this terrible crisis that your countrymen in South Africa went through during these eight long years ? You have said that I inspired those great men and women, but I cannot accept that proposition. It was they, the simple-minded folk, who worked away in faith, never expecting slightest reward, who inspired me, who kept me on the proper level, and who combined me by their great sacrifice by their great faith, by their great trust in the great God to do the work that I was able to do. It is my misfortune that I and my wife have been obliged to work in the lime light and you have magnified out of proportion this little work we have been able to do. Believe me, my dear friends, that if you consider whether in India or in South Africa it is possible for us, poor mortals, the same individuals, the same stuff of which you are made, if you consider that it is possible for us to do anything whatsoever with your assistance and without your doing the same thing that we would be prepared to do, you are lost, and we are also lost and our services will be in vain. I do not for one moment believe that the inspiration was given by us.

Inspiration was given by them to us, and we were able to be interpreters between the powers who called themselves the Governors and those men for whom redress was so necessary. We were simply links between the two parties and nothing more. It was my duty having received the education that was given to me by my parents, to interpret what was going on in our midst to those simple folk, and they rose to the occasion. They realised the importance of birth in India, they realised the might of religious force, and it was they who inspired us. Then let these who have finished their work, and who have died for you and me, let them inspire you and us. We are still living, and who knows that the devil will not possess us tomorrow and we shall not for sake the duty? But these three have gone for ever. An old man of 75 from the United Provinces, Harbat Singh, he has also joined the majority and died in gaol in South Africa, and he deserved the crown that you would seek to impose upon us. These young men deserve all these adjectives that you have so affectionately but blindly, lavished upon us. It was not only the Hindus who struggled, but there were Mohammedans, Parsis and Christians, and almost every part of India was represented in the struggle. They realised the common danger, and they realised also what their destiny was as Indians, as it was they, and they alone, who matched the soul-force against the physical forces.

Speech at Madras Law Dinner

[Speech delivered by Mr. M. K. Gandhi on the occasion of Madras Law Dinner held at Madras on April, 1915, *under the presidency of the Advocate-General]*

My Lord Chief Justice, Mr. Chairman and Gentlemen! During my three months' tour in India, as also in South Africa, I have been so often questioned how I, a determined opponent of modern civilisation, and avowed patriot, could reconcile myself to loyalty to the British Empire of which India was such a large part, how it was possible for me to find it consistent that India and England could work together for mutual benefit. It gives me the greatest pleasure this evening at this great and important gathering to redeclare my loyalty to the British Empire, and my loyalty is based upon, very selfish grounds. As a passive resistor I discovered that he has to make good his claim to passive resistance, no matter under what circumstances he finds himself, and I find that the British Empire had certain ideals, with which I have fallen in love, and one of these ideals is that every subject of the British Empire has the freest scope possible for his energies and for whatever he thinks is due to his conscience, I think that this is true of the British Empire, as it is not true of any other Government that we see. I feel, as you have, perhaps, known that I am no lover of any Government and I have more than once said that the Government is best which governs that least; and I have found that it is possible for me to be governed least under the British Empire hence my loyalty to the British throne.

Speech for Advice to Students

[Speech delivered at the YMCA Madras on April, 1915, *Hon'ble Mr. V. S. Srinivasa Shastry presiding]*

Mr. Chairman and Dear Friends! Madras has well-nigh exhausted the English vocabulary in using adjectives of virtue with reference to my wife and myself and if I may be called upon to give an opinion as to where I have been smoothered with kindness, love and attention, I would have to say it is Madras. (Applause). But as I have said so often, I believed it of Madras. So it is no wonder to me that you are lavishing all these kindnesses with unparalled generosity, and now the worthy President of the Servants of India Society, under which Society I am now going through a period of probation, has, if I may say so, capped it all. Am I worthy of these things? My answer from the innermost recess of the heart is an emphatic "No". But I have come to India to become worthy of every adjective that you may use, and all my life will certainly be dedicated to prove worthy of them if I am to be a worthy servant. In India's beautiful national song (Bande Mataram) the poet has lavished all the adjectives that he possibly could to describe Mother India. Have we a right to sing that hymn? The poet no doubt gave us a picture for our realisation, the words of which remain simply prophetic, and it is for you, the hope of India, to realise every word that the poet has said in describing this Motherland of ours. Today I feel that these adjectives are very largely misplaced in his description of the Motherland.

You, the students of Madras as well as the students all over India, are you receiving an education which will make you worthy to realise that ideal, and which will draw the best out of you ? Or is it an education which has become a factory for making Government employees, or clerks in commercial offices ? Is the goal of the education that you are receiving for mere employment whether in Government department or in other departments ? If that be the goal of your education, if that is the goal that you have set before yourselves, I feel, I fear, that the vision that the poet pictured for himself is far from being realised. As you have heard me say, perhaps, or as you have read, I am, and I have been, a determined opponent of modern civilisation. I want you to turn your eyes today upon what is going on in Europe, and if you have come to the conclusion that Europe is today groaning under the heels of that modern civilisation, then you and your elders will have to think twice before you emulate that civilisation in our Motherland. But I have been told: "How can we help it, seeing that our Rulers bring that culture to our Motherland?" Do not make any mistake about it. I do not for one moment believe that it is for our Rulers to bring that culture to you, unless you are prepared to accept it and if it be that the Rulers bring that culture before us, I think that we have forces for ourselves to enable us to reject that culture without having to reject the Rulers themselves. I have said on many a platform that the British race is with us. I decline to go into the reasons why that race is with us, but I do not believe that it is possible for India, if it would live up to the traditions of the Sages of whom you have heard from our worthy President, to transmit a message through this great race, a message not of physical might but a message of love. And then, it will be your privilege to conquer the conquerors not by shedding blood but by sheer force of spiritual predominance. When I consider what is going on in India, I think it is necessary for us to see what our opinion is in connection with the political assassinations and political dacoities. I feel that these are purely a foreign importation, which cannot take root in this land. But you, the student world, have to beware lest, mentally, or morally, you give one thought of approval to this kind of terrorism. I as a passive resister will give you another thing very substantial for it. Terrorise yourself; search within; by all means resist tyranny where ever you find it; by ail means resist encroachment upon your liberty; but not by shedding the blood of the tyrant. That is not what is taught by our religion. Our religion is based upon Ahimsa which in its active form is nothing but love, love not only to your neighbours, not only to your friends, but love even to those who may be your enemies.

One word more in connection with the same thing. I think that if we were to practise truth, to practise Ahimsa, we must immediately see that we also practise fearlessness. If our Rulers are doing what in our opinion is wrong, and if we feel it our duty to let them hear our advice, even though it may be considered sedition, I urge you to speak sedition — but at your peril, you must be prepared to suffer the consequences. And when you are ready to suffer the consequences and not hit below the belt, then I think you will have made good your right to have your advice heard even by the Government.

I ally myself to the British Government, because I believe that it is possible for me to claim equal partnership with every subject of the British Empire. I today claim that equal partnership. I do not belong to a subject race. I do not call myself a subject race. But there is this thing: it is not for the British Governors to give you, it is for you to take the thing. That I want only by discharging my obligations. Max Muller has told us — we need not go to Max Muller to interpret our own religion — but he says our religion consists in four letters D-U-T-Y and not in the five letters R-I-G-H-T. And if you believe that all that we want can go from a letter, discharge of our duty then think always of your duty, and fighting along these lines you will have no fear of any man, you will only fear God. That is the message that my Master too, Mr. Gokhale, has given to us, what is that message then ? It is in the Constitution of the Servants of India Society, and that it is that message by which I wish to be guided in my life. The message is to spiritualise political life and political institutions of the country. We must immediately set about realising it in practice. Then students cannot be away from politics. Politics is as essential to them as religion. Politics cannot be divorced from religion.

My views may not be acceptable to you I know. All the same, I can only give you what is stirring me to my very depths. On the authority of my experience in South Africa, I claim that your countrymen who had not that modern culture, but who had that strength of the Rishis of old, who have inherited the Tapasyacharya performed by the Rishis, without having known a single word of English literature, and without having known anything whatsoever of the present modern culture, were able to rise to their full height. And what has been possible for the uneducated and illiterate countrymen of ours in South Africa is ten times possible for you and for me today in this sacred land of ours.

Speech on Brahmins and Panchamas

[Mr. and Mrs. Gandhi on their way to Tranquebar arrived at Mayavaram on 2nd May, 1915, and they were presented with an address by the citizens of the town. In the course of his reply Mr. Gandhi said]

It was quite by accident that I had the great pleasure, of receiving an address from my 'Panchama brethren and there, they said that they were without convenience for drinking water, they were without convenience for living supplies, and they could not buy or hold land. It was difficult for them even to approach courts. Probably, the last is due to their fear, but a fear certainly not due to themselves, and who is then responsible for this state of things? Do we propose to perpetuate this state of things? Is it a part of Hinduism? I do not know. I have now to learn what Hinduism really is. In so far as I have been able to study Hinduism outside India, I have felt that it is no part of real Hinduism to have in its fold a mass of people whom I would call "untouchables". If it was proved tome that this is an essential part of Hinduism, I, for one, would declare myself an open rebel against Hinduism itself.

Are the Brahmins in Mayavaram equiminded towards the Pariah and will they tell me, if they are so equiminded and if so, will they tell me if others will not follow? Even if they say that they are prepared to do so but others will not follow, I shall have to disbelieve them until I have revised my notions of Hinduism. If the Brahmins themselves consider they are holding high position by penance and posterity, then they have themselves much to learn, then they will be the people who have cursed and ruined the land.

My friend, the Chairman, has asked me the question whether it is true that I am at war with my leaders. I say that I am not at war with my leaders. I seemed to be at war with my leaders because many things I have heard seem to be inconsistent with my notions of self-respect and with self-respect to my Motherland. I feel that they are probably not discharging the sacred trust they have taken upon their shoulders; but I am not sure I am studying or endeavouring to take wisdom from them, but I failed to take that wisdom. It may be that I am incompetent and unfit to follow them. So, I shall revise my ideas. Still I am in a position to say that I seem to be at war with my leaders. Whatever they do or whatever they say does not somehow or other appeal to me. The major part of what they say does not seem to be appealing to me.

English and the Vernaculars: I find here words of welcome in the English language. I find in the Congress programme a Resolution on Swadeshi. If you hold that you are Swadeshi and yet print these in English, then I am not a Swadeshi. To me it seems that it is inconsistent. I have nothing to say against the English language. But I do say that, if you kill the vernaculars and raise the English language on the tomb of the vernaculars, then you are not favouring Swadeshi in the right sense of the term. If you feel that I do not know Tamil, you should pardon me, you should excuse me and teach me and ask me to learn Tamil and by having your welcome in that beautiful language, if you translate it to me, then I should think you are performing some part of the programme. Then only I should think I am being taught Swadeshi.

Swadeshi Enterprise: I asked when we were passing through Mayavaram whether there have been any handlooms here and whether there were handloom weavers here. I was told that there were 50 handlooms in Mayavaram. What were they engaged in? They were simply engaged chiefly in preparing "Sarees" for our women. Then is Swadeshi to be confined only to the women ? Is it to be only in their keeping? I do not find that our friends, the male population also have their stuff prepared for them in these by these weavers and through their handlooms, (a voice there are a thousand hand looms here). There are, I understand, one thousand handlooms so much the worse for the leaders! If these one thousand handlooms are kept chiefly in attending to the wants of our women, double this supply of your handlooms and you will have all your wants supplied by your own weavers and there will be no poverty in the land. I ask you and ask our friend the President how far he is indebted to foreign goods for his outfit and if he can tell me that he has tried his utmost and still has failed to outfit himself or rather to fit himself out with Swadeshi clothing and therefore he has got this stuff, I shall sit at his feet and learn a lesson. What I have been able to learn today is that it is entirely possible for me, not with any extra cost to fit myself with Swadeshi clothing. How am I to learn through those who move or who are supposed to be movers in the Congress, the secret of the Resolution. I sit at the feet of my leaders, I sit at the feet of Mayavaram people and let them reveal the mystery, give me the secret of the meaning, teach me how I should behave myself and tell me whether it is a part of the National Movement that I should drive off those who are without dwellings, who cry for water and that I should reject the advances of those who cry for food. These are the questions which I ask my friends here. Since I am saying something against you, I doubt whether I shall still enjoy or retain the affection of the student population and whether I shall still retain the blessings of my leaders. I ask you to have a large heart and give me a little corner in it. I shall try to steal into that corner. If you would, be kind enough to teach me the wisdom, I shall learn the wisdom in all humility and in all earnestness.

Speech at Nellore Conference

[Replying to a complimentary Resolution moved at the Madras Provincial Conference at Nellore. Mr. Gandhi said]

It was an accident that this Resolution followed on two Resolutions, one with reference to his revered master and the other with reference to the noble Viceroy to whom a fitting tribute had been paid by the President. He was there free to acknowledge the indebtedness of his countrymen in South Africa to the noble Viceroy. If his wife and he were worthy of anything that had been said on this platform and on many a platform, he had repeated, and he was there again to repeat, that they owed all to the inspiration they derived from Indian sources, for it was Mr. Gokhale, his love, and his message, that had been his guiding star, and would still remain his guiding star. He would appeal to them not to spoil him and his wife by taking away from the services they had to render by over-praising them. He would make this simple, but humble, appeal. Let what he and his wife had done in South Africa be buried there. Their countrymen in South Africa would know what had been done. It was impossible for any one, much less for them, to trade on any reputation made in South Africa. He feared that by overpraising them, they might raise enormous expectations about him and his wife that they might in the end, he would not say it was hardly likely, meet with disappointment.

Speech before Bangalore Public

[An address was presented to Mr. and Mrs. Gandhi by the Citizens of Bangalore, on 8th May, 1915, to which Mr. Gandhi replied as follows]

Mr. Chairman and My Friends! I think it is simply impertinent to tell you that I thank you most sincerely on behalf of my wife and on my own behalf for the signal honour you have shown me. Words fail me, and one thought oppresses me all the more. Am I, are we, worthy of the honour? Are we worthy of the oriental generosity of this love ? The Chairman has furnished this ground for the love, and quoted Mr. Gokhale. Let me not bask in that reputation. See me please in the nakedness of my working, and in my limitations, you will then know me. I have to tread on most delicate grounds, and my path is destined to be through jungles and temples. The glamour produced by the saintly politician has vanished, and let us be judged eye to eye. So many have assembled here to do honour. This morning, you did greater honour. Greater honour was shown by the Reception Committee in arranging for the conversation, in order to open my heart to you and to understand the innermost thoughts in you by quiet conversation between my countrymen and myself.

I did not want to be dragged. There is a meaning. Let us not be dragged. Let them work silently. We should not encourage the thought that workers will be honoured similarly. Let public men feel that they will be stoned, that they will be neglected, and let them feel they still love the country. A charge has been brought against us that we are too demonstrative and lack business-like methods. We plead guilty to the charge. Are we to copy modern activities, or are we to copy the ancient civilisation, which has survived so many shocks ? You and I have to act on the political platform from the spiritual side, and if this is done, we shall then conquer the conquerors. The day will dawn then, when we can consider an Englishman as a fellow-citizen (Cheers). That day will shortly come, but it may be difficult to conceive. I have had signal opportunities of associating myself with Englishmen of character, devotion, nobility and influence. I can assure you that the present wave of activity is passing away, and a new civilisation is coming shortly, which will be a nobler one.

India is a great dependency and Mysore is a great Native State. It must be possible for you to transmit this message to British Governors and to British statesmen; the message is: establish a Rama Rajya in Mysore and have your minister a Vashista, who will command obedience. My fellow countrymen, then you can dictate terms to the conquerors.

Speech on Gokhale

[In unveiling the portrait of Mr. Gokhale in Bangalore, Mr. Gandhi spoke as follows]

My Dear Countrymen! Before I perform this ceremony to which you have called me, I wish to say this to you that you have given me a great opportunity or rather a privilege on this great occasion. I saw in the recitation — the beautiful recitation that was given to me — that God is with them whose garment was dusty and tattered. My thoughts immediately went to the end of my garment; I examined and found that it is not dusty and it is not tattered; it is fairly spotless and clean. God is not in me. There are other conditions attached; but in these conditions too I may fail; and you, my dear countrymen, may also fail; and if we do tend this well, we should not dishonour the memory of one whose portrait you have asked me to unveil this morning I have declared myself his disciple in the political field and I have him as my Rajya Guru: and this I claim on behalf of the Indian people. It was in 1896 that I made this declaration, and I do not regret having made the choice.

Mr. Gokhale taught me that the dream of every Indian who claims to love his country, should be to act in the political field, should be not to glorify in language, but to spiritualise the political life of the country, and the political institutions of the country. He inspired my life and is still inspiring: and in that I wish to purify myself and spiritualise myself. I have dedicated myself to that ideal. I may fail, and to what extent I may fail, I call my- self to that extent an unworthy disciple of my master.

Spiritualising the Political Life: What is the meaning of spiritualising the political life of the country ? What is the meaning of spiritualising myself? That question has come before me often and often and to you it may seem one thing, to me it may seem another thing; it may mean different things to the different members of the Servants of India Society itself. It shows much difficulty and it shows the difficulties of all those who want to love their country, who want to serve their country and who want to honour their country. I think the political life must be an echo of private life and that there cannot be any divorce between the two.

I was by the side of that saintly politician to the end of his life and I found no ego in him. I ask you members of the Social Service League, if there is no ego in you. If he wanted to shine, he wanted to shine in the political field of his country, he did so not in order that he might gain public applause, but in order that his country may gain. He developed every particular faculty in him, not in order to win the praise of the world for himself but in order that his country may gain. He did not seek public applause, but they were showered upon him, they were thrust upon him; he wanted that his country may gain and that was his great inspiration.

There are many things for which India is blamed, very rightly, and if you should add one more to our failures the blame will descend not only on you but also on me for having participated in today's functions. But I have great faith in my countrymen.

You ask me to unveil this portrait today, and I will do so in all sincerity and sincerity should be the end of your life.

Speech on Banaras Incident

[There appeared in the New India' a charge against Mr. Gandhi as having spoken something to be taken an exception to by the public while addressing a large audience at the "Hindu University Pavilion," Banaras to which Mr. Gandhi replied as under]

Mrs. Besant's reference in New India and certain other references to the Banaras incident perhaps render it necessary for me to return to the subject, however disinclined I may be to do so. Mrs. Besant denies my statement with reference to her whispering to the Princes. I can only say that if I can trust my eyes and my ears I must adhere to the statement I have made. She occupied a seat on the left of the semi-circle on either side of the Maharaja of Darbhanga, who occupied the Chair, and there was at least one Prince, perhaps, there were two who were sitting on her side. Whilst I was speaking Mrs. Besant was almost behind me. When the Maharajas rose Mrs. Besant also had risen. I had ceased speaking before the Rajas actually left the platform. She was discussing the incident with a group round her on the platform. I gently suggested to her that she might have refrained from interrupting, but that if she disapproved of the speech after it was finished she could have then dissociated herself from my sentiments. But she, with some degree of warmth, said: "How could we sit still when you were compromising every one of us on the platform? You ought not to have made the remarks you did." This answer of Mrs. Besant's does not quite tally with her solicitude for me which alone, according to her version of the incident, prompted her to interrupt the speech. I suggest that if she merely meant to protect me she could have passed a note round or whispered into my ears her advice. And, again, if it was for my protection why was it necessary for her to rise with Princes and to leave the hall as I hold she did along with them?

So far as my remarks are concerned I am yet unable to know what it was in my speech that seems to her to be open to such exception as to warrant her interruption. After referring to the Viceregal visit and the necessary precautions that were taken for the Viceroy's safety I showed that an assassins death was anything but honourable death and said that anarchism was opposed to our Shastras and had no room in India. I said then where there was an honourable death it would go down to history as men who died for their conviction. But when a bomb thrower died, secretly plotting all sorts of things, what could he gain ? I then went on to state and deal the fallacy that, had not bomb throwers thrown bombs we should never have gained what we did with reference to the Partition Movement. It was at about this stage that Mrs. Besant appealed to the chair to stop me. Personally, I will desire a publication of the whole of my speech whose trend was a sufficient warrant for showing that I could not possibly incite the students to deeds of violence. Indeed it was conceived in order to carry on a rigorous self-examination.

I began by saying that it was a humiliation for the audience and myself that I should have to speak in English. I said that English having been the medium of instruction it had done a tremendous injury to the country, and as I conceive I showed successfully that, had we received training during the past 50 years in higher thought in our own vernaculars, we would be today within reach of our goal. I then referred to the self-government Resolution passed at the Congress and showed that whilst the All India Congress Committee and the All India Muslim League would be drawing up their paper about the future Constitution their duty was to fit themselves by their own action for self-government. And in order to show how short we feel of our duty I drew attention to the dirty condition of the labyrinth of lanes surrounding the great temple of Kashi Vishvanath and the recently erected palatial buildings without any conception as to the straightness or width of the streets. I then took the audience to the gorgeous scene that was enacted on the day of the foundation and suggested that if a stranger not knowing anything about Indian life had visited the scene he would have gone away under the false impression that India was one of the richest countries in the world — such was the display of jewellery worn by our noblemen. And turning to the Maharajas and the Rajahs I humorously suggested that it was necessary for them to hold those treasures in trust for the nation before we could realise our ideals, and I cited the action of the Japanese noblemen who considered it a glorious privilege even though there was no necessity for them, to dispossess themselves of the treasures and lands which were handed to them from generation to generation. I then asked the audience to consider the humiliating spectacle of the Viceroy's person having to be protected from ourselves when he was our honoured guest. And I was endeavouring to show that the blame for these precautions was also on ourselves in that they were rendered necessary because of the introduction of organised assassination in India. Thus, I was endeavouring to show on the one hand how the students could usefully occupy themselves in assisting to rid the society of its proved defects, on the other, to wean themselves even in thought from methods of violence.

I claim that with twenty year's experience of public life in the course of which I had to address on scores of occasions turbulent audiences. I have some experience of feeling the pulse of my audience. I was following closely how the speech was being taken and I certainly did not notice that the student world was being adversely affected. Indeed some of them came to me the following morning and told me that they perfectly understood my remarks which had gone home. One of them a keen debater even subjected to cross-examination and seemed to feel convinced by a further development of the argument such as I had advanced in the course of my speech. Indeed I have spoken now to thousands of students and others of my countrymen throughout South Africa, England and India; and by precisely the arguments that I used that evening I claimed to have weaned many from their approval of anarchical methods.

Finally, I observe that Mr. S. S. Setlur of Bombay, who has written on the incident to the Hindu in no friendly mood towards me, and who I think in some respects totally unfairly has endeavoured to tear me to pieces, and who was an eye witness to the proceedings, gives a version different from Mrs. Besant's. He thinks that the general impression was not that I was encouraging the anarchists but that I was playing the role of an apologist for the Civilian bureaucrat. The whole of Mr. Setlur's attack upon me shows that if he is right I was certainly not guilty of any incitement to violence and that the offence consisted in my reference to jewellery, etc.

In order that the fullest justice might be done both to Mrs. Besant and myself I would make the following suggestion. She says that she does not propose to defend herself by quoting the sentence which drove the Princes away and that would be playing into the enemy's hands; according to her previous statement my speech is already in the hands of the detectives so that so far as my safety is concerned her forbearance is not going to be of the slightest use. Would it not therefore be better that she should either publish a verbatim report if she has it or reproduce such sentiments in my speech as in her opinion, necessitated her interruption and the Princes' withdrawal.

I will therefore conclude this statement by repeating what I have said before; that but for Mrs. Besant's interruption I would have concluded my speech within a few minutes and no possible misconception about my views on anarchism would have arisen.

Speech on the Need of India

[Mr. M. K. Gandhi delivered an address to the students at the YMCA auditorium Madras (1916) with the Hon. Rev. G. Pittendrigh in the chair, in the course of which he said]

I did not know what subject to choose. A friend has handed me a slip here, asking me whether I would not enlighten the students on the Banaras incident. I fear that I shall have to disappoint that friend and those of you who associate yourselves with that view. I do not think you need lay any stress upon that incident. Those are the passing waves which will always come and go. I would rather this morning, if I can possibly do so, pour my soul out to you with reference to something which I treasure so much above everything else. To many students who came to me last year, I said I was about to establish an Ashrama somewhere in India, and it is about that place that I am going to talk to you today.

I have felt during the whole of my public life that what we need, what any Nation needs, but we perhaps of all the other Nations of the world need just now, is nothing else and nothing less than character-building. You know that Mr. Gokhale used so often to say that our average was less than the average of so many European Nations. I do not know whether that statement of him, whom with pride I consider to be my political Guru, has really foundation in fact. But I do believe that there is much to be said to justify that statement in so far as the educated India is concerned, not because the educated portion of the community blundered, but because we have been creatures of circumstances. Be that as it may; this is the maxim of life which I have accepted, namely, that no work done by any man, no matter how great he is, will really prosper unless it has a religious backing.

By religion, I do not mean the religion which you will get after reading all the scriptures of the world; it is not really a grasp by the brain but it is the heart-grasp. It is a thing which is not evident to us, but it is a thing which is evolved out of us; it is always within us, with some, consciously so, with the others quite unconsciously, but it is there, and whether we wake up this religious instinct in us through outside assistance or by inward growth, no matter how it is done, it has got to be done if we want to do anything in the right manner and anything that is going to persist. Our scriptures have laid down certain rules as maxims of life, which we have to take for granted, and believing in these maxims implicitly for all these long years and having actually endeavoured to reduce to practice those injunctions of the Shastras, I have deemed it necessary to seek the association of those who think with me in founding this Institution. I shall place before you this morning the rules that have been drawn up and that have to be observed by everyone who seeks to be a member of that Ashrama.

Vow of Truth: There are five rules known as Yamas, and the first is the vow of truth, not truth as we ordinarily understand it, but truth which means that we have to rule our life by the law of truth at any cost, and in order to satisfy the definition I have drawn upon the celebrated illustration of the life of Prahlada, who, for the sake of truth, dared to oppose his own father. In this Ashrama we make it a rule that we must say no when we mean no, regardless of consequences.

Vow of Ahimsa: The next rule is the vow of Ahimsa, which means non-killing. To me, it has a world of meaning, and takes me into realms much higher than the realms to which I would go if I merely understood Ahimsa to mean non-killing. Ahimsa really means that you may not offend anybody, you may not harbour an uncharitable thought even in connection with one who may consider himself to be your enemy. For one who follows the doctrine of Ahimsa, there is no room for the enemy. Under this rule, there is no room for organised assassination, and there is no room for murders even openly committed, and there is no room for violence even for the sake of your country and even for guarding the honour of precious ones that may be under your charge. This doctrine of Ahimsa tells us that we may guard the honour of those who are under our charge by delivering ourselves into the hands of the men who would commit the sacrilege, and that requires far greater physical and mental courage than delivering blows. You may have some degree of physical power — I do not 186 say courage — and you may use that power, but after it is expended, what happens ? The man is wild with wrath and indignation, and you have made him wilder by matching your violence against his, and when he has done you to death, the rest of his violence is delivered on to your charge; but if you do not retaliate but simply stand on your ground to receive all the blows and stand between your charge and the opponent, what happens ? I give you my promise that the whole violence will be expended on you, and your charge will be left sacred.

Vow of Celibacy: Those who want to perform National Service or those who want to have the glimpse of real religious life must lead a celibate life, whether married or unmarried. Marriage brings a woman close together with a man, and they become friends in a special sense, never to be parted either in this life or in the lives that are to come; but I do not think that into that plane of life our lusts should necessarily enter.

Control of Palates: Then there is the vow of the control of the palates. A man who wants to control his animal passion easily does so without even noticing that he does so. Without being a slave to his palate, he will master his palate. This is one of the most difficult vows to follow. I am just now coming from having inspected the Victoria Hostel, and I saw to my dismay that there are so many kitchens, not kitchens that are established in order to serve caste restrictions, but kitchens that have become necessary in order that we can have condiments and the exact weight of condiments, to which we were used in the respective countries or the places or provinces from which we have come. For the

Brahmans themselves there are different compartments and different kitchens catering after the delicate tastes of those different groups. I suggest to you that this is simply slavery to the palate rather than mastery of the palate. Unless we are satisfied with foods that are necessary for the proper maintenance of our physical health, and unless we are prepared to rid ourselves of those stimulating and heating and exciting condiments that we mix with our food, we will certainly not be able to control the over-abundant unnecessary exciting energy that we may have. Eating and drinking and indulging in passion, we share in common with the animals, but have you seen a horse, a cow indulging in palate to the excess that we do ? Do you suppose that it is a sign of civilisation, a sign of actual life that we should multiply our eatables so far that we do not know where we are V.

Vow of Non-thieving: The next rule is the vow of non-thieving. We are thieves in a way if we take anything that we do not need for immediate use, and keep it from some body else who needs it. It is a fundamental law of Nature, that Nature produces enough for our wants from day today, and if only every body took only enough for him and no more, there will be no poverty in the world, and there will be no man dying of starvation in this world. And so long as we have got this inequality, so long I shall have to say we are thieves. I am no socialist, and I do not want to dispossess those who have got possessions, but I do say that personally those of us who want to see darkness out of light have to follow this doctrine. In India, we have three millions of people having to be satisfied with only one meal consisting of a chapati containing no fat in it and a pinch of salt.

Vow of Swadeshi: The vow of Swadeshi is a necessary vow. I suggest to you that we are departing from one of the sacred laws of our being when we leave our neighbour and go somewhere else to satisfy our wants. If a man comes from Bombay here and offers you wares, you are not justified in supporting the Bombay merchant or trader so long as you have got a merchant at your very door born and bred in Madras. That is my view of Swadeshi. In your village, so long as you have a village barber, you are bound to support the village barber to the exclusion of the finished barber that may come to you from Madras. Train your village barber by ail means to reach the attainment of the barber from Madras, but until he does so, you are not justified in going to the Madras barber. When we find that there are many things we cannot get, we try to do without them. We may have to do without so many things which today we consider necessary, and believe me when you have that frame of mind, you will find a great burden taken off your shoulders even as the pilgrim did in that inimitable book Pilgrim's Progress.

Vow of Fearlessness: I found through my wanderings in India that all educated India is seized with a paralysing fear. We may not open our lips in public. We may not declare our confirmed opinions in public. We may hold those opinions, and we may talk about them secretly, and we may do anything within the four walls of a house, but those opinions are not for public consumption. If we took a vow of silence, I would have nothing to say, but when we open our lips in public we say things which we really do not believe. I do not know whether this is not the experience of almost every one who speaks in public. I then suggest to you that there is only one Being, if Being is the proper term to be applied, whom we have to fear, and that is God. If you want to follow the vow of truth in any shape or form, fearlessness is the necessary consequence.

Untouchables: We have also a vow in connection with the untouchables. There is an ineffaceable blot which Hinduism carries with it today. I have declined to believe that it has been handed to us from immemorial times. I think that these miserable, wretched, enslaving spirits of untouchables must have come to us when we were in a cycle of our lives at our lowest ebb, and that evil has stuck to us, and it remains with us. It is to my mind a curse that has come to us, and so long as it remains with us, we are bound to consider that every affliction that we labour under in this sacred land is a fit and proper punishment for the great crime that we are committing. That any person should be considered untouchable because of his calling passes one's comprehension, and you, the student world, who receive all this modern education, if you become a party to this crime, it were better that you receive no education whatsoever. We are labouring under a heavy handicap. You, although you may realise that there cannot be a single human being on this earth who should be considered to be untouchable, you cannot react upon your families and upon your surroundings, because all your thought is conceived in a foreign tongue. So we have introduced a rule in the Ashrama that we shall receive our education through the Vernaculars. In order to solve the problem of languages in India, we in the Ashram a make it a point of learning as many Indian Vernaculars as we possibly can, and I assure you that the trouble of learning these languages is nothing compared to the trouble that we have to take in mastering the English language. Even after all that trouble, it is not possible for us to express ourselves in the English language as clearly as in our own mother tongue. Education has enabled us to see the horrible crime in connection with the so-called untouchables, but we are seized with fear, and we have got our superstitious veneration for our family traditions and for the members of our families.

Politics: Last of all, when you have conformed to these rules, I think then, and not till then, you may come to politics and dabble in them to your heart's content. Politics divorced from religions, have absolutely no meaning, and if the student world crowd the political platforms of the country, to my mind, it is not necessarily a healthy sign of national growth; but that does not mean that we in student-life ought not to learn politics. Politics are also a part of our being. We want to understand our national institutions, we ought to understand our national growth. So, in the Ashrama, every child is taught to understand political institutions, and know how the country is vibrating with new emotions, with new aspirations, with new life; but we want also the infallible light of religious faith, not faith which merely appeals to the intelligence, but faith which is indelibly inscribed in the heart. Today what happens is that immediately young men cease to be students they sink into oblivion, and they seek miserable employments, carrying miserable emoluments, knowing nothing of God, knowing nothing of fresh air and fresh light, and knowing nothing of that real vigorous independence that comes out of obedience to those laws that I have placed before you.

Speech on Economic vs Moral Progress

[Mr. M. K. Gandhi delivered an instructive lecture on "Does economic progress clash with real progress?" At a meeting of the Muir Central College Economic Society held in the Physical Science Theatre. The Hon. Pandit Madan Mohan Malaviya presided]

When I accepted Mr. Kapildeva Malaviya's invitation to speak to you upon the subject of this evening, I was painfully conscious of my limitations. You are an economic society. You have chosen distinguished specialists for the subjects included in your syllabus for this year and the next. I seem to be the only speaker ill-fitted for the task set before him. Frankly and truly, I know very little of economics, as you naturally understand them. Only the other day, sitting at an evening meal, a civilian friend deluged me with a series of questions on my crankisms. As he proceeded in his cross-examination, I being a willing victim, he found no difficulty in discovering my gross ignorance of the matters I appeared to him to be handling with a cocksuredness worthy only of a man who knows not that he knows not. To his horror and even indignation, I suppose, he found that I had not even read books on economics by such well-known authorities as Mill, Marshall, Adam Smith and a host of such other authors.

In despair, he ended by advising me to read these works before experimenting in matters economic at the expense of the public. He little knew that I was a sinner past redemption. My experiments continue at the expense of trusting friends. For there come to us moments in life when about somethings we need no proof from without. A little voice within us tells, "you are on the right track, move neither to your left nor right, but keep to the straight and narrow way." With such help we march forward slowly indeed, but surely and steadily. That is my position. It may be satisfactory enough for me, but it can in no way answer the requirements of a society such as yours. Still it was no use my struggling against Mr. Kapildeva Malaviya. I knew that he was intent upon having me to engage your attention for one of your evenings. Perhaps you will treat my instruction as a welcome diversion from the trodden path. An occasional fast after a series of sumptuous feasts is often a necessity. And as with the body so, I imagine, is the case with the reason. And if your reason this evening is found fasting instead of feasting, I am sure it will enjoy with the greater avidity the feast that Rao Bahabur Pandit Chaddrika Prashad has in store for you for the 12th of January.

Before I take you to the field of my experiences and experiments it is perhaps best to have a mutual understanding about the title of this evening's address. Does economic progress clash with real progress ? By economic progress, I take it, we mean material advancement without limit and by real progress we mean moral progress, which again is the same thing as progress of the permanent element in us. The subject may therefore be stated thus: Does not moral progress increase in the same proportion as material progress ? I know that this is a wider proposition than the one before us. But I venture to think that we always mean the larger one even when we lay down the smaller. For we know enough of science to realise that there is no such thing as perfect rest or repose in this visible universe of ours, If therefore material progress does not clash with moral progress it must necessarily advance the latter. Nor can we be satisfied with the clumsy way in which sometimes those who cannot defend the larger proposition put their case. They seem to be obsessed with the concrete case of thirty millions of India stated by the late Sir William Wilson Hunter to be living on one meal a day. They say that before we can think or talk of their moral welfare we must satisfy their daily wants. With these, they say, material progress spells moral progress. And then is taken a sudden jump: what is true of thirty millions is true of the universe. They forget that hard cases make bad law. I need hardly say to you how ludicrously absurd this deduction would be. No one has ever suggested that grinding pauperism can lead to anything else than moral degradation. Every human being has a right to live, and therefore to find the where withal to feed himself and where necessary, to clothe and house himself. But for this very simple performance we need no assistance from economists or their laws.

Take no thought for the morrow "is an injunction which finds an echo in almost all the religious scriptures of the world. In well ordered society the securing of one's livelihood should be and is found to be the easiest thing in the world. Indeed the test of orderliness in a country is not the number of millionaries it owns, but the absence of starvation among its masses. The only statement that has to be examined is whether it can be laid down as a law of universal application that material advancement means moral progress.

Now let us take a few illustrations. Rome suffered a moral fall when it attained high material affluence. So did Egypt, and so perhaps most countries of which we have any historical record. The descendants and kinsmen to the royal and divine Krishna too fell when they were rolling in riches. We do not deny to the Rocksfellers and the Carnegies possession of an ordinary measure of morality but we gladly judge them indulgently. I mean that we do not even expect them to satisfy the highest standard of morality. With them material gain has not necessarily meant moral gain. In South Africa where I had the privilege of associating with thousands of our countrymen on most intimate terms, I observed almost invariably that the greater the possession of riches the greater was their moral turpitude. Our rich men, to say the least, did not advance the moral struggle of passive resistance as did the poor.

The rich men's sense of self respect was not so much injured as that of the poorest: If I were not afraid of treading on dangerous ground, I would even come nearer home, and show you that possession of riches has been a hindrance to real growth. I venture to think that the scriptures of the world are far safer and sounder treatises on laws of economics than many of the modern textbooks. The question we are asking ourselves this evening is not a new one. It was addressed to Jesus two thousand years ago. St. Mark has vividly described the scene. Jesus is in his solemn mood; he is earnest. He talks of eternity. He knows the world about him. He is himself the greatest economist of his time. He succeeded in economising time and space — he transcended them.

It is to him at his best that one comes running, kneels down, and asks: "Good Master, what shall I do that I may inherit eternal life ?" And Jesus said unto him: "Why callest thou me good ? There is none good but one, that is, God. Thou knowest the commandments. Do not commit adultery, Do not kill, Do not steal; Do not bear false witness, Defraud not, Honour thy father and mother.' And he answered and said unto him: 'Master, all these have I observed from my youth.' Then Jesus beholding him loved him and said unto him: One thing thou lackest. Go thy way, sell whatever thou hast and give to the poor, and thou shall have treasure in heaven — come take up the cross and follow me.' And he was sad at that saying and went away grieved — for he had great possessions. And Jesus looked round about and said unto his disciples: How hardly shall they that have riches enter into the Kingdom of God.' And the disciples were astonished at his words. But Jesus answereth again and saith unto them Children, how hard is it for them that trust in riches to enter into the Kingdom of God. It is easier for a camel to go through the eye of a needle than for a rich man to enter into the Kingdom of God !" Here you have an eternal rule of life stated in the noblest words the English language is capable of producing. But the disciples nodded unbelief as we do even to this day. To him they said as we say today; But look how the law fails in practice. If we sell all and have nothing we shall have nothing to eat. We must have money or wo cannot even be reasonably moral. So they state their cause thus! "And they were astonished out of measure, saying among themselves: Who then can be saved'. And Jesus looking upon them saith: With men it is impossible but not with God, for with God all things are possible'. Then Peter began to say unto him: 4 Lo, we have left all, and have followed thee. And Jesus answered and said: ' Verily I say unto you there is no man that has left housa or brethren or sisters, or father or mother, or wife or children or lands for my sake and the Gospel's but he shall receive one hundredfold now in this time houses and brethren and sisters and mothers and children and lands with persecutions, and in the world to come eternal life. But many that are first shall be last and the last first.'" You have here the result or reward, if you prefer the term, of following the law. I have not taken the trouble of copying similar passages from the other non-Hindu scriptures and I will not insult you by quoting in support of the law stated by Jesus passages from the writings and sayings of our own sages, passages even stronger if possible than the Biblical extracts. I have drawn your attention to, perhaps the strongness of all the testimonies in favour of the affirmative answer to the question before us are the lives of the greatest teachers of the world. Jesus, Muhammad, Buddha, Nanak, Kabir, Chaitanya, Shankara, Dayanand, Ramakrishna were men who exercised an immense influence over and moulded the character of thousands of men. The world is the richer for their having lived in it. A.nd they were all men who deliberately embraced poverty as their lot.

I should not have laboured my point as I have done, if I did not believe that, in so far as we have made the modern materialistic craze our goal, in so far are we going down hill in the path of progress. I hold that economic progress in the sense I have put it is antagonistic to real progress. Hence, the ancient ideal has been the limitation of activities promoting wealth. This does not put an end to all material ambition. We should still have as we have always had in our midst people who make the pursuit of wealth their aim in life. But we have always recognised that it is a fall from the ideals. It is a beautiful thing to know that the wealthiest among us have often felt that to have remained voluntarily poor would have been a higher state for them. That you cannot serve God and Mammon is an economic truth of the highest value. We have to make our choice. Western Nations are to day groaning under the heel of the monster god of materialism. Their moral growth has become stunted. They measure their progress in USD American wealth has become the standard. She is the envy of the other Nations. I have heard many of our countrymen say that we will gain American wealth but avoid its method, I venture to suggest that such an attempt if it were made is fore doomed to failure. We cannot be "wise, temperate and furious" in a moment. I would have our leaders to teach us to be morally supreme in the world.

This land of ours was once, we are told, the abode of the Gods. It is not possible to conceive Gods inhabiting a land which is made hideous by the smoke and the din of mill chimneys and factories and whose road ways are traversed by rushing engines dragging numerous cars crowded with men mostly who know not what they are after, who are often absent minded, and whose tempers do not improve by taking uncomfortably packed like sardines in boxes and finding themselves in the midst of utter strangers who would oust them if they could and, whom they would in their turn oust similarly. I refer to these things because they are held to be symbolical of material progress.

But they add not an atom to our happiness. This is what Wallace, the great scientist, has said as his deliberate judgement. "In the earliest records which have come down to us from the past, we find ample indications that general ethical considerations and conceptions, the accepted standard of morality, and the conduct resulting from these, were in no degree inferior to those which prevail today." In a series of chapters he then proceeds to examine the position of the English Nation under the advance in wealth it has made. He says, "This rapid growth of wealth and increase of our power over nature put too great a strain upon our crude civilization, on our superficial Christianity, and it was accompanied by various forms of social immorality almost as amazing and unprecedented." He then shows how factories have risen on the corpses of men, women and children, how as the country has rapidly advanced in riches it has gone down in morality. He shows this by dealing with insanitation, life destroying trades, adulteration, bribery, and gambling. He shows how with the advance of wealth justice has become immoral, deaths from alcoholism and suicide have increased, the average of premature births and congenital defects has increased and prostitution has become an institution. He concludes his examination by these pregnant remarks:

> "The proceedings of the divorce courts show other aspects of the result of wealth and leisure while a friend who had been a good deal in London society assured me that both in country houses and in London various kinds of orgies were occasionally to be met with which would hardly have been surpassed in the period of the most dissolute Emperors. O War, too, I need say nothing. It has always been more or less chronic since the rise of the Roman Empire; but there is now undoubtedly a disinclination for war among all civilized peoples. Yet the vast burden of armaments taken together with the most pious declarations in favour of peace, must be held to show an almost total absence of morality as a guiding principle among the governing classes."

Under the British aegis we have learnt much, but it is my firm belief that there is little to gain from Britain's intrinsic morality that if we are not careful, we shall introduce all the vices that she has been a prey to, owing to the disease of materialism. We can profit by that connection only if we keep our civilisation, and our morals straight, i.e. if instead of boasting of the glorious past, we express the ancient moral glory in our own lives and let our lives bear witness to our past. Then we shall benefit her and ourselves. If we copy her because she provides us with rulers, both they and we shall suffer degradation. We need not be afraid of ideals or of reducing them to practice even to the utter- most. Ours will only then be a truly spiritual nation when we shall show more truth than gold, greater fearlessness than pomp of power and wealth, greater charity than love of self. If we will but clean our houses, our palaces and temples of the attributes of wealth and show in them the attributes of morality, we can offer battle to any combinations of hostile forces without having to carry the burden of a heavy militia. Let us seek first the Kingdom of God and His righteousness and the irrevocable promise is that everything will be added to us. These are real economics. May you and I treasure them and enforce them in our daily life.

Speech on Education, Ancient and Modern

[Mr. Gandhi addressed in Hindi a public meeting at Allahabad at Munshi Ram Prashad's garden under the chairmanship of the Hon. Pandit Madan Mohan Malaviya. The gathering was a record one even for Munshi Ram Prashad's garden where some of the largest public meetings have been held]

Mr. Gandhi who on rising was greeted with loud and prolonged cheers, said that he should have felt difficulty — of which he was ashamed — in addressing the meeting in Hindi was a striking commentary on the system of modern education which was a part of the subject of his lecture that evening. He would, however, prefer to speak in Hindi although he had greater facility of expression in English. Describing the modern system of education he said that real education was considered to have begun at the college at the age of 16 or 17. The education received in school was not useful. For instance, an Indian student, while he knew well the geography of England, did not possess a sufficient knowledge of the geography of his own country. The history of India which they were taught was greatly distorted, Government service was the aim of their education. Their highest ambition was to become members of the Imperial Legislative Council. The boys abandoned their hereditary occupations, and forsook their mother tongue. They were adopting the English language, European ideas and European dress. They thought in English, conducted all their political and social work and all commercial transactions, etc. in English and thought that they could not do without the English language. They had come to think that there was no other road. Education through English had created a wide gulf between the educated few and the masses. It had created a gulf in the families also. An English educated man had no community of feelings and ideas with the ladies of his family. And, as had been said, the aspirations of the English educated men were fixed on Government service and at the most on membership of the Imperial Legislative Council. He for one could never commend a system of education which produced such a state of things and men educated under such system could not be expected to do any great service to the country. Mr. Gandhi did not mean that the English educated leaders did not feel for the masses. On the other hand, he acknowledged that the Congress and other great public movements were initiated and conducted by them. But, at the same time, he could not help feeling that the work done during all these years would have been much more and much greater progress would have been made if they had been taught in their mother tongue. It was unfortunate, said the speaker, that a feeling had come over them that there was no path to progress other than that which was being followed. They found themselves helplees. But it was not manliness to assume an attitude of helplessness.

Mr. Gandhi then described the ancient system of education and said that even elementary education imparted by the village teacher taught the student all that was necessary for their occupations. Those who went in for higher education became fully conversant with the science of wealth Artha Shastra, ethics and religion Dharma Shastra. In ancient times there were no restrictions on education. It was not controlled by the State but was solely in the hands of the Brahmans who shaped the system of education solely with an eye to the welfare of the people. It was based on restraint and Brahmacharya. It was due to such a system of education that Indian civilization had outlived so many vicissitudes through thousands of years, while such ancient civilization as those of Greece, Rome and Egypt had become extinct. No doubt the wave of a new civilization had been passing through India. But he was sure that it was transitory, it would soon pass away and Indian civilization would be revivified. In ancient times the basis of life was self-restraint but now it was enjoyment. The result was that people had become powerless cowards and forsook the truth. Having come under the influence of another civilization it might be necessary to adapt our own civilization in certain respect to our new environments but we should not make any radical change in a civilization which was acknowledged even by some western scholars to be the best. It might be urged that it was necessary to adopt the methods and instruments of western civilization to meet the material forces of that civilization. But the forces born of spirituality, the bedrock of Indian civilization, were more than a match for material forces. India was pre-eminently the land of religion. It was the first and the last duty of Indians to maintain it as such. They should draw their strength from the Soul, from God. If they adhered to that path Swarajya which they were aspiring to and working for would become their hand-maid.

Speech at Gujarat Educational Conference

[The second Gujarat Educational Conference was held at Broach, in October 20, 1917, when Mr. M. K. Gandhi read his presidential address in Gujarati a translation of which reads as under]

After thanking the conference for the honour bestowed on him he said the selection fell on him simply because he would yield to none in his love and devotion for the Gujarati language. He then congratulated the last conference on the good work done by them and for publishing a very valuable report in time. He then highly regretted the premature loss of Mr. Ranjitram Vavabhai, one of the most active secretaries of the conference. Recapitulating the three objects of the Gujarat Kalavani Mandai under whose auspices the conference was held, he proceeded to treat them in detail.

Medium of Instruction: He regarded the question of the medium of instruction of the highest importance and as one on which the whole edifice of education rested. He referred to the two views held on this question. There is one party that wants the mother tongue Gujarati to be the medium. The other party supports English. Both are prompted by pure motives. Both have the good of the country at heart but purity of motives alone is not sufficient for the achievement of the desired end. Experience of the world shows that often a pure motive lands us on impure around. Let us therefore examine the merits or otherwise of the two views and see if we can arrive at unanimity on this point. This difficult question concerns the whole of India. But that does not mean that each province cannot solve it for itself, but must wait for general unanimity.'

Of course, it would help us to some degree in the solution of this problem if we review the agitation and efforts of other provinces. Bengal during the excitement of the 'partition' days tried to impart instruction in Bengali. Schools were established, funds poured in but the experiment failed. In my humble opinion it failed, because the organisers and teachers had not sufficient faith in their own experiment. The educated Bengali could not get out of the fascination of the English language. It was suggested that Bengali literature owes its development to the command the Bengalis have over the English language. In answer Mr. Gandhi instanced the wonderful Bengali of Sir Rabindranath Tagore which is in no way indebted to the knowledge of English. He owes inspiration to the very atmosphere of India. He has imbibed it from the Upanishads. The same can be said of Mahatma Munshi Ram and Pandit Madan Mohan Malaviya. The service which Swami Dayanand Sarasvati rendered to Hindi literature owed nothing to English. Tukaram and Ramdas who have enriched the Marathi language were not in the least under the obligation of the English language. English cannot claim any credit for the contribution to Gujarati literature of poets from Parmanand and Samel Bhat down to Dalpatram. When we consider how languages grow, we come to the conclusion that a language is but the reflection of the character of the people that speak it. Language depends upon the peculiar genius and occupation of a people. The inordinate use of polished and courtly forms of speech indicate that we have been under subjection for generations together. The English language abounds in nautical terms. We cannot import them in the Gujarati language, but if we take to navigation nautical phraseology will frame of itself.

[Mr. Gandhi then proceeded to give a quotation from Rev. Taylor's grammar of the Gujarati language in support of the above].

He then referred to the laudable efforts of the Arya Samaj in making Hindi the medium of instruction in their Gurukul; and of the Telugu people in using Telugu as the vehicle of education. In Maharashtra Professor Karve and Prof. Naick both work in the same direction. In Professor Bijapurkar's school they had already prepared suitable textbooks in Marathi. They are all hopeful about the success of their work. In Gujarat there was a movement already for imparting instruction through Gujarati. Prof. Gajjar and the late Dewan Bahadur Manibhai Jarbhai may be regarded as the pioneers and it now remains with us to consider whether we shall water the plant sown by them or allow it to wither away.

Experienced teachers say that what takes sixteen years to learn through English can perfectly be acquired in ten years at the most through the vernaculars. If thousands of our students save six years each of their precious life, what a great national saving it would be.

The excessive burden of having to learn through a foreign medium has sapped the strength, enthusiasm and vitality of our young men. Sickly and pale they can at best be mere imitators. All power of initiative, originality and enterprise; courage, discrimination and fearlessness dwindle away as years pass by. What they commence they cannot carry out. The few that show some spirit die young. The Negroes of South Africa are a stalwart and sober race. Social evils like child-marriage are unknown amongst them but they too have suffered like ourselves because they accepted Dutch as the medium of their education. They have grown impotent imitators of the west. With the loss of their mother tongue they lost all vigour and originality. We who have received English education cannot measure the loss we have sustained. If we consider what little hold we have upon our masses we can have some idea of that loss. We are proud of a Bose or a Ray amongst us but I dare say that had we received instruction through the vernacular for the last fifty years we would have had amongst us — so many Boses and Rays that their existence would not have been a matter of surprise to us.

Leaving aside the question whether Japan's activities are in the right direction or not we can say that the extraordinary enterprise and progressive life they have shown is due to their education being given in Japanese. Their education has infused a new life among the people which has been a wonder to the gaping world. Instruction through a foreign medium brings about untold evils.

There must be a correspondence between the impressions and expressions we receive with our mother's milk and the education we receive at school. A foreign medium destroys the correspondence, and whosoever helps this destruction, however pure his motives, is an enemy of his country. The evil does not stop here. The foreign medium has created an unnatural gulf between the educated classes and the masses at large. We do not understand the masses and the masses do not understand us. They regard us as foreigners and they fear and distrust us. If this state of things continues for long, Lord Curzon's charge that we do not represent the masses will some day prove to be true- Fortunately the educated classes have gradually come to realise the difficulty of reaching the masses. They see now that they have over reached the expectations of Lord Macaulay. We took to

English because it led to the acquisition of wealth, and some cultivated the ideas of nationalism through English.

If we were in power we could see the danger of the spread of English at the cost of the vernacular. Even the Government officers have not dispensed with the vernaculars. In offices and law courts they still use the vernaculars. If pleaders conducted their cases in the vernaculars, the clients would gain a great deal, and the language would be enriched.

It is argued that only the English knowing Indians have evinced patriotism. Recent events prove otherwise, but even accepting the assertion we can say that others had no opportunity whatsoever. The patriotism of the English educated has not spread amongst the masses. English may be kept as an optional subject for those who want to study it for political purposes or for the acquisition of wealth by the help of western sciences. Not only should they acquire a good command over the English language but it is also our duty to make facilities for imparting such education.

Before closing this topic he referred to the two pamphlets published by Dr. P. J. Mehta and recommended the audience to peruse them. He then suggested a number of ways and means for preparing a ground for making Gujarati as the medium of instruction such as the use of Gujarati language only in mutual intercourse among the Gujaratis, preparation of Gujarati textbooks, opening schools, etc.

National Language: After dealing with the medium of instruction he dealt at length upon the subject of National language. He gave an able reply to those who suggest that English ought to become the *lingua franca* of India. He said a National language should satisfy the following conditions:

- It must be easy for the official.
- It must be the vehicle of religious, social and political intercourse of the people.
- It must be spoken by a large number.
- It must be easy of acquisition by the masses.

Speech before the Merchants

[In reply to the address given to him by the merchants of Broach, Mr. Gandhi said]

Merchants always have the spirit of adventure, intellect and wealth, as without these qualities their business cannot go on. But now they must have the fervour of patriotism in them. Patriotism is necessary even for religion. If the spirit of patriotism is awakened through the religious fervour, then that patriotism will shine out brilliantly. So it is necessary that patriotism must be roused in the mercantile community.

The merchants take more part in public affairs nowadays than before. When merchants take to politics through patriotism, Swaraj is as good as obtained. Some of you might be wondering how we can get Swaraj. I lay my hand on my heart and say that, when the merchant class understands the spirit of patriotism, then only can we get Swaraj quickly. Swaraj then will be quite a natural thing.

Amongst the various keys which will unlock Swaraj to us, the Swadeshi Vow is the golden one. It is in the hands of the merchants to compel the observance of the Swadeshi Vow in the country, and this is an adventure which can be popularised by the merchants. I humbly request you to undertake this adventure, and then you will see what wonders you can do.

This being so, I have to say with regret that it is the merchant class which has brought ruin to the Swadeshi practice, and the Swadeshi Movement in this country. Complaints have lately risen in Bengal about the increase of rates, and one of them is against Gujarat. It is complained there that the prices of Dhotis have been abnormally increased and Dhotis go from Gujarat. No one wants you not to earn money, but it must be earned righteously and not be ill-gotten. Merchants must earn money by fair means. Unfair means must never be used.

Continuing, Mr. Gandhi said: India's strength lies with the merchant class. So much does not lie even with the army. Trade is the cause of war, and the merchant class has the key of war in their hands. Merchants raise the money and the army is raised on the strength of it. The power of England and Germany rests on their trading class. A country's prosperity depends upon its mercantile community. I consider it as a sign of good luck that I should receive an address from the merchant class. Whenever I remember Broach, I will enquire if the merchants who have given me an address this day have righteous faith and patriotism.

If I receive a disappointing reply, I will think that merely a wave of giving addresses had come over India and that I had a share in it.

Speech on Income and Expenditure Account

[Mr. M. K. Gandhi in submitting an account of the Indian Committee of the income and expenditure up to the January, 1915, in connection with the Passive resistance in South Africa made the following observations]

This struggle had defined principles and removed disabilities which were in the shape of a national insult. The larger question of the treatment of British Indians who come from outside can be dealt with here. For the question of the local disabilities still unredressed, the Indian Committee will have to exercise a ceaseless watch and assist, as heretofore, the efforts of our countrymen in South Africa. I feel that I ought to place on record my strong conviction based upon the close personal observation extending over a period of twenty years that the system of indentured emigration is an evil which cannot be mended, but can only be ended. No matter how humane employers may be, it does not lend itself to the moral well-being of the men affected by it. I, therefore feel that your committee should lose no time in approaching the Government of India with a view to securing the entire abolition of the system for every part of the Empire. I am bound to mention that the struggle would not have ended so soon or even as satisfactorily as it did, but for the generous support rendered by the Motherland under the leadership of the great and saintly patriot, the late Mr. Gokhale, and but for the very sympathetic and firm attitude taken by the nobleman who at present occupies the Viceregal chair.

Speech at Humanitarian Meeting

[A public meeting under the auspices of the Bengal and Bombay Humanitarian Funds was held in October, 1917, at the University Institute, College Square, where Mr. M. K. Gandhi presided. There was a good gathering and the name of Mr. Gandhi was sufficient to attract a pretty large audience. Babu Nilananda Mukherjeet, in a neat title speech proposed Mr. Gandhi to the chair. Mr. Gandhi in opening the meeting asked the audience whether he should speak in English or Hindi and there having been a preponderance of opinion on the side of English, he spoke in English]

Mr. Gandhi regretted that there should be a lack of the understanding and knowledge of Hindi by Indians. All were eager, he said, to do national service, but there could be no National service without a National tongue. He regretted that his Bengali friends were committing National suicide by Omitting to use their National tongue, without which one cannot reach the hearts of the masses. In that sense the wide use of Hindi would come within the purview of humanitarism. Mr. Gandhi next passed to another phase of humanitarism, viz. sacrifice of animals before Goddesses, and slaughter for food. The Hindu Shastras do not really advocate animal sacrifice. This current practice is one of the many things which have passed under the name of Hinduism. The Hindu religion aptly finds expression in the two aphorisms — 44 harmlessness is the best form of religion "and" there is no force higher than Truth," and these principles are incompatible with the cruel practice of animal sacrifice.

Speech at All India Social Service Conference

[On Monday, 31st December, 1917, at 3 p.m. the All-India Social Service Conference was held at the YMCA Hall College Street Calcutta. A large number of ladies and gentlemen were present. Sir Krishna Govinda Gupta in the absence of the Lord Bishop of Calcutta, who was unavoidably absent proposed that Mr. Gandhi should take the chair and in doing so said that Mr. Gandhi lived with the South Africans and suffered with them and he had done so much in Champaran lately and which would be followed in other parts. Mr. Gandhi in taking the chair, spoke as follows]

If I want to hear music, I must come to Bengal. If I want to listen poetry, I must come to Bengal, India is contained in Bengal, but not Bengal in India. I heard some Marvari boys singing songs. It was like jargon. I told them to associate with the Bengalis. [He then delivered the following presidential address].

Friends I thank you for the honour you 'have conferred upon me. I was totally unprepared for the invitation to preside over the deliberations of this assembly. I do not know that I am fitted for the task. Having fixed views about the use of Hindi at national gatherings, I am always disinclined to speak in English. And I felt that the time was not ripe for me to ask to be allowed to deliver the presidential speech in Hindi. Moreover, I have not much faith in conferences. Social Service to be effective has to be rendered without noise. It is best performed when the left hand know not what the right is doing. Sir Gibbie's work told because nobody knew it. He could not be spoiled by praise or held back by blame. Would that our service were of this nature. Holding such views, it was not without considerable hesitation and misgivings that I obeyed the summons of the Reception Committee. You will, therefore, pardon me if you find in me a candid critic rather than an enthusiast carrying the conference to its goal with confidence and assurance.

It seems to me then that I cannot do better than draw attention to some branches of Social Service which we have hitherto more or less ignored.

The greatest service we can render to society is to free ourselves and it from the superstitious regard we have learnt to pay to the learning of the English language. It is the medium of instruction in our schools and colleges. It is becoming the *'lingua franca'* of the country. Our best thoughts are expressed in it. Lord Chelmsford hopes that it will soon take the place of the mother tongue in high families. This belief in the necessity of English training has enslaved us. It has unfitted us for true national service. Were it not for force of habit, we could not fail to see that by reason of English being the medium of instruction, our intellect has been segregated we have been isolated from the masses, the best mind of the nation has become caged and the masses have not received the benefit of the new ideas we have received. We have been engaged these past sixty years in memorising strange words and their pronunciation instead of assimilating facts. In the place of building upon the foundation, training received from our parents, we have almost unlearnt it. There is no parallel to this in History. It is a national tragedy. The first and the greatest Social Service we can render is to revert to our vernaculars to restore Hindi to its natural place as the national language and begin carrying on all our provincial proceedings in our respective vernaculars and national proceedings in Hindi. We ought to rest till our schools and colleges give us instruction through the vernaculars. It ought not to be necessary even for the sake of our English friends to have to speak in English. Every English civil and military officer learns it because they need it for their business. The day must soon come when our legislatures will debate national affairs in the vernaculars or Hindi as the case may be. Hitherto the masses have been strangers to their proceedings. The vernacular papers have tried to undo the mischief a little. But the task was beyond them. The "Patrika" reserves its biting sarcasm, the "Bengali" its learning for ears turned to English. In this ancient land of cultured thinkers the presence in our midst of a Tagore or a Bose or a Roy ought not to excite wonder. Yet the painful fact is that there are so few of them. You will forgive me if I have tarried too long on a subject which in your opinion may hardly be treated as an item of Social Service. I have however taken the liberty of mentioning the matter prominently as it is my conviction that all national activity suffers materially owing to this radical defect in our system of education.

Coming to more familiar items of Social Service, the list is appalling. I shall select only those of which I have any knowledge.

Work in times of sporadic distress such as famine and floods is no doubt necessary and most praiseworthy. But it produces no permanent results. There are fields of Social Service in which there may be no renown but which may yield lasting results.

In 1914, cholera, fevers and plague together claimed 4,639,663 victims. If so many had died fighting on the battlefield during the war that is at present devasting Europe we would have covered ourselves with glory and lovers of Swaraj would need no further argument in support of their cause. As it is 4,639,663 have died a 'lingering death unmourned and their dying has brought us nothing but discredit. A distinguished Englishman said the other day that Englishman did all the thinking for us whilst we sat supine. He added that most Englishmen basing their opinions on their English experience presented impossible or costly remedies for the evils they investigated. There is much truth in the above statement. In other countries reformers have successfully grappled with epidemics. Here Englishmen have tried and failed. They have thought along western lines ignoring the vast differences, climatic and other, between Europe and India. Our doctors and physicians have practically done nothing. I am sure that half a dozen medical men of the front rank dedicating their lives to the work of eradicating the triple curse would succeed where Englishmen have failed. I venture to suggest that the way lies not through finding out cures but through finding or rather applying preventive methods. I prefer to use the participle 4 applying' for I have it on the aforementioned authority that to drive out plague (and I add cholera and malaria) is absurdly simple. There is no conflict of opinion as to the preventive methods. We simply do not apply them. We have made up our minds that the masses will not adopt them. There could be no greater calumny uttered against them. If we would but stoop to conquer, they can be easily conquered. The truth is that we expect the Government to do the work. In my opinion in this matter, the Government cannot lead, they can follow and help if we could lead. Here then, there is work enough for our doctors and an army of workers to help them. I note that you in Bengal are working some what in this direction. I may state that a small but earnest band of volunteers are at the present moment engaged in doing such work in Champaran. They are posted in different villages. There they teach the village children, they give medical aid to the sick and they give practical lessons in hygiene to the village folk by cleaning their wells and roads and showing them how to treat human excreta. Nothing can yet be predicted as to results as the experiments is in its infancy. This Conference may usefully appoint a committee of doctors who would study rural conditions on the spot and draw up a course of instructions for the guidance of workers and of the people at large.

Nothing perhaps affords such splendid facility to every worker, whole time or otherwise, for effective service as the relief of agony through which the 3rd class railway passengers are passing. I feel keenly about this grievance not because I am in it but I have gone to it as I have felt keenly about it. This matter affects millions of our poor and middle class countrymen. This helpless toleration of every inconvenience and insult is visibly deteriorating the nation even as the cruel treatment to which we have subjected the so-called depressed classes has made them indifferent to the laws of personal cleanliness and the very idea of self-respect. What else but down-right degradation can await those who have to make a scramble always like mad animals for seats in a miserable compartment, who have to swear and curse before they can speak through the window in order to get standing room, who have to wallow in dirt during their journey, who are served their food like dogs and eat it like them, who have ever to bend before those who are physically stronger than they and who being packed like sardines in compartments have to get such sleep as they can in a sitting posture for nights together. Railway servants swear at them, cheat them. On the Howrah Lahore service our friends from Kabul fill to the brim the cup of the misery of the 3rd class travellers. They become lords of the compartments they enter. It is not possible for any one to resist them. They swear at you on the slightest pretext, exhaust the whole of the obscene vocabulary of the Hindi language. They do not hesitate to belabour you if you retort or in any way oppose them. They usurp the best seats and insist on stretching themselves full length even in crowded compartments. No compartment is deemed too crowded for them to enter. The travellers patiently bear all their awful impertinence out of sheer helplessness. They would, if they could, knock down the man who dared to swear at them as do these Kabulis. But they are physically no match for the Kabulis and every Kabuli considers, himself more than a match for any number of travellers from the plains. This is not right. The effect of this terrorising on the national character cannot but be debasing. We, the educated few ought to deliver the travelling public from this scourage or for ever renounce our claim to speak on its behalf or to guide it. I believe the Kabulis to be amenable to reason. They are a God-fearing people. If you know their language, you can successfully appeal to their good sense. But they are spoilt children of nature. Cowards among us have used their undoubted physical strength for our nefarious purposes. And they have now come to think that they can treat poor people as they choose and consider them- selves above the law of the land. Here is work enough for Social Service Volunteers for this class of work can board trains and educate the people to a sense of their duty, call in guards and other officials in order to remove over crowding see that passengers leave and board trains without a scramble. It is clear that until the Kabulis can be patiently taught to behave themselves, they ought to have a compartment ail to themselves and they ought not to be permitted to enter any other compartment. With the exception of providing additional plant, every one of the other evil attendant on railway travelling ought to be immediately redressed. It is no answer that we have suffered the wrong so long. Prescriptive rights can not accrue to wrongs.

No less important is the problem of the depressed classes. To lift them from the position to which Hindu society has reduced them is to remove a big blot on Hinduism. The present treatment of these classes is a sin against religion and humanity.

But the work requires service of the highest order. We shall make little headway by merely throwing schools at them. We must change the attitude of the masses and orthodoxy. I have already shown that we have cut ourselves adrift from both. We do not react on them. We can do so only if we speak to them in their own language. An anglicised India cannot speak to them with effect. If we believe in Hinduism we must approach them in the Hindu fashion. We must do 'tapsya ' and keep oar Hinduism undefiled. Pure and enlightened orthodoxy must be matched against superstitious and ignorant orthodoxy. To restore to their proper status a fifth of our total population is a task worthy of any Social Service organisation.

The bastis of Calcutta and the chawls of Bombay badly demand the devoted services of hundreds of social workers. They send our infants to an early grave and promote vice, degradation and filth.

Apart from the fundamental evil arising out of our defective system of education I have hitherto dealt with evils calling for service among the masses. The classes perhaps demand no less attention than the masses. It is my opinion that all evils like diseases are symptoms of the same evil or disease. They appear various by being refracted through different media. The root evil is loss of true spirituality brought about through causes I cannot examine from this platform. We have lost the robust faith of our forefathers in the absolute efficacy of 'Satya' (truth) 'Ahimsa' (love) and 'Brahmacharya' (Self-restraint). We certainly believe in them to an extent. They are the best policy but we may deviate from them if our untrained reason suggests deviation. We have not faith enough to feel that though the present outlook seems black, if we follow the dictates of truth and exercise self restraint, the ultimate result must be sound. Men whose spiritual vision has become blurred mostly look to the present rather than conserve the future good. He will render the greatest social service who will reinstate us in our ancient spirituality. But humble men that we are, it is enough for us if we recognise the loss and by such ways as are open to us prepare the way for the man who will infect us with his power and enable us to feel clearly through the heart, things we are today unable to perceive through our reason.

Looking then at the classes I find that our Rajahs and Maharajahs squander their resources after the so-called useless sport and drink. I was told the other day that the cocaine habit was sapping the nation's manhood and that like the drink habit it was on the increase and in its effect more deadly than drink. It is impossible for a social worker to blind himself to the evil. We dare not ape the West. We are a nation that has lost its prestige and its self-respect. Whilst a tenth of our population is living on the verge of starvation, we have no time for indulging ourselves. What the West may do with impunity is likely in our case to prove our ruin. The evils that are corroding the higher starta of society are difficult for an ordinary worker to tackle. They have acquired a certain degree of respectability. But they ought not to be beyond the reach of this Conference.

Equally important is the question of the status of women both Hindu and Mohammedan. Are they or are they not to play their full part in the plan of regeneration alongside of their husband? They must be enfranchised. They can no longer be treated either as dolls or slaves without the social body remaining in a condition of social paralysis. And here again I would venture to suggest to the reformer that the way to woman's freedom is not through education but through the change of attitude on the part of men and corresponding action. Education is necessary but it must follow the freedom. We dare not wait for literary education to restore our womanhood to its proper state. Even without literary education our women are as cultured as any on the face of the earth. The remedy largely lies in the hands of husbands.

It makes my blood boil as I wander through the country and watch lifeless and fleshless oxen with their ribs sticking through their skins, carrying loads or ploughing our fields. To improve the breed of our cattle, to rescue them from the cruelty practised on them by their cow worshipping masters and to save them from the slaughter house is to solve half the problem of our poverty . . . We have to educate the people to a humane use of their cattle and plead with the government to conserve the pasture land of the country. Protection of the cow is an economic necessity. It cannot be brought about by force. It can only be achieved by an appeal to the finer feelings of our English friends and our Mohammedan countrymen to save the cow from the slaughter house. This question involves the overhauling of the management of our Pinjra — poles and cow protection societies. A proper solution of this very difficult problem means establishment of perfect concord between Hindus and Mohammedans.

I have glanced at the literature kindly furnished at my request by the several Leagues who are rendering admirable Social Service. I note that some have included in their pro- gramme many of the items/mentioned by me. All the Leagues are non-sectarian and they have as their members the most distinguished men and women in the land. The possibilities for services of a far reaching character are therefore great. But if the wirk is to leave its impress on the nation, we must have workers who are prepared, in Mr. Gokhale's words — to dedicate their lives to the cause.

Speech on Kaira Distress

[An influential and largely attended meeting of Bombay merchants and traders was held (February 1918) at the Mooljijetha Market under the presidency of Mr. Jamnadas Dwarkadas, when Mr. M. K. Gandhi who had specially come to Bombay, explained to the audience the situation in the Kaira district. Mr. Gandhi, in a brief but lucid speech, narrated the whole story with the fervour and conviction so characteristic of him. Mr. Gandhi on rising to speak was greeted with loud cheers from all sides. He said:]

I do not want to say much. I have received a letter asking me to be present at tomorrow's deputation that is going to wait on his Excellency the Governor, and I am sure I will be able to explain to him the true facts. Still I must make it clear here that the responsibility of the notice issued by the Gujarat Sabha lies on me. I was at Ahmedabad before that notice was issued, where the matter of Kaira district was being discussed, when it was decided that the Gujarat Sabha ought to take part in the matter. I think that as regards this notice, a mountain has been made out of a molehill. Every one knew what the notice was when it was being framed. Nobody then even dreamt that Government would misinterpret it. The Sabha had with it sufficient data about the plight of the people. They came to know that Government officials were collecting taxes and the people were even selling their cattle to pay the taxes. The matter had come to such a pass, and, knowing this, the Sabha thought it better to issue a notice to console the people who braved these hardships. And the notice was the result of that information, and I have every hope that in the deputation that is going to wait on the Governor, the result of the deliberations will end in the success of the people.

Commissioner's Wrath: If the Commissioner had not been angry with us, and had talked politely with the deputation that waited on him, and had not misinstructed the Bombay Government, such a grave crisis would not have eventuated, and we would not have had the trouble of meeting here this evening. The Sabha's request was to suspend the collection of dues till the negotiations were over. But Government did not take this proper course and issued an angry Press Note. It was my firm belief — and even now I firmly believe — that the representatives of the people and Government could have joined together and taken the proper steps. I regret to have to say that Government has made a mistake. Perhaps subordinate officers of Government would say to Government that the notice was issued not from a pure motive, but from some other ulterior motive. If Government are impressed with this erroneous belief, those who have stood by the people, I hope, will continue to stand by them to the end and will not retreat. Any responsible right-thinking man could have given them the same advice. People possess the same rights as the authorities have, and public men have every right to advise the people of their rights. The people that do not fight for their rights are like slaves, and such people do not deserve Home Rule. When authorities think that they can take anything from the people and can interfere, a difficult situation arises. And if such a situation arises, I must plainly say that those who have given the people the right advice, will stand by them till the end.

Two Weapons: I have not yet come to any conclusion, and I sincerely trust that those who understand the responsibility, will not hesitate to undergo hardships in order to secure justice. And in such an eventuality I hope you will not beat an ignominious retreat. The first and the last principle of passive resistance is that we should not inflict hardships on others, but put up with them ourselves in order to get justice, and Government need not fear anything if we make up our mind, as we are bent on getting sheer justice from it and nothing else. To get that justice we must fight with the authorities and the people that do not so fight are but slaves. We can have only two weapons on occasions like this: Revolt or passive resistance, and my request is for the second remedy always. The right of suffering hardships, and claiming justice and getting our demands is from one's birth. Similarly we have to get justice at the hands of Government by suffering hardships. We must suffer hardships like brave men. What I have to say is, resort to the right means, and that very firmly, in order to remove the distress through which the Gujarat people are passing. It is my conviction that if we tell the truth to the British Government it can ultimately be convinced, and if only we are firm in our resolve, rest assured that Kaira people shall suffer wrongs no more.

Speech on Fight to Maintain Truth

[On 18th April, 1918, Mahatma Gandhi and company visited Ras — a large village in Borsad Taluka. A meeting of two thousand and five hundred cultivators was held at which agriculturists from the villages of Jantrah Banijari, Kanabha, Amiyad, Divel, Dabhasi, Gorel Sajpur, Khanpur, Vadeli and Kathana were present]

Mahatmaji in his address said that he had full knowledge of the responsibility he had undertaken by giving them the advice he did. He was also aware that it was increasing day by day. And yet he said he did not think he ever dreamt that he should withdraw the advice. As days passed by he felt that had he not given them the advice he had, he would have been untrue to the salt of Gujarat, and there would have been a gap in his service which he was peacefully rendering to it.

He then pointed out the two reasons why he advised them so. Firstly, that men as well as women would be ennobled by it. Secondly, to assert the right of the people to be heard when there was difference of opinion between the people and the Government. Mr. Gandhi said: "The Government has been acting till now as if the people's opinions count for nothing. Such is the experience of members of legislative councils and municipalities. We have got no scope there to assert our opinions." He then described how people lived in fear of Government officials. He said: "Such a condition of yours is even worse than that of brutes." He then asked them to give up fear, if they wanted to be ' men.'

Proceeding, he said that the nature of our struggle was twofold. Firstly, it will teach us to be fearless. He said, "We are not going to be insolent in our fight. We desire to fight by means of soul-force. We are not going to win success in our struggle by giving pains to others. We shall obtain success enduring pain ourselves. Our 'shastras' say that to obtain happiness we have to endure pain. What did 'Dashrath' do to obtain such sons as Bharat, Ram, Laxman and Shatrughna? He performed penances. What did Nala do? Austerities. He endured a great deal of pains for the sake of his self-respect, for preserving Truth. Damyanti also endured pain for the same. That is why we remember them in our morning prayer. Such men have left us a heritage of that virtue truth, and we are going to add to it by enduring more pain for the same. By enduring pain shall we able to remove it?"

He then pointed the twofold benefit involved in the struggle. First, it was that of suspension; second, that of teaching the Government to respect popular opinions. Finally he said: From things so ' Satyagraha ' will remove" all pains. It is a "panacea of all evils."

Speech on Sense of Duty

[The following exhortation was addressed by Mr. M, K. Gandhi to the Tamil community of South Africa]

Remember that we are descendants, of Prahlad and Sudhanva, both passive resisters of the purest type. They disregarded the dictates even of their parents, when they were asked to deny God. They suffered extreme torture rather than inflict suffering on their persecutors. We in the Transvaal are being called upon to deny God, in that we are required to deny our manhood, go back upon our oath, and accept an insult to our nation Shall we, in the present crisis, do less than our forefathers?

10

Golden Words of the Mahatma

- Live as if your were to die tomorrow. Learn as if you were to live forever.
- If you don't ask, you don't get.
- Poverty is the worst form of violence.
- The history of the world is full of men who rose to leadership, by sheer force of self-confidence, bravery and tenacity.
- Prayer is not an old woman's idle amusement. Properly understood and applied, it is the most potent instrument of action.
- The difference between what we do and what we are capable of doing would suffice to solve most of the world's problems.
- Why do blacks identify with the Christian religion of their oppressors?
- Indolence is a delightful but distressing state; we must be doing something to be happy. Action is no less necessary than thought to the instinctive tendencies of the human frame.

- Adaptability is not imitation. It means power of resistance and assimilation.
- It is unwise to be too sure of one's own wisdom. It is healthy to be reminded that the strongest might weaken and the wisest might err.
- As human beings, our greatness lies not so much in being able to remake the world - that is the myth of the atomic age - as in being able to remake ourselves.
- Anger and intolerance are the enemies of correct understanding.
- A "No" uttered from deepest conviction is better and greater than a "Yes" merely uttered to please, or what is worse, to avoid trouble.
- You must be the change you wish to see in the world.
- Love the sinner but hate the sin.
- Seven sins of life: Politics without principle. Commerce without morality. Wealth without work. Education without character. Science without humanity. Pleasure without conscience. Worship without sacrifice.
- God alone is the judge of true greatness because He knows men's hearts.
- The only tyrant I accept in this world is the still voice within.
- Fear has its use but cowardice has none.
- Cowards can never be moral.
- All crime is a kind of disease and should be treated as such.
- No culture can live, if it attempts to be exclusive.
- Culture of the mind must be subservient to the heart.
- Honest differences are often a healthy sign of progress.
- In this age of the rule of brute force, it is almost impossible for anyone to believe that any one else could possibly reject the law of the final supremacy of brute force.

- If we practice and eye for an eye and a tooth for a tooth, soon the whole world will be blind and toothless.
- The weak can never forgive. Forgiveness is the attribute of the strong.
- Freedom is not worth having if it does not connote freedom to err.
- Good government is no substitute for self-government.
- If I had no sense of humour, I would long ago have committed suicide.
- When I despair, I remember that all through history the way of truth and love has always won. There have been tyrants and murderers and for a time they seemed invincible but in the end, they always fell - Think of it, Always.
- In a gentle way, you can shake the world.
- God comes to the hungry in the form of food.
- To believe what has not occurred in history will not occur at all, is to argue disbelief in the dignity of man.
- The best way to find yourself is to lose yourself in the service of others.
- They cannot take away our self-respect if we do not give it to them.
- Consciously or unconsciously, every one of us does render some service or other. If we cultivate the habit of doing this service deliberately, our desire for service will steadily grow stronger and we will make not only our own happiness, but that of the world at large.
- It is the quality of our work which will please God and not the quantity.
- There is more to life than increasing its speed.
- Intolerance betrays want of faith in one's cause.
- I am prepared to die, but there is no cause for which I am prepared to kill.

- My life is my message.
- The good man is the friend of all living things.
- A coward is incapable of exhibiting love; it is the prerogative of the brave.
- I first learned the concepts of non-violence in my marriage.
- Increase of material comforts, it may be generally laid down, does not in any way whatsoever conduct to moral growth.
- I believe in equality for everyone, except reporters and photographers.
- It is better to be violent, if there is violence in our hearts, than to put on the cloak of nonviolence to cover impotence.
- Cowards can never be moral.
- Unity to be real must stand the severest strain without breaking.
- The greatness of a nation can be judged by the way its animals are treated.
- To believe in something, and not to live it, is dishonest.
- Among the many misdeeds of the British rule in India, history will look upon the act of depriving a whole nation of arms as the blackest.
- President means chief servant.
- Purity of mind and idleness are incompatible.
- Our life is a long and arduous quest for Truth and the soul requires inward restfulness to attain its full height.
- Patience means self-suffering.
- Personally, I hold that a man, who deliberately and intelligently takes a pledge and then breaks it, forfeits his manhood.
- Prayer is a confession of one's own unworthiness and weakness.
- Prayer is the key of the morning and the bolt of the evening.

- Non-violence is the article of faith.
- Remember that there is always a limit to self-indulgence, but none to self-restraint.
- The mice which helplessly find themselves between the cats' teeth acquire no merit from their enforced sacrifice.
- Satisfaction lies in the effort, not in the attainment, full effort is full victory.
- Not to have control over the senses is like sailing in a rudderless ship, bound to break to pieces on coming in contact with the very first rock.
- Strength does not come from physical capacity. It comes from an indomitable will.
- Those who know how to think need no teachers.
- Unity to be real must stand the severest strain without breaking.
- I have known many meat eaters to be far more nonviolent than vegetarians.
- A vow is fixed and unalterable determination to do a thing, when such a determination is related to something noble which can only uplift the man who makes the resolve.
- Your capacity to keep your vow will depend on the purity of your life.
- There is nothing that wastes the body like worry, and one who has any faith in God should be ashamed to worry about anything whatsoever.
- A policy is a temporary creed liable to be changed, but while it holds good it has got to be pursued with apostolic zeal.

11

Mahatma Gandhi's Life at a Glance

1869, October , 2: Born at Porbandar, Kathiawad, son of Karamchand (Kaba) and Putlibai Gandhi.

1876: Attended primary school in Rajkot, where his family moved. Betrothed to Kasturbai (called Kasturba in her old age), daughter of Gokuldas Makanji, a merchant.

1881: Entered high school in Rajkot.

1883: Married to Kasturba.

1885: Father died at age of 63.

1887: Passed matriculation examination at Ahmedabad and entered Samaldas College, Bhavnagar, Kathiawad, but found studies difficult and remained for only one term.

1888: First of four sons born.

1891, September: Sailed from Bombay for England to study law.

1892: Returned to India after being called to bar. Began practice of law in Bombay and Rajkot.

1893, April: Sailed for South Africa to become lawyer for an Indian firm. Found himself subjected to all kinds of colour discrimination.

1894: Prepared to return to India after completing law case, but was persuaded by Indian community to remain in South Africa and do public work and earn a living as a lawyer. Drafted first petition sent by the Indians to a South African legislature.

May: Organised Natal Indian Congress.

1896: Returned to India for six months to bring back his wife and two children to Natal.

December: Sailed for South Africa with family. Was mobbed when he disembarked at Durban for what Europeans thought he wrote about South Africa when he was in India.

1899: Organised Indian Ambulance Corps for British in Boer War.

1901: Embarked with family for India, promising to return to South Africa if Indian community there needed his services again.

1901-02: Travelled extensively in India, attended Indian National Congress meeting in Calcutta, and opened law office in Bombay.

1902: Returned to South Africa after urgent request from Indian community.

1903: Opened law office in Johannesburg.

1904: Established the weekly journal, Indian Opinion. Organised Phoenix Settlement near Durban, after reading Ruskin's "Unto This Last".

1906, March: Organised Indian Ambulance Corps for Zulu "Rebellion". Took vow of continence for life.

September: First satyagraha campaign began with meeting in Johannesburg in protest against proposed Asiatic ordinance directed against Indian immigrants in Transvaal.

October: Sailed for England to present Indians' case to Colonial Secretary and started back to South Africa in December.

1907, June: Organised satyagraha against compulsory registration of Asians (The Black Act).

1908, January: Stood trial for instigating satyagraha and was sentenced to two months' imprisonment in Johannesburg jail (his first imprisonment). Was summoned to consult General Smuts at Pretoria; compromise reached; was released from jail.

February: Attacked and wounded by Indian extremist, Mir Alam, for reaching settlement with Smuts.

August: After Smuts broke agreement, second satyagraha campaign began with bonfire of registration certificates.

October: Arrested for not having a certificate, and sentenced to two months' imprisonment in Volksrust jail.

1909, February: Sentenced to three months' imprisonment in Volksrust and Pretoria jails.

June: Sailed for England again to present Indians' case.

November: Returned to South Africa, writing "Hind Swaraj" *en route.*

1910, May: Established Tolstoy Farm near Johannesburg.

1913: Began penitential fast (one meal a day for more than four months) because of moral lapse of two members of Phoenix Settlement.

September: Helped campaign against nullification of marriages not celebrated according to Christian rites, with Kasturba and other women being sentenced for crossing the Transvaal border without permits.

November: Third satyagraha campaign begun by leading "great march" of 2,000 Indian miners from Newcastle across Transvaal border in Natal. Arrested three times in four days (at Palmford, Standerton, and Teakworth) and sentenced at Dundee to nine months' imprisonment; tried at Volksrust in second trial and sentenced to three months' imprisonment with his European co-workers, Polak and Kallenbach. Imprisoned in Volksrust jail for a few days and then taken to Bloemfontein in Orange Free State.

December: Released unconditionally in expectation of a compromise settlement, C. F. Andrews and W. W. Pearson having been sent by Indians in India to negotiate.

1914, January: Underwent fourteen days' fast for moral lapse of members of Phoenix Settlement. Satyagraha campaign suspended, with pending agreement between Smuts, C. F. Andrews, and Gandhi, and with ultimate passage of Indian Relief Act.

July: Left South Africa sailing from Cape Town for London with Kasturba and Kallenbach, arriving just at beginning of World War I. Organised Indian Ambulance Corps in England, but was obliged to sail for India because of pleurisy.

1915: Secured removal of customs harassment of passengers at Viramgam; first incipient satyagraha campaign in India.

May: Established Satyagraha Ashram at Kochrab, near Ahmedabad, and soon admitted an untouchable family; in 1917 moved Ashram to new site on Sabarmati River.

1916, February: Gave speech at the opening of Hindu University at Banaras.

1917: Helped secure removal of recruiting of South African indenture workers in India. Led successful satyagraha campaign for rights of peasants on indigo plantations in Champaran. Defied an order to leave area in April, was arrested at Motihari and tried, but case was withdrawn. Mahadev Desai joined him at Champaran.

1918, February: Led strike of mill workers at Ahmedabad. Mill owners agreed to arbitration after his three-day fast (his first fast in India).

March: Led satyagraha campaign for peasants in Kheda. Attended Viceroy's War Conference at Delhi and agreed that Indians should be recruited for World War I. Began recruiting campaign, but was taken ill and came near death; agreed to drink goat's milk and learned spinning during convalescence.

1919: Rowlatt Bills (perpetuating withdrawal of civil liberties for seditious crimes) passed, and first all-India satyagraha campaign conceived.

April: Organised nationwide hartal — suspension of activity for a day — against Rowlatt Bills.

Arrested at Kosi near Delhi on the way to Punjab and escorted back to Bombay, but never tried. Fasted at Sabarmati for three days in penitence for violence and suspended satyagraha campaign, which he called a "Himalayan Miscalculation" because people were not disciplined enough. Assumed editorship of English weekly, Young India, and Gujarati weekly, Navajivan.

October: After five months' refusal, authorities allowed him to visit scene of April disorders in Punjab. Worked closely with

Motilal Nehru. Conducted extensive enquiry into violence in many Punjab villages.

1920, April: Elected president of All-India Home Rule League.

June: Successfully urged resolution for a satyagraha campaign of non-cooperation at Muslim Conference at Allahabad and at Congress sessions at Calcutta (Sept.) and Nagpur (Dec.).

August: Second all-India satyagraha campaign began, when he gave up Kaisar-e-Hind medal.

1921: Presided at opening of first shop selling homespun (khadi) in Bombay.

August: Presided at bonfire of foreign cloths in Bombay.

September: Gave up wearing shirt and cap and resolved to wear only a loin-cloth in devotion to homespun cotton and simplicity.

November: Fasted at Bombay for five days because of communal rioting following visit of Prince of Wales (later Edward VIII and Duke of Windsor).

December: Mass civil disobedience, with thousands in jail. Gandhi invested with "sole executive authority" on behalf of Congress.

1922, February: Suspended mass disobedience because of violence at Chauri Chaura and undertook five-day fast of penance at Bardoli.

March: Arrested at Sabarmati on charge of sedition in Young India. Pleaded guilty in famous statement at the "great trial" in Ahmedabad before Judge Broomfield. Sentenced to six years' imprisonment in Yeravda jail.

1923: Wrote "Satyagraha" in South Africa and part of his autobiography in prison.

1924, January: Was operated on for appendicitis and unconditionally released from prison in February.

September: Began 21-day "great fast" at Muhammad Ali's home at Delhi as penance for communal rioting (between Hindus and Muslims), especially at Kohat.

December: Presided over Congress session at Belgaum as president.

1925, November: Fasted at Sabarmati for seven days because of misbehaviour of members of Ashram.

December: Announced one-year political silence and immobility at Congress session at Kanpur.

1927: No-tax satyagraha campaign launched at Bardoli, led by Sardar Patel.

1928, December: Moved compromise resolution at Congress session at Calcutta, calling for complete independence within one year, or else the beginning of another all-India satyagraha campaign.

1929, March: Arrested for burning foreign cloths in Calcutta and fined one rupee.

December: Congress session at Lahore declared complete independence and a boycott of the legislature and fixed January 26 as National Independence Day. Third all-Indian satyagraha campaign began.

1930, 12 March: Set out from Sabarmarti with 79 volunteers on historic salt march for 200 miles to sea at Dandi.

6-April: Broke salt law by picking salt up at seashore as whole world watched.

May: Arrested by armed policemen at Karadi and imprisoned in Yeravda jail without trial. One hundred thousand persons arrested. There was no Congress session in December because all leaders were in jail.

1931, January: Released unconditionally with 30 other Congress leaders.

March: Gandhi-Irwin Pact signed, which ended civil disobedience.

August: Sailed from Bombay accompanied by Desai, Naidu, Mira, etc. for the Second Round Table Conference, arriving in London via Marseilles, where he was met by C. F. Andrews. Resided at Kingsley Hall in London slums, broadcast to America, visited universities, met celebrities, and attended Round Table Conference sessions.

December: Left England for Switzerland, where he met Romain Rolland, and Italy, where he met Mussolini. Arrived in India. Was authorised by Congress to renew satyagraha campaign (fourth nationwide effort).

1932, January: Arrested in Bombay with Sardar Patel and detained without trial at Yeravda prison.

September, 20: Began "perpetual fast unto death" while in prison in protest of British action giving separate electorates to untouchables.

September, 26: Concluded "epic fast" with historic cell scene in presence of Tagore after British accepted "Yeravda Pact".

December: Joined fast initiated by another prisoner, Appasaheb Patwardhan, against untouchability; but fast ended in two days.

1933: Began weekly publication of Harijan in place of Young India.

8 May: Began self-purification fast of 21 days against untouchability and was released from prison by government on first day. Fast concluded after 21 days at Poona.

July: Disbanded Sabarmati Ashram, which became centre for removal of untouchability

August: Arrested and imprisoned at Yeravda for four days with 34 members of his Ashram. When he refused to leave Yeravda village for Poona, he was sentenced to one year's imprisonment at Yeravda.

August, 16: Began fast against refusal of government to grant him permission to work against untouchability while in prison; on fifth day of fast he was removed to Sassoon Hospital; his health was precarious; he was unconditionally released on eighth day.

November: Began ten-month tour of every province in India to help end untouchability. Kasturba arrested and imprisoned for sixth time in two years.

1934: Three separate attempts made on his life.

July: Fasted at Wardha Ashram for seven days in penance against intolerance of opponents of the movement against untouchability.

October: Launched All-India Village Industries Association.

1935: Health declined; moved to Bombay to recover.

1936: Visited Seagon, a village near Wardha in the Central Provinces, and decided to settle there... (This was renamed Sevagram in 1940 and eventually became an Ashram for his Disciples).

1937, January: Visited Travancore for removal of untouchability.

1938: Tour of Northwest Frontier Province with Khan Abdul Ghaffar Khan.

1939, March: Began fast unto death as part of satyagraha campaign in Rajkot; fast ended four days later when Viceroy appointed an arbitrator.

1940, October: Launched limited, individual civil-disobedience campaign against Britain's refusal to allow Indians to express their opinions regarding World War II — 23,000 persons imprisoned within a year.

1942: Harijan resumed publication after being suspended for 15 months.

March: Met Sir Stafford Cripps in New Delhi but called his proposals "a post-dated cheque"; they were ultimately rejected by Congress.

August: Congress passed "Quit India" resolution — the final nationwide satyagraha campaign — with Gandhi as leader.

August, 9: Arrested with other Congress leaders and Kasturba and imprisoned in Agha Khan Palace near Poona, with populace revolting in many parts of India. He began correspondence with Viceroy. Mahadev Desai, his secretary and intimate worker died in Palace.

1943, February, 10: Began 21-day fast at Agha Khan Palace to end deadlock of negotiations between Viceroy and Indian leaders.

1944, February 22: Kasturba died in detention at Agha Khan Palace at the age of seventy-four.

6 May: After decline in health, was released unconditionally from detention (this was his last imprisonment; he spent 2,338 days in jail during his life time).

September: Important talks with Jinnah of Muslim League in Bombay. on Hindu-Muslim unity.

1946, March: Conferred with British Cabinet Mission in New Delhi.

November: Began four-month tour of 49 villages in East Bengal to quell communal rioting over Muslim representation in provisional government.

1947, March: Began tour of Bihar to lessen Hindu-Muslim tensions. Began conferences in New Delhi with Viceroy (Lord Mountbatten) and Jinnah.

May: Opposed Congress decision to accept division of the country into India and Pakistan.

August, 15: Fasted and prayed to combat riots in Calcutta as India was partitioned and granted independence.

September: Fasted for three days to stop communal violence in Calcutta. Visited Delhi and environs to stop rioting and to visit camps of refugees (Hindus and Sikhs from Punjab).

1948, January, 13: Fasted for five days in Delhi for communal unity.

January, 20: Bomb exploded in midst of his prayer meeting at Birla House, Delhi.

January, 30: Assassinated in 78th year at Birla House by Nathuram Vinayak Godse.

the [illegible] duty of Indians to maintain it as such. They should draw their strength from the Soul, from God. If they adhered to that path Swarajya which they were aspiring to and working for would become their hand-maid.

Speech at Gujarat Educational Conference

[The second Gujarat Educational Conference was held at Broach, in October 20, 1917, when Mr. M. K. Gandhi read his presidential address in Gujarati a translation of which reads as under]

After thanking the conference for the honour bestowed on him he said the selection fell on him simply because he would yield to none in his love and devotion for the Gujarati language. [illegible] the last conference on the good work [illegible] publishing a very valuable report in time. He [illegible] the premature loss of Mr. Ranjitram [illegible] one of the [illegible] secretaries of the conference. Recapitulating [illegible] the Gujarat Kelavani Mandal under whose auspices the conference was held, he proceeded to treat them in detail.

Medium of Instruction: He regarded the question of the medium of instruction of the highest importance and as one [illegible]

[illegible]

Bibliography

Acharlu, K. S.: *The Story of Mahatma Gandhi*, Academy of Gandhian Studies, Hyderabad, 1990.

Afaque, K. M.: *Gandhian Approach to Communal Harmony: A Critical Study*, Ajanta, Delhi, 1986.

Ali, S. S.: *Gandhi and South Africa*, Hind Pocket Books, Delhi, 1994.

Alter, Joseph S.: *Gandhi's Body: Sex, Diet and the Politics of Nationalism*, University of Pennsylvania Press, Philadelphia, 2000.

Ambedkar, B. R.: *What Congress and Gandhi Have Done to the Untouchables*, K. Santhanam's Ambedkar's Attack Lahore, 1977.

Andrews, C. F.: M. K. *Gandhi: A Sketch of his Life and Work*, In Speeches and Writings of M. K. Gandhi, G.A. Natesan, 1933.

Archarya, N. V. R. K.: *The Gandhian Era*, Cauvery Publications, Hyderabad, 1990.

Ashe, G.: *Gandhi: A Study in Revolution*, Heinemann, London, 1968.

Athyle, D. V.: *The Life of Mahatma Gandhi*, Swadeshi Publishing Co., Poona, 1923.

Attenborough, R.: *In Search of Gandhi, Piscataway*, New Century Publishers, New Jersey, 1982.

Bakshi, S. R.: *Gandhi and Champaran Satyaqraha*, Akashdeep, Delhi, 1988.

Balvantsinha: *Under the Shelter of Bapu*, Navjivan, Ahmedabad, 1962.

Bernays, R.: *Naked Faquir*, Henry Holt, New York, 1932.

Bhana, S. and Brain, J. B.: *Setting Down Roots: Indian Immigrants in South Africa*, Witwatersrand University Press, Johannesburg, 1990.

Bhana, Surendra and Goolam Vahed: *The Making of a Political Reformer: Gandhi in South Africa*, Manohar, New Delhi, 2005.

Bharathi, K. S.: Gandhi and Nehru, Indus, New Delhi, 1990.

Bhattacharya, B. C.: *Mahatma Gandhi*, Gulab Vazirani, New Delhi, 1977.

Bhattacharyya, S. N.: *Mahatma Gandhi: The Journalist*, Asia Publishing, Bombay, 1965.

Bishop, D. H.: *Thinkers of the Indian Renaissance*, Wiley, New Delhi, 1982.

Bolton, G.: *The Tragedy of Gandhi*, Allen & Unwin, London, 1934.

Bondurant, Joan, V.: *Conquest of Violence: The Gandhian Philosophy of Conflict*, Princeton UP, 1988.

Borman, William: *Gandhi and Non-Violence*, State University of New York Press, New York, 1986.

Brock, P.: *The Mahatma and Mother India: Essays on Gandhi's Non-violence and Nationalists*, Navjivan, Ahmedabad, 1983.

Brookes, E. H.: *South Africa in a Changing World*, Oxford University Press, Cape Town, 1953.

Brown, J. M.: *Gandhi: Prisoner of Hope*, Yale University Press, New Haven, 1989.

Byles, M. B.: *The Lotus and the Spinning Wheel*, Allen & Unwin, London, 1963.

Catlin, G. E. G.: *In the Path of Mahatma Gandhi*, Macdonald, London, 1948.

Chadha, Yogesh: *Gandhi: A Life*.

Chakrabarti, M.: *Gandhian Spiritualism: A Quest or the Essence of Excellence*, Concept Publishing, New Delhi, 1993.

Chakravarty, A.: *Mahatma Gandhi and the Modern World*, The Book House, Calcutta, 1945.

Chandra, B.: *Freedom Struggle*, National Book Trust, New Delhi, 1972.

Chatterjee, B. L.: *Gandhi: Champion of the Proletariat*, Prakashani, Calcutta, 1944.

Chatterjee, Margaret: *Gandhi's Religious Thought*, University of Notre Dame Press, 1983.

Chaudhury, P. C. R.: *Gandhi and His Contemporaries*, Sterling, New Delhi, 1986.

Chernus, Ira: *American Nonviolence: The History of an Idea.*

Copley, A. R. H.: *Gandhi: Against the Tide*, Blackwell, Oxford, 1987.

Cursons, W. E.: *Joseph Poke: The Missionary Hearted*, Christian Literature Depot, Johannesburg, 1929.

Dalton, Dennis: *Mahatma Gandhi: Nonviolent Power in Action*, Columbia University Press, New York, 1993.

————: *Mahatma Gandhi: Selected Political Writings*, Hackett Publishing Company, Indianapolis/Cambridge, 1996.

Desai, V. G.: *A Gandhi Anthology*, Navjivan, Ahmedabad, 1952.

Devanessen, C. D. S.: *The Making of the Mahatma*, Longmans, London, 1969.

Dhavan, Gopinath: *The Political Philosophy of Mahatma Gandhi*, Delhi, 1990.

Diwakar, R. R.: *Satyagraha: Its Technique and History*, Hind Kitabs, Bombay, 1946.

Dore, F. and Prevost, M.: *Selected Letters of Romain Rolland*, Indira Gandhi National Centre for the Arts, Delhi, 1990.

Easwaran, E.: *Gandhi the Man*, Nilgiri Press, California, 1978.

Erikson, Erik, H.: *Gandhi's Truth: On the Origins of Militant Nonviolence*, W. W. Norton, New York, 1969.

Ferguson-Dave, C. J.: *The Early History of Indians in Natal*, South African Institute of Race Relations, Johannesburg, 1951.

Fischer, Louis: *The Essential Gandhi: An Anthology of His Writings on His Life, Work and Ideas*, New York, Vintage, 2002.

————: *The Life of Mahatma Gandhi*, Harper & Row, New York, 1950.

Fox, Richard: *Gandhian Utopia: Experiments with Culture*, Beacon Press, Boston, 1989.

Freeman, J. B.: *Gandhiji in South Africa: An Historical Drama in Five Acts*, Viswanathan, Madras, 1950.

Gandhi, E.: *Mohandas Gandhi: The South African Years*, Maskew Miller Longman, Cape Town, 1994.

Gandhi, M. K.: *An Autobiography or The Story of My Experiments With Truth*, Navajivan Publishing House, Ahmedabad, 1940.

————: *The Gandhi Reader: A Sourcebook of His Life and Writings*, Homer Jack, Grove Press, New York, 1956.

————: *The Collected Works of Mahatma Gandhi*, Ministry of Information and Broadcasting, New Delhi, 1994.

————: *Patel: A Life*, Navajivan Publishing House, 1990.

————: *Satyagraha in South Africa: Translated from the Gujarati by Valji Govindji Desai*, Navjivan, Ahmedabad, 1928.

Gangal, S. C.: *Gandhian Thoughts and Techniques in the Modern World*, Criterion Publications, New Delhi, 1988.

Gordon, Haim: *A Rejection of Spiritual Imperialism: Reflections on Buber's Letter to Gandhi, Journal of Ecumenical Studies*, 1999.

Green, Martin: *Gandhi: Voice of a New Age Revolution*, Continuum, New York, 1993.

————: *The Origins of Nonviolence: Tolstoy and Gandhi in their Historical Settings*, Pennsylvania State University Press, New Jersey, 1986.

Grenier, Richard: *The Gandhi Nobody Knows*, Commentary, 1983.

Hancock, W. K.: *Smuts, the Fields of Force: 1919-1950*, Cambridge University Press, London, 1968.

Horsburgh, H. J. N.: *Nonviolence and Aggression: A Study of Gandhi's Moral Equivalent of War,* Oxford University Press, London, 1968.

Hunt, James, D.: *Gandhi in London,* Promilla & Co., New Delhi, 1978.

Hutchins, Francis, G.: *India's Revolution: Gandhi and the Quit India Movement,* Harvard UP, Cambridge, 1973.

Huttenback, R. A.: *Gandhi in South Africa: British Imperialism and Indian Question,* Cornell University Press, New Jersey, 1971.

Iyer, R. N.: *The Moral and Political Thought of Mahatma Gandhi,* Oxford University Press, Oxford, 1973.

Jordens, J. T. F.: *Gandhi's Religion: A Homespun Shawl,* St. Martin's Press, New York, 1998.

Joshi, P.: *Gandhi on Women: Collection of Mahatma Gandhi's Writings and Speeches on Women,* Navjivan, Ahmedabad, 1988.

Kalarthi, M.: *Ba and Bapu: Translated from the Original in Gujarati by Gurdial Mallik,* Navjivan, Ahmedabad, 1962.

Kapur, Sudarshan: *Raising Up a Prophet: The African-American Encounter with Gandhi,* Beacon Press, Boston, 1992.

Kataria, S.: *Gandhi's Reaction to World Affairs,* Kanishka Publishing House, Delhi, 1990.

Kendall, P.: *Mr. Gandhi in Africa and India: In her India and the British a Quest for Truth,* C. Scribner's Sons, London, 1931.

Khanna, Suman: *Gandhi and the Good Life,* Gandhi Peace Foundation, New Delhi, 1985.

Kishwar, Madhu: *Gandhi and Women,* Manushi Prakashan, Delhi, 1986.

Kuper, H.: *Indian People in Natal,* Greenwood Press, Wesport, 1974.

Lester, M.: *Gandhi: World Citizen,* Kitab Mahal, Allahabad, 1945.

Lewin, J.: *Politics and Law in South Africa: Essays on Race Relations,* Merlin, London, 1963.

Lewis, M. D.: *Gandhi: Maker of Modern India,* D. C. Heath and Co., Massachusetts, 1965.

Mahadevan, T. K.: *The Year of the Phoenix,* Gulab Vazirani, New Delhi, 1982.

Malkani, N. R.: *Ramblinqs and Reminiscences of Gandhiji,* Navjivan, Ahmedabad, 1972.

Mani, M. P.: *Foundations of Gandhian Thought,* Dattsons, Sadar, 1987.

Mann, Bernhard: *The Pedagogical and Political Concepts of Mahatma Gandhi and Paulo Freire,* International Studies in Political Socialization and Education, Hamburg, 1996.

Mashruwalla, K. G.: *Towards Sarvodaya Order,* Navjivan, Ahmedabad, 1971.

Nanda, B. R. R.: *Gandhi: A Pictorial Biography,* Government of India, New Delhi, 1972.

Nayar, P. S.: *In Gandhiji's Mirror,* Oxford University Press, Delhi, 1991.

Pachai, B.: *Mahatma Gandhi in South Africa,* South African Institute of Race Relations, Johannesburg, 1969.

Palmer, M.: *The History of Indians in Natal,* Oxford University Press, Cape Town, 1957.

Parekh, Bhikhu: *Gandhi's Political Philosophy: A Critical Examination,* Macmillan, London, 1996.

Patel, Jehangir, P. and Marjorie Sykes: Rasulia, Madhya Pradesh: Friends Rural Centre, 1987.

Patil, V. T.: *Mahatma Gandhi and the Civil Disobedience Movement: A Study in the Dynamics of Mass Movement,* Renaissance Publishing House, Delhi, 1988.

Pinto, Vivek: *Gandhi's Vision and Values: The Moral Quest for Change in Indian Agriculture,* New Delhi, 1998.

Pouchepadass, Jacques: *Champaran and Gandhi: Planters, Peasants and Gandhian Politics,* Oxford UP, New Delhi, 1999.

Prasad, Nageshwar: *Hind Swaraj: A Fresh Look,* Gandhi Peace Foundation, Delhi, 1985.

Radhakrishnan, S.: *Mahatma Gandhi: Essays and Reflections on his Life and Work,* Jaico, Bombay, 1964.

Rao, Seshagiri, K. L.: *Mahatma Gandhi and Comparative Religion,* Motilal Banarsidass, New Delhi, 1978.

Reddy, E. S.: *Gandhi, Nehru and Freedom Struggle in South Africa,* New Delhi, 1988.

Satyaprakash: *Gandhiana 1962-1976,* Indian Documentation Centre, New Delhi, 1977.

Schimlek, F.: *Against the Stream: Life of Father Bernard Huss,* Mariannhill Mission Press, Mariannhill, 1949.

Sharp, Gene: *Gandhi as a Political Strategist with Essays on Ethics and Politics,* Extending Horizon Books, Boston, 1979.

Shridharani, K.: *War without Violence: A Study of Gandhi's Method and its Accomplishments,* London Victor Gollancz, 1939.

Singh, Col. G. B. and Watson, Dr. Tim: *Gandhi Under Cross Examination,* Sovereign Star Publishing, 2008.

Swaminathan, K. and Patel, C. N.: *A Gandhi Reader,* Orient Longman, Madras, 1988.

Swan, Maureen: *Gandhi: The South African Experience,* Ravan Press, Johannesburg, 1985.

Tahtinen, U.: *Ahimsa: Non-violence in Indian Tradition,* Navjivan, Ahmedabad, 1976.

Terchek, Ronald, J.: *Gandhi: Struggling for Autonomy,* Rowman & Littlefield, Lanham, 1999.

Tiwari, K. N.: *World Religions and Gandhi,* Classical Publishing, New Delhi, 1988.

Togni, L. S.: *The Struggle for Human Rights and International and South African Perspective,* Juta, Kenwyn, 1994.

Upaddhyaya, H.: *Bapu Katha,* Sarva Seva Sangh Prakashem, Varanasi, 1987.

Venkatesananda, S.: *The Voice of Truth,* Sanathcin Dharma of Ladysmith, Ladysmith, 1990.

Verbeek, J. Nathanson, M. and Peel, E.: *Webb's Guide to the Official Records of the Colony of Natal,* University of Natal Press, Pietermaritzburg, 1984.

Verma, M. M.: *Gandhi's Technique of Mass Mobilisation,* R. K. Gupta, New Delhi, 1990.

Verma, S. L.: *On the Grounds of Gandhian Polity: Leadership, Relevance and Problems,* RBSA Publishers, Jaipur, 1990.

Virasai, B.: *The Emergence and Making of a Mass Movement Leader: Portrait of Mahatma Gandhi in South Africa, 1893-1914,* University Microfilms, Ann Arbor, 1968.

Walker, R.: *Sword of Gold: A Life of Mahatma Gandhi,* Indian Independence Union, London, 1945.

Weber, T.: *Conflict Resolution and Gandhian Ethics,* Peace Publishers, New Delhi, 1991.

Index

□□□

Commissioner's Wrath: If the Commissioner had not been angry with us, and had talked politely with the deputation that waited on him, and had not misinstructed the Bombay Government, such a grave crisis would not have eventuated, and we would not have had the trouble of meeting here this evening. The Sabha's request was to suspend the collection of dues till the negotiations were over. But Government did not take this proper course and issued an angry Press Note. It was my firm belief — and even now I firmly believe — that the representatives of the people and Government could have joined together and taken the proper steps. I regret to have to say that Government has made a mistake. Perhaps subordinate officers of Government would say [illegible] that the notice was issued not from a pure motive but from some other [illegible] with [illegible] those who have stood by the people, I hope, will continue to stand by them to the end [illegible] relief. Any responsible right-thinking man would have given them the same advice. People possess the same rights as the [illegible] men have every right to advise the [illegible]